T0327683

Semi-Organic Growth

Semi-Organic Growth

Tactics and Strategies behind Google's Success

GEORGE T. GEIS

WILEY

Library of Congress Cataloging-in-Publication Data:

Geis, George T.
  Semi-organic growth + website : tactics and strategies behind Google's success /
George T. Geis.
      pages cm
   Includes bibliographical references and index.
   ISBN 978-1-118-93322-0 (hardback)
1. Consolidation and merger of corporations. 2. Google (Firm) I. Title.
II. Title: Semi-organic growth.
   HD2746.5.G447 2015
   658.4'012—dc23
                                                                    2015005928

10 9 8 7 6 5 4 3 2 1

To George S. Geis, Terri L. Geis, and Anne L. Geis—three ongoing sources of semi-organic growth

Contents

Preface

A round 1995, I became intrigued with developing a methodology and related visualization technology to systematically analyze company acquisitions, minority equity investments, alliances, and other corporate development activities. At the time, I was concentrating on companies that included Microsoft, Intel, and Cisco.

Then along came Google. Starting with the early days of Google, acquisitions appeared to play a particularly important role in the strategic unfolding of this iconic company. Google was becoming an experimental lab, not only for products and services but also in utilizing M&A to further its purposes.

I wanted to understand in depth why Google was engaging in what was an unprecedented level and type of M&A activity.

As of 2015, Google had acquired some 200 companies. But there's much more to the story than numbers. The major thesis of this book is that early in the company's existence, a playbook for M&A activity (which I dub *semi-organic growth*) was established, and that this pattern became a core element of Google's success.

Semi-Organic Growth presents a unique analysis of Google's distinctive expertise in the area of mergers and acquisitions. The book provides insights derived from the many Google acquisitions completed over the company's brief history. While organizational revenue growth has traditionally been characterized as organic (internally generated) or inorganic (from acquisition), this book features Google's use of a blended, semi-organic strategy to accelerate product and service revenue.

Google's extensive use of M&A during its period of rapid growth has been in sharp contrast to rivals such as Apple. In addition, Google's overall success in M&A further contrasts with the failures of many other companies in this area of corporate business development. All readers will gain distinctive insights from the M&A expertise and practices of this iconic company.

Semi-Organic Growth illustrates how Google's M&A moves can be explained through a unique sector/subsector classification scheme that dynamically maps the media, Internet, and technology platform markets. Market modeling dynamics are illustrated with some 50 infographics to help understand important categorical M&A dimensions and visualize deal constellations. These market-modeling techniques are applicable to any company.

The book examines Google's practices in disclosing M&A deal structure (such as valuation and form of consideration) and in using contingent consideration in the form of earn-outs and stay bonuses.

But perhaps most importantly, we examine how Google has integrated its acquisitions, thereby accelerating the growth of its array of products and services.

Chapter 1 describes the challenges of building a successful M&A program in domains that include strategy, economic valuation, organizational design, and deal dynamics. This chapter discusses each of these activities, emphasizing approaches linked to positive outcomes.

Chapter 2 features Google's acquisition of Applied Semantics, a watershed transaction in that it imprinted on Google a methodology for revenue acceleration through semi-organic growth. This chapter provides a history of the Applied Semantics deal and how the acquisition led to the creation of AdSense, which grew into a highly significant service within Google.

Chapter 3 contrasts Apple and Google, two companies that have had dramatically different corporate philosophies with respect to the role of M&A in strategy. Until 2012, Apple engaged in M&A only sparingly, believing that innovation should essentially originate from within. In contrast, Google was acquiring companies at a rapid clip and using technology and talent from the purchases as a major part of its innovation efforts.

Chapter 4 introduces marketing modeling, which involves connecting knowledge chunks comprised of three elements: market segments, companies, and deals. The chapter illustrates market modeling by developing a sample model for Google in the MIT (media, Internet, and technology infrastructure) spaces.

Chapter 5 highlights advertising as Google's core business. The chapter develops a market model for media and then analyzes Google's acquisitions in sectors such as online content and advertising.

Chapter 6 analyzes numerous acquisitions that Google has made to strengthen its position in Internet search, as well as accelerate its move into a range of additional Internet products and services. This chapter develops a market model to explain Google's Internet-related purchases.

Chapter 7 explains how acquisitions have played a key role in extending Google beyond its core search/advertising business to an ever-expanding technology platform for new products and services. The chapter explores acquisitions that relate to subsectors of this platform, including smartphone, smart home, robotics, and artificial intelligence.

Chapter 8 illustrates that although Google is regarded as having developed the most successful technology M&A program in history, certainly not all of its deals have done well. This chapter examines some of Google's abortive transactions and suggests reasons for these failures. We also provide an analysis of gains and losses associated with the purchase of Motorola Mobility.

Chapter 9 examines when a publicly traded company such as Google announces an acquisition. When must the company disclose deal valuation and other key terms? This chapter focuses on the M&A disclosure practices of Google and Apple and explores possible motives for deal disclosure or secrecy.

Chapter 10 describes how an acquirer can pay for a target using accumulated free cash flow, using cash raised from a new debt or stock offering, exchanging shares of its stock for shares of the target, or combining these forms of payment. How often has Google used stock in purchasing a company? What are the motives for using stock as opposed to cash? How does Google's consideration choices in its M&A transactions compare to those of other major technology companies such as Apple or Facebook?

Chapter 11 highlights that for some M&A transactions, not all consideration is paid out by an acquirer at the close of the transaction. Earn-out consideration contingent on the target meeting performance metrics can be used. Or retention bonus consideration (in cash or in stock) can be provided to motivate target employees to stay on with the acquirer for a period of time. We'll explore how these forms of contingent consideration have been used by Google and other leading technology and media companies.

Chapter 12 stresses that successfully integrating an acquisition is vital if M&A value is to be captured. This chapter explores some classic strategic dimensions that provide a high-level framework for M&A integration. We examine how Google's semi-organic form of acquisitions fits into this scheme and how Google has learned to be more effective in executing a challenging integration strategy. We also describe some notable Google failures in M&A integration.

Chapter 13 highlights that a substantial amount of M&A activity is undertaken to support specific products or services that can reach customers. This chapter uses Google as an example to illustrate a market model that maps a company's products and services and how a particular acquisition might enhance these offerings. We also identify four major types of acqui-hires, talent/technology purchases designed to accelerate sales of both existing and new products and services. Finally, we explore career moves by a number of Google M&A alumni, company founders who sold organizations to Google, worked to add value to a Google offering, and subsequently made significant career changes.

Chapter 14 examines how competitive contests such as the Amazon/ Google struggle for market control in e-commerce and advertising can be understood by developing M&A deal constellations. We next illustrate the concept of ecosystem synergy and demonstrate how this type of synergy can strengthen competitive positioning and add value to a company. We show how a number of Google's acquisitions have achieved this higher order of synergy.

I hope you enjoy and benefit from this journey through the land of Google's semi-organic M&A!

Watch the Videos

This book is accompanied by a companion website that includes a short introductory video, together with 14 additional online videos, each about 10 minutes in length. The content of each video is designed to add to your understanding of key concepts found in a given chapter. You'll find these videos referenced at the end of each chapter.

For the URL and access code for your online videos, please refer to the instructions at the end of this book.

Acknowledgments

I have greatly benefited from the insights and support of many colleagues, friends and students in writing this book.

Debbie Foster, Olaf Westheider, and Steven O'Toole provided inspiration and outstanding technical support in the development of the concept of market modeling.

Sean Carr, Executive Director of the Batten Institute at the Darden School of Business, University of Virginia, suggested that I give a talk while on campus as a visiting professor. The talk, which involved Google's acquisition strategy, was uploaded to YouTube and subsequently viewed by Bill Falloon, Executive Editor of Finance and Investment at Wiley. Bill encouraged me to write a book expanding upon the talk. Thus the origin of *Semi-Organic Growth*.

My special thanks to Bill Falloon and Meg Freeborn, Development Editor at Wiley, for their encouragement throughout this project. I also appreciate the assistance of the entire Wiley team for their support in completing this effort.

I regard the M&A writings of Bob Bruner, Dean of the Darden School, as foundational to a number of ideas that appear in this book. I've benefited from my ongoing conversations with Bob.

I am indebted to many students and research collaborators for insight and assistance. These include James Biskey, Debadutta Bhattacharyya, Neelima Clark, Tom Crow, Zubin Davar, John Dearing, Reggie Hall, Kevin Hopkins, Ahreum Hong, Kyle Jansen, Joey Lei, K. Burns McNamee, Alisa Sommer, Emily Scadden, Renu Senjalia, Joshua Schachter, Jacqueline Sutro, and Miao Wang. Please forgive any omissions.

I am not writing this book as a Google insider. However, I have benefited from interviews with numerous present and past Google employees, conducted as reality checks. I am extremely grateful for the insights provided.

I deeply appreciate the entire UCLA Anderson environment for decades of support. Special thanks to Al Osborne, Elaine Hagan, Martin Lieberman, and George Ingersoll.

Finally, I'd like to thank my wife, Penny, who graciously postponed getting our new Springer Spaniel until the first draft of this book was completed. Now it's time for many more long walks along the Cambria ocean bluffs.

CHAPTER 1

M&A Success and Failure

K onrad Lorenz's classic experiment with graylag geese captures the attention of many college freshman enrolled in an introductory psychology class. Lorenz found that geese would *imprint* on the first movable object within a *critical period* occurring 13 to 16 hours after hatching. It didn't matter whether the "parent" object was Lorenz's boots or a box placed on a toy train moving around a circular track.

Imprinting involves phase-sensitive learning whereby an animal or person establishes a pattern of attachment to another animate or inanimate object. Business ventures can also experience imprinting events during the early stages of development.

The notion that a corporation's early experiences can have lasting impact on future development has long been noted.[1] A firm commonly experiences an inertial impulse very early in its history that persists for a significant duration.[2] This initial organizational experience can involve corporate development activity. For example, Milanov and Fernhaber presented evidence that the initial alliance experiences of a venture affect future alliance formation patterns.[3]

Similarly, the acquisition of Applied Semantics early in Google's history (before going public in 2004) imprinted upon the company not only a proclivity to do mergers and acquisitions (M&A), but also to favor a certain style of *M&A activity*. Indeed, over its relatively brief corporate history, Google has acquired some 200 companies. In addition, Google has enjoyed an unusual degree of achievement in its dominant style of M&A activity, in 2012 asserting success in two-thirds of purchases,[4] significantly higher than commonly cited acquisition statistics.

However, before we examine strategies and tactics that Google has employed in its transactions, let's examine how M&A performance has traditionally been measured, as well as some of the most common reasons for M&A failure and success.

M&A Activities

Developing a successful M&A program is a major challenge for any organization, arguably significantly more difficult than operational functions.
Nevertheless, the pace and volume at which technology firms have been
buying is staggering. For example, according to Thomson Reuters, the total
spent on technology M&A worldwide during the first quarter of 2014 was
$65.2 billion. This represented the largest dollar volume for any equivalent
period since 2000.

Consider the breadth of activities that must be considered in doing a
deal (Table 1.1).

Strategy

First of all, a compelling strategic rationale for a transaction must be developed. This may involve responding to an opportunity or shock in a market.
Or it may be based on a creative vision whereby the company desires to
establish new positioning in a market or even attempts to create a new market. For example, Google's cluster of eight robotics acquisitions in 2013
clearly signaled that the company saw significant market opportunity in
areas that could range from robotic manufacturing to android-assisted home
health care. Although to be successful such strategic thinking necessarily
must involve senior executives, a company such as Google also has strategy
leads engaging in analysis to support the growth of each major business
division, including areas such as search, social, mobile, and YouTube.

TABLE 1.1 Deal Activities

Strategy	Economics	Organization	Deal Dynamics
Responding to opportunity or threat	Doing valuation/ NPV analysis	Establishing best practices for integration	Designing the deal, including tax strategy
Determining attractiveness of industry position	Determining synergies	Building acquisition teams	Engaging in negotiation and bidding
Establishing strategic deal system	Estimating revenues, costs and cash flows	Merging corporate cultures, as necessary	Handling legal concerns
Determining optimal type of transaction	Determining effects of deal financing		Engaging in negotiation and bidding

Strategy also involves establishing a systematic approach to M&A activity. Organizations have established systems for virtually every activity of the firm—from HR management to supply chain management—but typically lag in thinking systematically about M&A and other corporate business development activities. There are some notable exceptions, such as GE Power Systems (later renamed GE Energy), as documented by Robert Bruner.[5] We'll later examine Google's systematic approach to M&A.

In addition, deal strategy involves determining the optimal type of transaction. This includes knowing when not to acquire a company, but instead designing an alternative form of partnership relationship. For example, in 2003, as Apple was in the process of launching its iTunes platform, the *Los Angeles Times* reported that Apple was considering the purchase of Universal Music (a global player in recorded music) owned at the time by Vivendi.[6] Apple correctly decided against the purchase. Doing so, among other things, would have created supply-channel conflict with other music providers that it needed to launch iTunes into a platform with a broad music library. Instead, Apple licensed music from Universal (and other music companies) in order to build an extensive collection for users to download using iTunes. (In 2014, Apple was facing different challenges as it attempted to maintain a leadership position in digital music and, as we'll see in Chapter 3, decided to engage in a major M&A activity to do so.)

Deal Economics

Second, deal economics must be evaluated. This involves conducting a valuation analysis that is appropriate for a given M&A transaction. This may require obtaining a constellation of values using methodologies such as discounted cash flow analysis, revenue, or earnings-related multiples using public company comparables, multiples from past M&A transactions, or multiples of *something-or-other* in early-stage ventures, There is rarely one North Star valuation metric. The constellation approach is intended to provide an acquirer with perspective regarding an appropriate range of value.

Jaw-dropping valuations have not been uncommon for deals in technology markets, including some Google transactions. Although not as staggering as the estimated $350 million/employee multiple that Facebook paid in its $19 billion acquisition of WhatsApp in 2014, Google has spent $1 billion or more for newly minted companies such as YouTube, Waze, and Nest.

Such valuations subject a company to critics who characterize the purchase as an irrational spending spree, but a deal might be later dubbed as brilliant if the target's platform proves out as a core asset in the acquirer's growth.

Synergy analysis is an essential ingredient in valuation, although *synergy* is perhaps one the most misused terms in corporate strategy. The word *synergy* has a most interesting origin as part of business jargon, according to the following account.

Professor J. Fred Weston was a giant in the field of M&A.[7] He arrived at UCLA from the University of Chicago in 1949 and over his career wrote 32 books and 147 journal articles, many of which dealt with M&A. He mentored many outstanding graduate students, including Nobel Laureate Bill Sharpe. I worked with Fred, taking over as faculty director for UCLA Anderson's *Executive Program on Mergers & Acquisitions* from him in 2005. Fred continued to speak in the program. When I introduced him as the "John Wooden of M&A" (referring to UCLA's legendary basketball coach), it was scarcely an overstatement.

Fred told the story about how the term *synergy* came to be used in corporate deal making. The year was 1950, and Fred was at lunch in Westwood, California, with executives from a nascent industry that would later become aerospace. Fred saw a drink menu on the table that promoted *Irish coffee, The Perfect Synergy* (Irish coffee blends coffee and Irish whiskey). Not knowing what synergy meant, Fred looked up the term after he returned to his office at UCLA and saw that *synergy* equals the interaction of two or more agents so that their combined effect is greater than the sum of their individual effects. "Now that's what an M&A is supposed to do," thought Fred. He began using *synergy* in his writings to characterize successful deals, and the term became a cornerstone of academic and professional thinking.

Many of Google's deals involve estimating *revenue synergy* that is believed will occur sometime in the future. Only rarely does a Google M&A transaction center on cost savings resulting from the combination of Google and the target company. Much of this anticipated revenue synergy involves creating or accelerating new products or services—rather risky synergy goals, but we'll see how Google considers and attempts to manage such risk.

Organizational Design

Third, organizational design plays a crucial role in M&A activity. For example, it's widely understood that unless deal integration efforts succeed, the premium or even the basic consideration paid for a target can evaporate. Some executives feel that this implies that integration efforts must necessarily be concluded rapidly, certainly within a year. After all, cash flows associated with an acquisition have *time value*, so the sooner positive flows are realized, the more valuable they will be.

Although rapid assimilation is the correct path for some deals, we'll see that one size doesn't fit all with M&A integration. In fact, there are numerous styles for successful integration, some of which require that targets be left alone for a considerable period of time after the deal closes.

Google has come to understand that there is not a holy-grail path to integration and utilizes numerous styles for its acquisitions in attempting to make a deal work. For example, consider Google's 2012 acquisition of Wildfire Interactive. Wildfire's technology enabled advertisers to serve campaigns on social websites such as Facebook, Google+, Twitter, Pinterest, YouTube, and LinkedIn. When Google acquired Wildfire, Jason Miller, a Google product manager, made this blog posting: "With Wildfire, we're looking forward to creating new opportunities for our clients to engage with people across all social services ... social presence can complement all marketing campaigns—search, display, video, mobile, offline ads and more."

As part of the deal terms, Google established a significant retention bonus in order to motivate Wildfire co-founders Victoria Ransom and Alain Chuard to continue leading the company's 400-employee team. Wildfire was left alone in an attempt to pursue key enterprise social marketing metrics that Google felt could be better achieved without immediate tight integration into a Google product group. There certainly was no guarantee that this integration approach would yield desired results, but Google apparently believed it would maximize the chances that it would.

In contrast, other acquisitions have been immediately associated with product groups within Google. For example, in 2011, Google purchased Green Parrot Pictures, a developer of tools for the manipulation of digital video and images. Almost immediately, Green Parrot's technology and team was attached to the YouTube group with the goal of helping users make flicker-free videos, particularly for videos taken with mobile phones.

Still other acquisitions become part of a collection with the goal of introducing a series of new product introductions. Consider the cluster of robotics acquisitions mentioned earlier. Google initially placed these acquisitions and its robotics initiative under Silicon Valley veteran Andy Rubin to explore greenfield opportunities based on the collective technologies from these deals.

There is much more subtlety in Google's approach to integration. Many of these efforts have been successful, but there are also notable failures. We'll devote Chapter 12 to exploring acquisition integration in detail.

Deal Dynamics

Finally, consider the deal dynamics dimension of M&A. This dimension includes designing the terms and structure of the deal. Will the consideration of the transaction involve cash, stock, or some combination? Will there be contingent consideration, payable to the target only if certain milestones are met? How about retention or stay bonuses for key talent? Will the employees of the acquired company need to relocate, or can they stay in place?

Consider some dynamics issues relating to Google deals. When Google purchased Waze, an Israeli crowd-sourced mapping and navigation company, the consideration was $966 million in cash. (Retention bonuses could increase this amount.) Google would use the technology to enhance its Google Maps with Waze's real-time traffic information. In closing this deal, Google allowed Waze personnel to remain in Israel. This concession was reportedly an important factor in Waze's decision to agree to the acquisition.

Google rarely uses its stock in making acquisitions, although it has done so in certain key purchases (such as Applied Semantics AdMob, and YouTube). However, going forward, Google might use stock more often in M&A transactions. After a stock split in 2014, the company has nonvoting stock to use as a potential acquisition currency.

Taking all four of these major activities (strategy, economics, organization, and deal dynamics) into consideration, the bottom line is that successful M&A activity is an intricate challenge. It is no small undertaking for a company such as Google to succeed in building an acquisition program that becomes a core strategic capability.

Evaluating Performance

M&A success rates for corporations are generally considered poor, although just how poor has been the subject of some disagreement. Some studies report the rate at which acquisitions fail to create value range to be 40 to 60 percent, while others assert a failure rate within an even higher range of 70 to 90 percent.[8]

Abstracting from a wide range of studies, Robert Bruner concluded: "The buyer in M&A transactions must prepare to be disappointed. The distribution of announcement returns is wide and the mean close to zero. There is no free lunch."[9] (Announcement returns involve *event studies* that examine abnormal returns to shareholders in the period of time surrounding transactions.) Bruner went on to further assert that negative performance post-merger is troubling, but suggested that more rigorous testing is necessary to draw firm conclusions about the returns after an acquisition is completed.

M&A activity performance has been studied extensively, with various schools of thought emerging.[10] First, the *financial economic* school measures value creation and stock market returns around the time of a transaction. These studies are prominent in academic thinking, but are of limited use when the acquirer is private or when the acquirer engages in a small transaction (or series of small transactions) relative to its market capitalization. And such small acquisitions have long dominated for Google and other leading technology companies, as reflected in the practice known as *acqui-hiring*. Acqui-hiring, in general, involves the process of acquiring a company to recruit its talent, with or without being interested in the target's technology, products, and services. We'll examine various forms of the acqui-hiring phenomenon in Chapter 13.

A second school of thought involves evaluating the effects of *strategic relatedness* on M&A performance. Traditionally, this line of thought has argued that acquisitions enjoyed a higher likelihood of success if they were in some way related to the acquirer's current products or markets. Significant evidence has been presented that acquisitions involving unrelated diversification commonly result in lower financial returns than nondiversifying deals.[11] Peter Lynch, well known as a mutual fund investor, went so far as to coin the term *diworsification,* implying that an organization that diversifies too widely risks destroying its original business, given the management energy and firm resources that are diverted from core activities.

The concept of strategic relatedness is highly relevant to our study of Google's M&A activity. While many of the company's targets have been related to its core ad-tech activities, other deals, such as Google's $3.2 billion acquisition of Nest Labs in 2014, offering smart home products such as smart thermostats and smoke alarms, might be considered as taking Google afield from its advertising center.

Not all companies that have used M&A to diversify have failed in this effort. For example, Berkshire Hathaway has been a notable success. We'll evaluate the likely performance impact of Google's diversification deals as we explore its expanding market footprint.

A third school of thought used to evaluate M&A effectiveness involves *organizational behavior.* Here, a host of questions are asked. What role do organizational variables such as acquisition experience play in M&A results? How can cultural distance between two companies be measured, and what is the impact of cultural distance on M&A success? What are the styles of post-acquisition integration, and how quickly and to what degree should the target be integrated?

As mentioned earlier, conventional wisdom argues for rapid integration. After all, the sooner positive cash flow from cost or revenue synergies is realized, the higher the present value to the acquirer. However, consider Facebook's $2 billion acquisition of Oculus, a developer of virtual reality technology. Immediately following the announcement of the acquisition in 2014, Oculus founder Palmer Luckey was astounded at the outpouring of negativity received by the company and stunned that some employees had even received death threats. Luckey was forced to respond to dozens of questions involving privacy concerns now that his company would be owned by Facebook. Rapid integration was not likely to work well for this deal!

As we've illustrated, Google employs a range of integration speeds and styles in its acquisition program. And the company continues to learn from integration successes and failures as it attempts to build a strategic core competency in the organizational behavior domain. In order to succeed, the organizational behavior practices of any acquirer must involve active knowledge management.

Target Financial Performance

Overall *M&A target performance* has varied across the decades. For example, average abnormal returns (above what an investor would expect to return given comparable risk level) averaged 25.1 percent during the 2000s, up from 18.5 percent during the 1990s.[12]

Furthermore, in any given period, the range of premiums paid to acquire a company has a large variance. For example, Bloomberg reported a spread of premiums paid to shareholders of target firms for a sample of deals during the second quarter of 2013. Of these, 49 deals had premiums between 0 to 10 percent, 54 had premiums between 10 and 25 percent, 52 carried premiums between 25 and 50 percent, and 19 enjoyed premiums of 50 to 100 percent. Finally, 13 had hyper-premiums of greater than 100 percent.[13]

Also, the trend for premiums paid can be increasing or decreasing. In 2013, U.S. companies were paying on average a premium of only 19 percent above their target's trading price one week before the deal was announced.[14] This reflected the lowest takeover premium since at least 1995, according to Dealogic. Given the uncertainty of macroeconomic conditions, executives and corporate boards were being cautious.

Nevertheless as suggested earlier, wide variance across deals in premiums typically occur, especially when the premiums paid to rapidly growing private high-tech companies are included. (Private company premiums are harder to measure than those associated with public companies, but are often based on the most recent private valuation.) Using another metric, WhatsApp's $19 billion price tag implied a multiple of approximately 100 times revenue and a huge premium over previous valuations.

It's not always possible to know the premium paid for an acquisition, For example, we'll see in Chapter 9 that Google discloses the valuation and terms for only a small number of its deals. Third parties provide estimates for a larger set of Google acquisitions.

The bottom line? M&A pays for almost all targets across industries. But in hot technology areas, the payoff can be off-the-charts.

Acquirer Financial Performance

As we've seen, classic research findings suggest that acquirers on average do not have much room for optimism, given that the distribution of announcement returns has a mean close to zero. Thus, a pressing question facing an acquirer is: How can my company do better than average?

More recent research involving large-scale samples provides a little more room for optimism. Abnormal returns to acquirer shareholders are modestly positive (about 1 percent) if large public company deals and deals involving stock-for-stock exchanges are filtered out.[15]

Post-merger returns typically analyze cash flow or operating profit over a period of time (typically three-to-five years) after an acquisition. However, there's a major problem with these analyses. The longer the period of study, the greater the likelihood that confounding factors (extraneous to the deal) impact financial performance.

In addition, it is not possible to analyze how the company would have performed had it passed up the acquisition. In an attempt to address this problem, some studies compare the performance of two similar companies, only one of which made an acquisition. But here again, confounding variables swamping the M&A dimension can enter into play.

Complexity in the M&A performance analysis is taken to an even higher level when a company is a serial acquirer or focuses on smaller acquisitions that are rounding errors in its market capitalization. Google is a prime example of such a company.

The bottom line is that research studies on acquirer performance face substantial methodological hurdles. With this caveat in mind, one study of studies analyzed 26 studies of post-merger performance, 14 of which showed a decline of operating returns, 7 showed positive (but not significant) returns, and 5 showed positive (statistically significant) returns.[16] This is hardly a confident, conclusive picture of M&A performance results.

Numerous studies show acquirers of privately owned firms realize positive returns of 1.5 to 2.6 percent.[17] Such higher returns are generally attributed to factors such as a limited number of bidders and the relative illiquidity of private companies, resulting in an associated liquidity discount. But such discounts may not apply to venture-backed companies that Google attempts to acquire—ventures where other deep-pocketed bidders may also be in pursuit. For example, reportedly both Apple and Facebook were interested in Waze's crowd-sourced traffic technology.

Some evidence exists that high-tech firms realize positive value by acquiring small, but related ventures to fill in gaps in their product offerings.[18] This is one likely reason why successful high-tech companies persist in being very active deal makers. There will be more about this in our next chapter.

Several studies have shown that publicly traded acquirers using cash for transactions tend to do better long term than those that use stock.[19] One rationale for this observation is that executives tend to use stock when they believe their shares are overvalued.[20] Hence, it's not surprising that the acquirer's share price drops after the acquisition. (AOL's stock-for-stock merger with Time Warner is often cited as a classic example of this phenomenon.)

On the other hand, a company may genuinely believe its stock is an attractive currency (certainly not overvalued) and use the appeal of its shares to woo a target and close a deal. Consider Google's stock-for-stock acquisition of YouTube, where Google's shares were likely to have been regarded by both acquirer and target as a very desirable currency.

Acquisitions such as the Google purchase of YouTube argue against the superior acquirer performance when doing cash deals. Herd and McManus[21] further support this argument in stating, "Historically, acquirer may have been keen to use equity to finance a deal when they've believed their equity was overvalued. But during the last decade, they've come to realize that equity is often more dear than cash in an era of plentiful and cheap credit."

Given all of this, we can conclude that the motives for using equity in an M&A transaction vary across acquirers. Equity can be used when the purchaser feels its currency is *Weimar-Republic* hyperinflated. However, the use of equity may also signal a deal's importance if the acquirer is demonstrating to the target a willingness to use a tender that both believe has significant potential to appreciate.

When Berkshire Hathaway uses it stock, the company signals that it views the acquisition as having special value. As Warren Buffett quipped at a shareholders meeting about issuing stock in a transaction: "Charlie [Munger] and I like using stock about as much as preparing for a colonoscopy."

Perhaps here's the key takeaway regarding M&A financial performance for acquirers. Average returns across all companies may not be all that exciting. But the real issue is, how does a company outperform these averages? How does a company move into the top quartile of performers? How does a company build a core strategic advantage via M&A? Throughout this book, we'll explore what we can learn about these questions from Google.

Reasons for M&A Failure

In other to provide context for understanding M&A success, let's highlight three major reasons for *M&A failure*. Not surprisingly, these reasons closely connect to the broad areas of M&A activity discussed earlier.

Flawed Strategy

The strategic rationale for an acquisition must be soundly based on a company's *core competencies*. Growth opportunities should be centered in areas where a firm has some distinctive advantage, not on areas of overt weakness. The chances that M&A will solve a company's problems have about the same likelihood of success as a marriage resolving the difficulties of two troubled people.

Consider an example. If a product or service is unable to obtain distribution by clearly providing value, acquiring distribution is unlikely to be the solution.[22] In 1987, during the early days of personal computing, Atari was struggling to convince retailers to sell its PCs. In an attempt to solve the problem, Jack Tramiel, then chairman of Atari, bought the Federated Group chain of consumer electronics stores for $67.3 million. Tramiel reasoned that the network of 65 Federated stores in California, Arizona, Texas, and Kansas would successfully move his computers.

Other retailers were reluctant to carry Atari's machines, given that customers viewed Atari as a video-game manufacturer and not a serious PC provider. But using its newly obtained captive distribution, Atari graced its computer line with prime shelf space at Federated. And yet, Atari and Federated soon faltered. As the adage goes, *you won't improve buoyancy by strapping together two leaky canoes.*

For a corporate business development effort to succeed, it must be connected to a company's core competency and not try to solve a company's fundamental flaw.

Attempting to move too early into a market can be another source of seriously flawed strategy. When AOL and Time Warner attempted to create the world's first global digital media company, the vision was splendid. The timing was not. Although numerous explanations can be given for what is considered by many to be the worst business combination ever, one prominent reason is a flawed timing strategy. After all, in 2000 broadband capacity was still in its infancy in the United States.

Overpayment

Just as numerous factors can lead to flawed M&A strategy, overpayment can spring from many sources. Overestimating synergy is one of most common overpayment drivers.

Recall that the origin of the word *synergy* in M&A activity arises from Fred Weston's encounter with Irish coffee on a restaurant drink menu. So perhaps it's not surprising that corporate executives may appear somewhat inebriated in asserting the amount of synergy (particularly revenue synergy) that will arise from transactions. It's no wonder that Wall Street believes and values cost synergies much more than revenue synergies as vehicles for wealth creation. Cost synergies are viewed to be much more in control of an acquirer. Revenue synergies can be quite fanciful.

Nevertheless, a company can build a reputation for knowing how to generate revenue synergies. Indeed, very few Google deals can be described as driven by cost-reduction synergies. Google's ability to use M&A for *semi-organic growth* derives from continuous organizational learning relating to how to create revenue synergy that blends existing with newly acquired resources.

Associated with overestimating synergy is a phenomenon known as the *winner's curse*.[23] Simply stated, the winner's curse implies that in an auction the winner tends to overpay.

Consider the experiment I've run numerous times in an executive program at UCLA. It's called the pitcher experiment. Put a collection of currency into a water pitcher, with dollar bills, some fives, some tens, and perhaps a twenty-dollar bill visible. Then ask the participants to bid on the contents. The winning bidder will pay the amount bid and will receive, in turn, the contents of the pitcher. Only once in the many times I've run this experiment has the winning bidder benefited. All other bidders fell trap to the winner's curse, paying more for the contents of the pitcher than the value obtained.

Certainly, the winner's curse is one reason when Warren Buffett described his acquisition criteria this way in Berkshire Hathaway's annual report: "We don't participate in auctions."

Integration Pace and Style

As previously mentioned, the sooner enhanced cash flows from deal cost or revenue synergies are realized, the larger will be their present value. For some deals, this is absolutely appropriate. Furthermore, rapid integration can provide organizational clarity and minimize the uncertainty felt by company stakeholders, from employee to customer. However, for other deals, rapid absorption of the target into the mother ship will be the catalyst for the departure or suboptimal performance of key human assets acquired in the transaction.

Given the need for tight controls, especially in its defense contacting businesses, as a practice Honeywell Aerospace quickly and efficiently absorbed the people, assets, and systems of the companies it acquired into the corporate parent. But when it discovered a superb center of excellence somewhat hidden in one of its acquisitions, Honeywell realized that it would be a mistake to dismantle the creative talent and distinctive technology the unit possessed. Rightly so, the company not only preserved the unit, but worked hard to nurture and spread its capabilities throughout the entire company.

Similarly, it would have been completely counterproductive for Walt Disney to absorb Pixar into existing Disney animation operations. Far better to let the Pixar talent, technology, and culture permeate Disney, thereby creating a new Disney animation operation in a rich amalgamation with Pixar being the primary element.

Style of integration involves identifying the key dimensions of strategy that frame how the integration should proceed. For example, we've highlighted three such styles in this section—absorption, preservation, and amalgamation. These styles and others will be more fully illustrated in Chapter 12.

Pace of integration involves designing the timing at which the execution of a given style should take place and when (if necessary) that style should modified. Pace also includes the realization that the target's talent, technology, and distinct business functions may need to be integrated using different clocks.

Semi-organic growth at its core involves a highly stylistic blend of existing internal capabilities and acquired external resources. Such growth requires artistically crafted integration design and implementation to succeed.

Semi-Organic Growth: Beginnings

Despite research findings that show M&A does not build value for most companies, Google (certainly one of the most successful companies over the past 10 years) is among the most active deal makers.

Has Google succeeded, despite its torrid M&A activity? Are Google's leaders merely engaging in Montessori-like experimentation within a company that has mounds of cash to play around with? Or are most Google transactions driven by strategic design that indeed adds value, perhaps even when a significant premium is paid for a target?

Numerous studies argue that in the high-tech arena, deal making is essential, and in order to succeed, a company must view corporate business development as fundamental as product development, marketing, or any other aspect of operations.[24] The planks of this argument go like this:

- The pace of change in tech is furious, implying that assets must be managed aggressively or even destructively.
- High-tech markets are often winner-take-all, with network effects that can create dominant positions lasting a decade or longer. (Consider Microsoft in office software, Google in search, Apple in consumer

electronics.) In spite of this, a company must move decisively to retain that position, and transactions take less time to bring needed talent or technology in-house. Google, for example, has made at least 10 acquisitions specifically related to improving its search technology. Microsoft has made numerous acquisitions in building the core of its Office suite, including Forethought, a $14 million deal that brought PowerPoint into the company.

- Deal making is a necessity as important as R&D. Certainly the risk of failure is pervasive in both activities, but such risk should never be allowed to undermine what is required for a technology enterprise to progress.
- A high volume of transactions can build M&A know-how into an organization's DNA. The busiest surgeons are likely to be among the best. Likewise, subtle M&A knowledge accumulates over time in areas such as target identification, valuation, due diligence, and integration, thereby increasing the odds of deal success.

If a company is fortunate and hits a home run in one of its early deals, M&A imprinting can take place. Let's examine how this happened with Google.

An Imprint

In April 2003, Google purchased Applied Semantics for $41.5 million in cash plus stock and stock options valued at $60.9 million. This acquisition took place before Google went public in 2004. Applied Semantics' 45-person organization and its core technology (AdSense) is one of the best acquisitions in Google's history. AdSense technology positions text ads all over the Internet by semantically scanning the contents of a page and displaying relevant ads.

Over the next 10 years, AdSense grew to contribute over 25 percent of Google's advertising revenue, some $13 billion. As the technology evolved, the Applied Semantics team, working with other Google engineers and related Google technology, was instrumental in helping AdSense become a cornerstone of Google's paid advertising platform. (AdSense growth rates started to slow in 2013, but the technology still remained central to Google advertising offerings.)

The infographic in Figure 1.1 is the first of many such visuals we'll use to display deal information. Companies are represented by sector icons, with Google represented by a search sector icon and Applied Semantics by an advertising sector icon. Although this representation is quite simple, we'll see how more complex infographics can provide insight into meaningful patterns that reflect past and potential future business development activity.

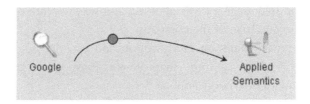

FIGURE 1.1 Google acquires Applied Semantics

In acquiring Applied Semantics, Google obtained key assets including patents, technology, and people that greatly contributed to the revenue acceleration of one of its key product offerings. But perhaps even more importantly, we'll next examine how this deal imprinted on Google a way of thinking about M&A activity that persists to this day.

Watch the Video

www.wiley.com/go/semiorganicgrowth
   To view videos relating to the content of this chapter, refer (1) *Introductory Video: Semi-Organic Growth and Corporate Business Development;* and (2) *When Not To Do an Acquisition. Apple and Digital Music,* which accompany this book as a supplemental resource.

Notes

1. See Stinchcombe (1965).
2. Boeker (1989).
3. Milanov and Fernhaber (2009).
4. See, for example, Matt Lynley, "Google's M&A Boss: with Larry Page in Charge, Only a Third of Our Acquisitions Are Busts," *Business Insider* (March 6, 2012).
5. Bruner (2004), "Corporate Development as a Strategic Capability: The Approach of GE Power Systems," Chapter 37. This chapter provides an excellent case study of a systematic approach to M&A.
6. Chuck Philips, "Apple Reportedly in Talks to Buy Universal Music," *Los Angeles Times* (April 11, 2013). More likely than not, Steve Jobs feigned

acquisition interest in Universal Music and was not interested in completing the purchase of the company.

7. For additional details on Fred Weston and synergy, see my posting on *M&A Professor* at http://maprofessor.blogspot.com/2009/07/j-fred-weston-origin-of-synergy.html.

8. For a summary of research related to M&A success, see Bauer, Florian, and Matzler (2014).

9. Bruner (2004), p. 63.

10. See Bauer and Matzler (2014) for a discussion of the major threads of M&A performance research.

11. Akbulut and Matsusaka (2010).

12. Netter, Stegemoller, and Wintoki (2011).

13. "Global Financial Advisory Mergers & Acquisitions Rankings H1 2013," *Bloomberg* (July 2, 2013).

14. Vipal Monga, "Why Are Takeover Prices Plummeting?" *Wall Street Journal* (November 26, 2013).

15. See, for example, Netter, et al. (2011).

16. Martynova and Renneborg (2008).

17. See, for example, Fuller, Netter, and Stegemoller (2002).

18. Frick and Torres (2002).

19. Fuller, Netter, and Stegemoller (2002).

20. Akbulut (2013).

21. Herd and McManis (2012).

22. Rajendra S. Sisodia, "A Goofy Deal," *Wall Street Journal* (August 4, 1995).

23. Thaler (1988).

24. Frick and Torres (2002).

CHAPTER 2

Imprinting Semi-Organic Growth

A fter Gil Elbaz graduated from Caltech in 1991, he took on data engineering roles for companies that included IBM, Sybase, and Silicon Graphics. After becoming convinced that data science was his future, in 1997 Gil and colleague Adam Weissman founded the company that later became Applied Semantics (ASI) in a Hollywood Hills, California, home.

Elbaz and Weissman initially were interested in developing a search engine that would focus on concepts rather than keywords.[1] With support from friends and family, the duo formed Oingo. They also filed for a patent on semantic search, one of several patents that would later prove valuable.

A little after Oingo was founded, Google was being launched in Susan Wojcicki's Menlo Park garage. Wojcicki had graduated from UCLA Anderson in 1998, purchased the Menlo Park home, and to help cover the mortgage rented her garage to Stanford students Larry Page and Sergey Brin. Susan would not only play an important role in the early history of Google, but also become a driving force in Google's expansion of advertising beyond search pages. And it's as a result of this expansion effort that Google and ASI would connect.

After exploring semantic-based search for a while and concluding that people preferred searching on Google, Elbaz and Weissman shifted gears to focus their technology on Internet advertising. They filed for another patent, this one relating to a concept-based advertising system. In May 2001, the company name was changed from Oingo to Applied Semantics in order to "better reflect Oingo's altered business model."

ASI flushed out what it called CIRCA technology (Conceptual Information Retrieval and Communication Architecture) in a series of white papers. The technology was described as understanding, organizing, and extracting "knowledge from websites and information repositories in a way that mimics human thought."

Applied Semantics deployed its technology in a system known as AdSense, in that companies would be paid "cents" for clicks resulting from ads placed on their webpages based on "sensed-base" analysis performed by AdSense.[2]

Inside Google, Susan Wojcicki was championing the notion that Google should expand beyond search-based advertising using a strategy that was very similar to what Applied Semantics was doing. Wojcicki and others believed that the entire Web could become an advertising canvas for Google. Websites would be able to develop content and then leave it to Google to determine the best ads for the sites.

But Applied Semantics and its patents appeared to stand in the way of this Google initiative.

Applied Semantics Deal

In 2003, timing was good to explore a potential deal between Google and Applied Semantics. ASI's exclusive deal with Overture (another pay-for-placement search service) was expiring. Google was developing its own technology, code-named Phil, which matched keywords to webpages, and was eager to start placing ads on content pages all over the Internet.

After a lukewarm meeting with Overture to establish a more strategic relationship, Applied Semantics presented its business opportunity to Google in Mountain View. Although Gil Elbaz knew Sergey Brin, Gil coyly had waited for an invitation to pitch Applied Semantics to Google.

Brin was very enthusiastic about the deal, so much so that in the meeting he listened to what Applied Semantics described as a billion-dollar opportunity, and on the spot passionately doubled it to a *two-billion-dollar opportunity*.[3]

On April 23, 2003, Google announced its acquisition of Applied Semantics. Brin stated in a posting: "Applied Semantics is a proven innovator in semantic text processing and online advertising. This acquisition will enable Google to create new technologies that make online advertising more useful to users, publishers, and advertisers alike."

According to a Google S-1 filed later, the consideration for the Applied Semantics acquisition consisted of $102.4 million, including $41.5 million in cash plus stock and stock options valued at $60.9 million; $84.2 million of the transaction was allocated to goodwill. At the time, it was Google's largest acquisition.

Applied Semantics' investors wanted to cash out, not eager to receive the stock of some privately held, high-risk technology venture. Gil Elbaz and his associates saw the pieces of the consideration very differently. Gil viewed himself as a stock picker and grasped Google's enormous potential. Since Google was valued at the time at approximately $6 billion, the stock and stock option consideration in the transaction reflected about 1 percent of Google's value. Elbaz didn't hesitate to take his consideration in stock.

In 2014, 1 percent of Google would translate into billions of dollars in market value. And the $2 billion revenue opportunity that Brin enthusiastically proclaimed was generating well over $10 billion on an annual basis. Some two million content publishers were using AdSense, and Google was proud to announce that it was sending about 100,000 checks per month to its AdSense advertising partners.

AdSense Is Born

Applied Semantics' 45-person team was now part of Google, but would not move from its location in its Santa Monica, California. Google would adopt Applied Semantics' catchy name for its new advertising offering. The Google product would become AdSense, and over the years that followed, engineers from Google and the former-ASI would work together to take the product through many revisions refining the technology. AdSense software would be scanning millions of webpages for meaning. After parsing content, it could tell businesses what kind of ads would work well on a particular page.

Although no one used the term at the time, an *acqui-hire* had taken place, and Google's use of *semi-organic growth* was about to fan the flames of revenue growth.

As we noted in the Chapter 1, acqui-hiring involves the process of acquiring a company to recruit its talent, with or without being interested in the target's technology, products and services. In the case of ASI, Google was interested in both talent and technology.

Let's examine the value that came with the Applied Semantics acquisition:

- *People*. Google added top-quality engineering and managerial talent that had been working for years on context-sensitive ad placement on the Web.
- *Technology*. ASI had launched AdSense in 2002, using its CIRCA technology to extract core concepts that occur on webpages.
- *Intellectual property*. ASI had obtained patents related to CIRCA. If Google had launched its own technology to do context-sensitive advertising, it potentially faced serious IP roadblocks.
- *Customer base/sales*. ASI was a profitable company with a significant customer base at the time of the acquisition.
- *Regional beachhead*. The Santa Monica office of ASI not only become Google's offices in the Los Angeles area. It also became a base from

which Google continued to recruit talent as the company expanded its physical presence in the region.

Although there has been some debate over whether Google's own technology (Phil) or ASI's AdSense was dominant as the new AdSense progressed, such debate should not be the focal issue. As AdSense moved through updates and revisions, technologies from both companies were blended, and engineers from the old Google and the new Google collaborated.[4]

As Hunter Walk, a former Google manager wrote: "Applied Semantics—in both team and technology—helped accelerate the AdSense product, one which today delivers billions of dollars in revenue to Google."[5]

Putting this all together, Google amalgamated ASI's people, technology, and other assets with its own and achieved a massive revenue acceleration in context-based advertising. Google had experienced the majesty of *semi-organic growth*.

What Distinguishes Semi-Organic Growth

In business, *organic growth* has little to do with producing organic fruit or vegetables. Organic growth comes from nurturing a company's existing businesses from within or internally developing new business lines.

For example, an organization can choose to develop its in-house sales and marketing competencies, to build inventory to enhance sales, to internally innovate new products or services through R&D efforts, or any of a number of other options that cause growth to come from within. For the first decade of the twenty-first century, Apple was a prime example of what was essentially organic growth, as it developed iPods, iPhones, and iPads without conducting major acquisition activity.

Inorganic growth occurs when a company acquires another company and starts selling the target's products or services in order to enhance its own growth. This type of growth comes from offerings that were essentially developed outside of the acquirer.

Investors often find it useful to differentiate between organic sales growth from inorganic in attempting to analyze how much of a company's growth is sustainable.

Despite makings scores of acquisitions, until December 2012 Google only provided one revenue line in its annual income statement. It did not attempt to distinguish between organic and inorganic growth. Only after the acquisition of Motorola Mobility did a second revenue line item (of some $4 billion) appear in its income statement.

But as we've already seen, Google did enjoy substantial revenue growth as a result of the blending the people and technology of the ASI acquisition (and many other deals) with preexisting Google resources.

In other words, much of Google's growth was *semi-organic*. Semi-organic growth is generated when revenue results from products or services that emerge when acquired technology-related assets attach to a company's existing capabilities in a complementary manner. The ASI acquisition is a clear illustration of semi-organic growth.

Semi-Organic Complementarity

Complementarity is key in stimulating semi-organic growth. Consider the research findings of Bauer and Matzler: "Despite the dominant logic that strategic similarity fosters value creation, there are fundamental arguments that complementary differences are more crucial for M&A success."[6] The authors go on to argue that while similarity is often important in obtaining efficiency-based synergies (such as scale or scope), complementarity can generate efficiency synergies *as well as* value created from differences that are mutually supportive (*enhancement-based synergies*).

Complementary acquisitions that yield *economies of fitness* are an essential element of semi-organic growth.

Sometimes an acquisition brings multiple opportunities for complementary of fit. Consider Google's acquisition of DeepMind in 2014. DeepMind is an artificial intelligence company that builds learning algorithms for a wide range of applications that include recommendation systems for e-commerce. The company was founded by neuroscientist Demis Hassabis (master gamer), Jaan Tallin (Skype and Kazaa developer), and Shane Legg (researcher).

The infographic in Figure 2.1 shows DeepMind placed in the context of Google's cluster of robotics acquisitions made one year earlier in 2013. While it was not entirely clear what Google would do with DeepMind's talent and technology, one area of potential complementarity was robotics.

The field of artificial intelligence (AI) has undergone several cycles of boom and bust since AI was christened and sent out the door with research momentum at The Dartmouth Conference of 1958 organized by Marvin Minsky and others. Periods of buoyant optimism for the technology have given way to AI winters.

But in 2014, an AI spring had returned. Google's purchase of DeepMind for estimates that ranged from $400 million to $625 million reflected a newfound confidence in what AI could accomplish in multiple business sectors of interest to Google.

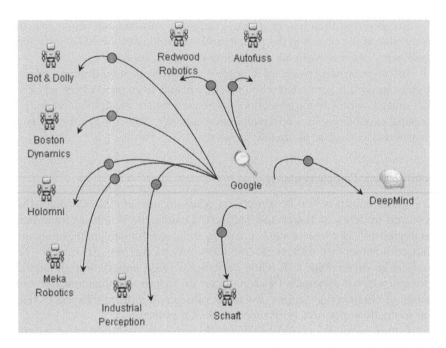

FIGURE 2.1 DeepMind and Robotics Acquisitions

Even before the DeepMind purchase, Google was in full experimentation mode with AI. In fact, DeepMind was reportedly competing with Google for talent in the field. In 2012, Google hired futurist Ray Kurzweil as a director of engineering to work on machine learning and language processing.

Furthermore, Google's acqui-hiring of DeepMind would help it compete against other players focusing on deep learning. Facebook had recruited Yann LeCunn (former NYU professor) to head its artificial intelligence lab. According to reports, Google competed against Facebook for DeepMind.[7] IBM was investing $1 billion in its Watson supercomputer division working on deep learning. And Yahoo had made its own acqui-hire of the LookFlow team to lead its deep learning initiative.

It was thought that DeepMind's technology would first be used to improve Google's core search systems, removing unwanted noise in results. Kurzweil had stated that he intended to develop a search engine so advanced that it would become a "cybernetic friend."

However, in addition to this search complementarity, consider potential add-on value that DeepMind could add the Google's nascent robotics initiative.

In 2013, Google's acquisition of eight robotics companies had garnered as much attention as Amazon's futuristic plan for package delivery via drones. Speculation was abounding regarding Google's goals for its robot menagerie—including the next generation of manufacturing outsourcing, humanoid elder care assistants, and driverless vehicles. Comedian Stephen Colbert quipped that Google intended to enslave humanity, and in response Colbert intended to breed an Ewok army to counter the forthcoming invasion.

An *acquisitions cluster* involves a series of company purchases in a highly related sector. This was not the first time Google has bunched deals in a specific sector, but this concentration of eight clustered acquisitions in such a short time was unprecedented.

Each of Google's acquisitions shown in Figure 2.1 had distinctive attributes. For example, Industrial Perception focuses on robotic "sight," Boston Dynamics emphasizes mobility, and Meta stresses humanoid features. But all companies fit cleanly in the robotic sector.

One could postulate potential complementarities between this robotics cluster and DeepMind talent and technology that would turn science fiction into reality. Imagine robots continuously improving their performance by observing humans or other mentor robots. Enter a new labor force for both blue-collar jobs as well as knowledge worker positions. Under such a scenario, the distinction between human and machine would come under new challenge.

Google could achieve M&A complementarity via DeepMind for a significant number of its existing or emerging products and services. In this sense, there is *combinatorial complementarity*. Search and robotics are only two possible areas where blending might occur. Value could be realized from achieving mutually supportive, enhancement-based synergies created not from the similarity of the targets but from the differences.

Semi-organic growth could be taken to new heights within Google in the decades ahead. But achieving such growth would not be without organizational challenges.

A Semi-Organic Deal Challenge

Putting aside for the moment the significant technology risk that can be associated with semi-organic growth, other major challenges come into play when executing this form of corporate development strategy. *Deal integration* looms large among these challenges.

When I began my study of Google's M&A activity, I hoped to find a company that had discovered and flawlessly implemented the illusive holy grail of acquisition strategy and tactics. However, as discussed in Chapter 1, highly successful corporate business development involves performing, to use a swimming analogy, a very difficult dive off of the high board. Strategy, valuation, integration, and deal structure must harmoniously come together.

Without a doubt, Google has achieved more than its fair share of M&A success. The company has beaten the averages. Nevertheless, Google's semi-organic growth has also seen major hiccups. We'll explore these stumbles in more detail in Chapter 8. For now, let's return to Applied Semantics, admittedly a semi-organic masterpiece, but not without some aggravating flaws.

The Google/Applied Semantics integration did not go totally smoothly, at least from the point of view of ASI. Gil Elbaz felt that his ASI management team had been running on all cylinders, and this team would be broken up. In 2003, Google was essentially organized along functional lines and felt that acquisitions should fit neatly into this structure. So, for example, Gil would report to the vice president of engineering in Mountain View. Similarly, finance, marketing, and other functional areas reported to their counterparts in Mountain View. The ASI team would no longer be able to operate as an integrated unit.

The ASI team would essentially be absorbed. Google's rationale for making this move was understandable. After all, the webpage content analysis and corresponding ad placement technologies of the two companies had to be tightly coupled. But knowing when to absorb as opposed to amalgamate is a vital decision in M&A integration, and Google may have moved too quickly into the absorption mode. While maintaining strategic control of ASI, some additional time to garner the benefits of allowing ASI to operate as a holistic team might have been better than tightly controlling operational functions too early on in the integration process.

Google noticed that the ASI integration did not go as well as hoped, and the company took action to try to improve post-acquisition success. In 2005, Google asked Brad Stein, formerly ASI's CFO, to assume a lead role in developing and executing more effective methods for integrating future acquisitions. Stein would remain in this role until 2011.

As we'll see in Chapter 12, Google would handle the acquisition of companies such as Android and YouTube very differently than ASI. The company learned how to establish, modify (if necessary), and monitor an array of integration approaches, as well as better establish success metrics essential for determining M&A success.

Gil Elbaz would leave Google in 2007 and a year later found his second major venture, Factual, which was developing technology that enabled organizations to share and mash open data. Gil was determined to build a company not only with great engineers but also with a culture that did its best to align personal motivations with organizational mission. Although Gil looked on his Google years with fondness, he also intended to build a company with more "emotional intelligence" than what he had experienced.

Deeper Look at Tech Complementarity

In spite of Google/ASI integration glitches that may have occurred, as we've stressed, the deal should be regarded as among the best in Google's history. After all, this acquisition was favorably positioned when evaluated by two important factors that determine success or failure in technology M&A transactions. These factors extend our earlier discussion of deal complementarity.

As described by Sears and Hoetker,[8] two critical complementary constructs are: (1) *target overlap*, the proportion of the target's knowledge base that the acquirer already possesses; and (2) *absorptive capacity*, the ability of the acquirer to recognize and recombine possibilities involving the target's knowledge base.

When target overlap is low, a significant proportion of the target's knowledge will be new to the acquirer, and there will be major opportunities for novel amalgamations of the target's technology with that of the acquirer. However, unless the acquirer has absorptive capacity (to appreciate and utilize the target's technology), it will not likely achieve these novel amalgamations. The technological resources of the target are more likely to be wasted.

When target overlap is high, the acquirer is likely to have necessary absorptive capacity, but there may be very limited creative combinations available, since much of the target's knowledge is already possessed by the acquirer. There will be fewer possibilities to create novel products and services.

Although absorptive capacity is related to deal integration capability, the two concepts should be distinguished. Absorptive capacity relates more to the ability of an organization to comprehend how the target's technology could be accommodated and utilized within the context of the acquirer's offerings. Integration capability relates more to the actual process of combining the sociotechnical systems of the target with the acquirer.

Now let's revisit the Google/Applied Semantics deal. Google unquestionably had considerable absorption capacity for ASI's AdSense initiative. Indeed, Google senior management, including Sergey Brin and Susan Wojcicki, were anxious to extend the company's advertising in the direction of contextual searches across the entire Web. In fact, Google had been working on its own system to do so.

Furthermore, we've seen that although there was technology overlap between the two companies, it was not so large that creative combinations would be overly challenging. Interestingly, there is evidence that a *curvilinear relationship* exists between the knowledge bases of acquirer/ target and innovative performances.[9] This implies that companies should target acquisitions that are neither too unrelated nor too similar in terms of their technology bases. The middle ground of knowledge-relatedness seems to be most promising.

Indeed, according to Elbaz, numerous iterative revisions of AdSense, starting with existing Phil and CIRCA technologies, were blended as standing and "acquired." Google engineers creatively advanced the offering by utilizing the overlapping technology bases of the companies.

Chaos Lurking beyond the Semi-Organic?

Much has been written about Google's broad diversification initiatives, with some advancing the notion that investment activity at the company may be too widely scattered—so-called moonshot initiatives include driverless cars, high-altitude balloons (Project Loon), jet-sized drones, and a mysterious Calico venture hoping to extend human life. And that's only a starter list.

Is Google taking in much more than it can chew? Has the company far exceeded its absorption capacity in entering too many areas that are too far afield from its search/advertising core? Is Google a chaotic laboratory, with senior management running from flower-to-flower like a hyper-kinetic butterfly?

Marisa Mayer, former Google executive and later CEO of Yahoo, stated that Google could not be understood unless one realized that Larry Page and Sergei Brin are both Montessori children.[10] Montessori, of course, refers to educational philosophy developed by Maria Montessori, an Italian physician and educator, who in the early 1900s established schools emphasizing independence and a deep respect for a child's internal curiosity and natural *rhythm of learning.*

As we'll see throughout this book, many Google acquisitions have had clear linkages to its roots as an ad-tech and search company. But starting in 2013 and 2014, an increasing number of deals were signaling that the Montessori lads were spending more of their time in new areas of the "classroom."

Google was attempting to become a media, Internet, and technology-centric conglomerate playing across industries that could range from automotive to health care to aerospace. And the entrée into many of these markets was accompanied with significant M&A activity.

Company chaos or unprecedented long-range diversification success— what would it be?

We've seen the central role that absorptive capacity plays in determining acquisition success. The truth is that some companies have very limited capacity to "recognize the value of new information, assimilate it, and apply it to commercial ends."[11] Others, by their very nature, are super-sponges, able to acquire, absorb, and achieve success in widely diverse industries.

Consider Berkshire Hathaway. Berkshire employs a holding company structure, having a mere couple of dozen employees at its Omaha headquarters. The company is highly dependent on empowered leaders running its diverse portfolio of companies. Buffett's uncanny capability to select, support, and motivate the management of these companies has led to outstanding financial performance over a long period of time. Given this core competency, Berkshire has shown huge absorption capacity, even though it doesn't actually *absorb* the target, but instead preserves (and enriches) the operating entities it acquires.

Could it be that Google's real core competency should be characterized as a Montessori-like curiosity and experimentation that is able to be fueled by fortuitous success in ad-tech? If so, this competency could provide another example of a company with an enormous capacity for absorption.

Nevertheless, Google must demonstrate the ability to turn at least some of its afield experimentation into vibrant commercial success. Only then can a final determination be made if what appears to be buckshot-investment chaos is, in fact, the genesis of breathtaking innovation in industries other than ad-tech.

If none of these moonshots is triumphant, then look for Google investors to start acting like many Apple investors in 2013. Google will be under intense pressure to return capital to shareholders. The playground of diversification-based M&A activity will start to close down.

Semi-Organic Acceleration

Moonshots aside, let's return to the safety and sensibility of more focused semi-organic growth and summarize what the Applied Semantics acquisition set in motion for Google.

By acqui-hiring the talent and technology of ASI, Google set in motion a dominant pattern of transactions that persists in the company to this day. Google had made other acqui-hires before the ASI deal.

For example, in February 2003, months before the ASI acquisition, Google had acquired Pyra Labs, the company that had developed Blogger, a Web service that helped fuel the growth of weblogs, or blogs. Over 10 years later, Blogger continued to exist as a free blog publishing platform for sharing text, photos, and video. And, of course, Blogger content also provided webpages that could contain advertising placed by Google.

Immediately after the acquisition, Evan Williams, Pyra's CEO, and six staff members were assigned to an existing Google engineering team, and semi-organic growth began. This integration was simple and direct. Although acquisitions such as Pyra certainly helped Google understand what the M&A process involved, these early deals were not transformative. The imprinting of semi-organic growth on Google would take more than a small "bolt-on" deal.

The acquisition of Applied Semantics and its multibillion potential for revenue synergy would be the pattern setter. ASI was the imprint for dozens and dozens of deals to follow that would propel Google's growth by combining the company's existing capabilities with those of an outside target.

The second-stage rockets of semi-organic growth would now be firing. And the volume and pace of these type of deals undertaken by Google would be unprecedented.

Watch the Video

www.wiley.com/go/semiorganicgrowth

To view a video on the concept of semi-organic growth described in this chapter, refer to *What's Distinctive about Semi-Organic Growth?* which accompanies this book as a supplemental resource.

Notes

1. See Bill Slawski, "Search Based on Concepts: Applied Semantics and Google," SEO by the Sea (March 30, 2010), for a discussion of the early history of Applied Semantics.
2. Steven Levy (2011) does an excellent job in describing the early relationship between Google and Applied Semantics in his book *In the Plex*. See pp. 103–104.
3. Levy (2011), p. 103.
4. For example, according to a February 28, 2014, interview the author conducted with Gil Elbaz, CIRCA technology allowed an advertiser to become more involved in selecting specific keywords that matched the content of websites.
5. See http://www.linkedin.com/today/post/article/20130313034305-7298 -early-employees-eva-ho-applied-semantics.

6. Bauer and Matzler (2014).
7. See, for example, https://www.theinformation.com/google-beat -facebook-for-deepmind-creates-ethics-board.
8. Sears and Hoetker (2014).
9. This "Goldilocks" relationship between technology overlap and innovative performance in M&A activity is described by Cloodt et al. (2006).
10. Levy (2011), p 121.
11. This description of absorptive capacity was first used by Cohen and Levinthal (1990), "Absorptive Capacity: A New Perspective on Learning and Innovation," *Administrative Science Quarterly* 35 (1): 128–152.

CHAPTER 3

Google versus Apple: M&A Paths Diverge, then Converge

Between the years 2001 and 2012, Google and Apple had strikingly different appetites for M&A transactions. The fact that these two superstar technology companies had vastly different patterns of acquisition activity is testimony to the reality that there's more than one corporate development road to value-building victory.

We've earlier indicted the frenetic acquisition pace that Google was undertaking during this period, in no small part triggered by the imprinting of the highly successful Applied Semantics deal. On the other hand, for most of this time the leadership of Apple seemed to be declaring that "real men don't do M&A." Apple was behaving as if it could do most the important innovation in-house and had little need to buy other company's technology and talent.

Google and Apple differed not only in the *number* of acquisitions, but also in the *rationales* for the deals that each company was doing. Overall, Apple was buying a relatively small number of companies to add specific software or hardware components to existing core products and services. In some of its deals, Google was doing likewise. But Google was also being much more expansive in its thinking as to how M&A activity could accelerate growth opportunities in a rapidly expanding number of markets.

Furthermore, after Google purchased Android in 2005, over time it became clearer that Google and Apple were destined to be competitors. This competition would lead a series of M&A *cascades*, whereby the two companies started to engage in blow-for-blow M&A combat. An acquisition by one company in a specific market segment would trigger a counter-acquisition by the other.

Starting around 2012 Apple would dramatically step up its deal pace. Had Apple decided to become more Google-like in elevating the role of

M&A in its corporate development strategy? Or were there other factors driving Apple's conversion to serial acquirer?

Let's begin our comparison of the M&A activity of these two companies by providing historical context.

Historical Perspective in M&A Activity

Table 3.1 provides data on the number of documented M&A transactions by Google and Apple during the years 2001 through 2013 as reported by Capital IQ. Neither Google nor Apple discloses all acquisitions, and targets do not always announce that they've been acquired. Third parties attempt to play "detective" and discover additional deals, but not all are discovered. Consequently, Capital IQ does not document all deals undertaken by the two companies. Nevertheless, the number of transactions shown in Table 3.1 can serve as a proxy for M&A activity.

Note that Google dominates Apple in documented M&A transactions for every one of the years shown in the table. In some years (such as 2010 and 2011), the disparity is strikingly large. However, in 2013 there is a clear indication that Apple was beginning to ramp up its acquisition volume.

TABLE 3.1 Documented M&A Transactions for Apple and Google (2001–2013)

Year	Apple	Google
2001	2	1
2002	2	0
2003	0	4
2004	0	5
2005	1	6
2006	2	9
2007	0	14
2008	1	3
2009	1	7
2010	4	28
2011	1	32
2012	3	14
2013	10	20
Totals	27	143

Source: Capital IQ, real estate transactions not included

Google M&A Infographic for 2010

Let's compare two M&A infographics to delve more deeply into a slice of this data. Figure 3.1 depicts a significant number of the acquisitions made by Google in 2010.

The number and range of these deals is breathtaking. Starting at the top and working around clockwise, companies with icons representing the following sectors are depicted:

- Media applications
- Audio, video, and graphics technologies
- Cloud, Web infrastructure
- Financial service apps
- Hardware components
- Entertainment software
- Internet retail
- Social media
- Advertising
- Travel applications
- Systems software
- Mobile apps
- Semiconductors
- Office application software
- Search
- Photography
- Mapping

Let's examine the 2010 deals in several of these sectors in order to provide some flavor for the types of acquisitions Google was making.

Audio, video and graphics technologies: Google acquired Phonetic Arts, comprised of researchers and engineers working on speech synthesis, including technology that generated natural computer speech from small samples of recorded voice. The company's technology converted lines of recorded dialogue into a speech library that could then piece together sounds to generate new sentences that sounded realistic. In making the deal, Google said Phonetic's technology could help it move closer toward a *Star Trek* future.

Entertainment software: Google purchased social games start-up SocialDeck Inc., a gaming company that had developed titles for Facebook and Apple's iPhone. Google was also reportedly in discussions with other developers to offer their games on its Google+ service. (Later on, Google moved its game services to Google Play.)

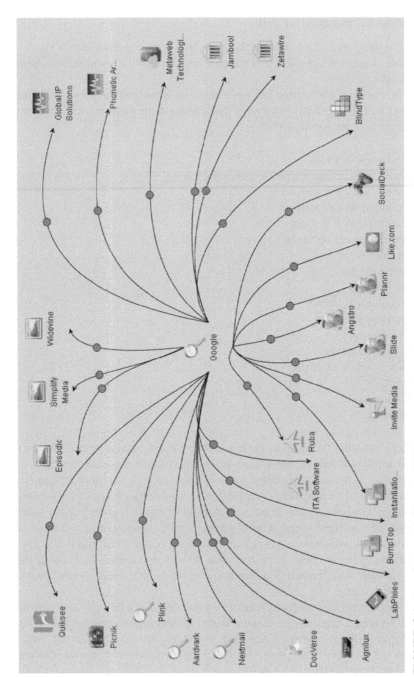

FIGURE 3.1 Google's acquisitions in 2010

Financial service applications: Google acquired Jambool Inc. in a deal reportedly valued at $70 million. Jambool offered a payment API that enabled micropayments in an online game or social network application. The company's currency (Social Gold) API allowed developers to establish a virtual currency for real commerce. Later, Social Gold was incorporated into Google's payment products and used in purchases on Android Market.

Travel applications: Google purchased ITA Software, Inc. for $676 million in cash. ITA offered Internet-based software to the airline industry. Google intended to develop search tools to help users find travel information more easily on the Web, including making it easier for travelers to comparison shop for flights and airfares. In order to receive antitrust clearance on its acquisition of ITA, conditions were imposed by the Department of Justice limiting how Google could use the company's technology. These conditions, which were to last until 2016, would require Google to license the software to other companies, to develop ITA products and offer them to competitors, and to erect a firewall so it cannot see sensitive information from competitors.

Advertising: Google acquired Invite Media, a company that developed and operated a media-buying platform which utilizes optimization technology for the display marketplace. Invite's demand-side platform was designed to facilitate navigation of high-volume display advertising exchanges for buyers. Initially, Invite would be maintained as a separate unit, but eventually Invite Media would be integrated with Google's DoubleClick for Advertisers. (Some two years after Google closed the deal, Nat Turner and Zach Weinberg, Invite co-founders, would leave Google to start a health-care company. Turner stated that ad tech was never his passion and that what truly motivated him was health care. We'll explore the afterlife of a number of *Google M&A Alumni*—entrepreneurs who sold their companies to Google and then moved on—in Chapter 13.)

Semiconductors: Google acquired Agnilux, a stealth chip design company founded by former employees of PA Semiconductor. PA was acquired by Apple to build custom chips for iPod, iPhone, and other mobile devices. Google intended to leverage Agnilux's technology to efficiently utilize Google platforms such as its Chrome and Android operating systems with devices such as tablets.

Office application software: Google acquired DocVerse, an online document and collaboration tool. Google would leverage DocVerse's technology to improve interoperations between Microsoft Office products and Google Apps, making it easier for Microsoft users to transition to cloud computing on the Google Apps platform.

This sample of Google deals suggests some core takeaways, which identify themes we'll see throughout this book:

- Unlike Apple at the time, Google was making a large number of acquisitions across an extremely broad range of sectors cutting across advertising, Internet services, and technology infrastructure.
- Some targets were initially left alone for a period following the deal close, but over time were absorbed into other Google services. For example, Invite Media was initially preserved, but later on its melding with DoubleClick would prove to be especially important in rounding out an online advertising ecosystem.
- Several transactions (such as Agnilux and DocVerse) involved a response to some of Google's key competitors, such as Apple and Microsoft.
- Although an initial deal rationale could be made for each transaction, Google would often experiment with the acquired technologies. And the technologies might wind up other than where originally envisioned. In addition, some technologies might not fit any product or service and end up being shuttered.
- A number of entrepreneurs that came with the acquisition would leave Google and found other companies, most often not in ad-tech but in sectors that they now felt driven to pursue. Hence, we see the emergence of a class of Google M&A alumni.

Apple M&A Infographic for 2010

Take a look at a comparable infographic (Figure 3.2) for known Apple acquisitions in 2010.

In contrast to the Google M&A activity in 2010, Apple's deal constellations looks comparatively sparse, with only six acquisitions shown. (Six deals are shown as opposed to the four deals listed in Table 3.1, as two additional acquisitions beyond those provided by Capital IQ have been identified.)

Most of Apple's acquisitions are tightly tied to components that enhance the company's consumer electronics products. The following sectors are depicted in clockwise order:

- Audio, video, and graphics technologies
- Semiconductors
- Biometrics
- Mapping and imaging
- Photography
- Mobile advertising

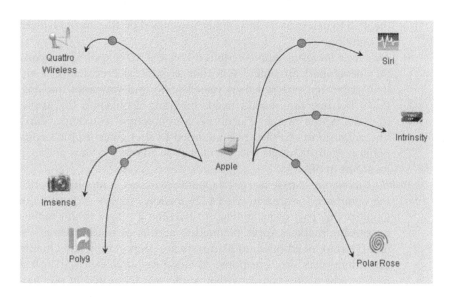

FIGURE 3.2 Apple's acquisitions in 2010

Let's examine several of these deals to explore how most do, in fact, involve adding components or functionality to Apple products.

Audio, video, and graphics technologies: Apple acquired Siri, Inc., a developer of a mobile search and virtual personal assistant that utilized voice recognition technology. Apple's acquisition of Siri was part of its mobile strategy to become more involved in the search market. Additionally, Apple valued Siri's voice recognition technology and wanted to keep it out of Google and its Android platform.

Semiconductors: Apple acquired Intrinsity for an estimated $121 million. Intrinsity technology enhanced mobile processors to improve performance and battery life by making faster processors that used less energy. Intrinsity engineers would join Apple. Formerly, Intrinsity had partnered with PA Semi (an earlier Apple acquisition) to design the A4 chip, which Apple intended to use in the iPad and future iPhones.

Biometrics: Apple acquired Polar Rose AB for an estimated $29 million. Polar Rose specialized in facial recognition technologies. Polar Rose allowed users to search, organize, and share digital media by using computer vision technology. Apple could use the face recognition technologies to enhance the iPhone's image search as well as enable the iPad to detect users and create customized profiles through facial recognition.

Mapping and imaging: Apple acquired Poly9, a 3D mapping company that developed an online GIS tool as well as Free Earth, a virtual globe that enabled map visualization and waypoint tracking. Poly9 became the second major mapping acquisition for Apple. In 2009, Apple bought Placebase, a competitor to Google Maps. The acquisition of Poly9 was intended to strengthen Apple's competition against Google Earth, which allowed users to view and map locations in 3D.

Mobile Advertising: Apple acquired Quattro Wireless, a mobile advertising company, for an estimated $275 million. Apple's acquisition of Quattro was part of its strategy to become a player in the mobile advertising market. Apple planned to add its own advertising system (iAd) to its iPhone and iPad software. Importantly, the Quattro acquisition was also a response to Google's purchase of AdMob, a mobile advertising company that Apple was interested in purchasing. Quattro Wireless competed with AdMob in mobile advertising.

A major subtheme behind this collection of Apple acquisitions stands out. A significant number of the deals were made in direct competitive response to Google. Let's take a more careful look at the Apple/Google deal competition dynamic.

Dyadic Cascading

Starting in 2009 and continuing thereafter, Apple and Google resembled the Coke and Pepsi of technology. Their competitive furor was clearly reflected in the two companies' merger and acquisition activity. From mobile ad systems to mapping, Apple and Google were engaging in blow-by-blow M&A combat.

Some strange antitrust dynamics were resulting from an "AppGoog" M&A competition battle. For example after a six-month investigation, the Federal Trade Commission in May 2010 approved Google's acquisition of AdMob. The commission stated that its fears that Google would dominate the mobile advertising market were allayed by Apple's emergence as a competitor in this space. Google could love its enemy, at least for this moment.

When an M&A by one company triggers a series of transactions by other companies (often competitors) in the same sector, we call this an *M&A cascade*. For example, during the first half of 2014, a flurry of deals

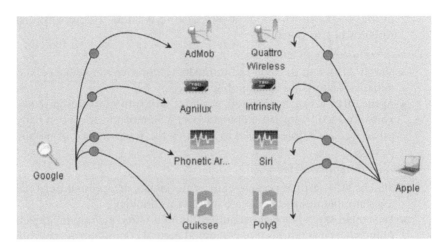

FIGURE 3.3 Apple/Google dyadic M&A cascading in 2010

in the pharmaceutical sector were occurring, often in response to an initial acquisition in the space.

When two companies engage in a series of tit-for-tat M&A deals, we deem this *dyadic M&A cascading.*

Figure 3.3 depicts an infographic of some of the dyadic Apple and Google M&A cascading that occurred during 2009-2010. We've seen some of these acquisitions in our earlier depiction of Apple's and Google's 2010 deals, but now want to portray some of these deals in a side-by-side con-figuration in order to highlight how often dyadic cascading was occurring. Our description of each acquisition will highlight the competitive nature of these transactions.

Let's describe four sectors in which a heated tit-for-tat deal-making showdown seen in Figure 3.3 was happening.

1. *Mobile advertising systems*
   - November 2009—Google announced plans to purchase mobile advertising start-up AdMob for $750 million in stock. AdMob sold ads that appear on websites geared for smartphones. The company was a first-mover in developing technology to deliver ads on Apple's iPhone, as well as on devices that used Google's Android mobile operating system.
   - January 2010—Apple acquired Quattro Wireless, a mobile advertis-ing company. Importantly, the Quattro acquisition was viewed as a

dyadic response to Google's purchase of AdMob, a company that Apple was also pursuing.

2. *Semiconductor efficiency*

- March 2010—Apple acquired Intrinsity to improve performance and enhance battery life in its mobile devices.
- April 2010—Google acquired Agnilux, a stealth chip design company founded by former employees of PA Semiconductor, a company purchased by Apple in 2008 to improve the performance of mobile devices.

3. *Speech recognition/synthesis*

- March 2010—Apple acquires Siri, a developer of a virtual personal assistant that utilized voice recognition technology.
- December 2010—Google acquired Phonetic Arts, a company developing speech synthesis that generated natural computer speech from small samples of recorded voice. (As time passes, Phonetic Arts enabled robo-voices to sound much more like human voices, and this technology was deployed in Google Now. Users claimed that the Google Now assistant voice was smoother than that of Apple's Siri.)

4. *Mapping technology*

- July 2010—Apple acquires Poly9, a 3D mapping company that had developed FreeEarth for map visualization. The Poly9 deal was viewed as an attempt to strengthen Apple's competition against Google Earth.
- September 2010—Google acquired Quiksee for an estimated $10 million. Quiksee developed solutions for creating location-based interactive videos and interactive video mapping technologies based on user-filmed videos. Quiksee's technology could be deployed in the Street View of Google Earth service.

Dyadic cascading between Google and Apple would continue beyond 2010. In addition, other players such as Facebook, Yahoo!, and Microsoft would join in an acquisition fray and engage in many responsive M&A transactions.

M&A Strategy Changes

The role of M&A in corporate strategy is hardly a static affair. In this section, we'll illustrate key changes made by Apple and Google in their acquisition activities.

Apple Changes Tunes

Starting around 2013, Apple accelerated its pace of acquisitions. In fact, at its annual meeting in February 2014, CEO Tim Cook made the surprising announcement that Apple has acquired 23 companies during the past 16 months.

Analysts and the media scrambled to identify these deals as an indicator of where the company may be heading. Uncovering Apple's acquisitions is not an easy task, as reflected by the company's notoriously cryptic statement that accompanies many deal *confirmations:* "Apple buys smaller technology companies from time to time, and we generally do not discuss our purpose or plans."

Given Apple's traditional M&A secrecy, why was Cook stressing the significant number of acquisitions his company was now making? Could he have dropped this stat in an attempt to signal that: (1) Apple was not just sitting on its huge pile of cash; or (2) market dynamics were changing, and, going forward Apple would not handicapped by a "not-invented-here" mentality? Was Cook implying that in addition to internal innovation, M&A would assume a much more important role as the company attempted to stay competitive in a post-Jobs era?

Figure 3.4 shows a number of Apple acquisitions in 2013. Deals were occurring in the following sectors: social media, semiconductors, application software, mapping, database software, media applications, audio/voice recognition, and mobile apps.

Of particular interest is the cluster of four acquisitions occurring in the mapping space. These included Broadmap (sorting and analyzing mapping data), Hopstop (local transit information), Embark (transit mapping), and Wifislam (microlocation technology). Data from HopStop and Embark would be combined in an updated version of Maps for iOS, Apple's mobile operating system. In 2012, when Apple ditched Google maps in favor of its own mapping service, the result was a widely publicized fiasco. Apple was now feeling the pressure to quickly improve its mapping offerings and would now rely more heavily on outside data and technology obtained via M&A to remain competitive.

Then in 2014, Apple's M&A tune changed even more dramatically when the company announced its plans for a $3 billion acquisition of Beats, a developer of high-end headphones as well as a music-streaming service.

The deal reflected a major discontinuity in Apple's M&A strategy, especially given the size of the transaction. Until now, the 1996 purchase of NeXT (bringing Steve Jobs back to Apple) for $429 million and 1.5 million Apple shares had been the company's largest deal. In fact, Apple had not

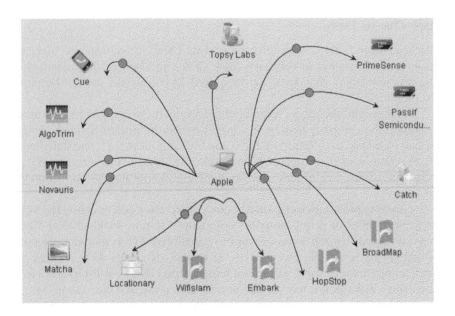

FIGURE 3.4 Select Apple acquisition in 2013

even formally disclosed in its annual 10-K the value of any specific M&A transaction since 2002.

The Beats deal would be a clean break from Apple's past corporate development activities. Why was the world's premium consumer electronics company paying such a hefty sum for a headphone company? Consider the following possibilities:[1]

- Wearable technology was emerging as the next big thing. To successfully play in this space, design would be essential. And the Beats headset was considered cool.
- Revenue synergy possibilities loomed. A customer could walk into an Apple store and leave not only with a pair of Beats headsets but also a new iPhone or Apple Watch to further enhance the music listening experience.
- Downloaded music sales on iTunes were drifting downward, and streaming appeared to be the future. Not wanting to cannibalize music downloads on iTunes, Apple had been late to streaming. Coupling iTunes Radio with Beats' streaming service could help Apple compete with streaming leaders such as Pandora or Spotify.

■ Beats' music industry veterans (Dr. Dre and Jimmy Iovine) were widely regarded as masters of music licensing and marketing. Owning Beats would bring both executives into the Apple fold as part of a large *acqui-hire*. Iovine, in particular, could become a particularly valuable resource in future Apple deals to obtain rights to digital music, video, or other types of content.

Here again, Apple's M&A playbook was looking like Google's. Just a few months earlier in 2014, Google had acquired Nest Labs, a developer of smart home appliances, for $3.2 billion in cash—a price tag remarkably coincident with the Beats' deal. And a key aspect of the Nest deal had been the vaunted design talent of Nest executives such as Tony Fadell, the company's CEO.

Google Retunes

Even before Apple's M&A awakening, Google had been retuning its own M&A processes. Around 2006, Google founders Larry Page and Sergey Brin were becoming concerned that the company was accumulating too many disparate products—a veritable menagerie of applications. According to David Lawee, former vice president of corporate development: "Sergey spread this mantra internally that he wanted more features, less products."[2]

Then when Larry Page became CEO in 2011, Google reorganized into six or seven core product areas, with each area having its own hiring targets. The goal was for Google to do fewer acqui-Hires and more Acqui-hires. In other words, acquisitions were to move beyond the mere hiring of talent and were to focus on buying companies that had a clear fit with Google's product areas. Obtaining talent was still considered important, but the talent should bring with it technology that would accelerate a designated Google core product or service.

Given Google's innate appetite for ongoing experimentation, not all future deals would tightly fit into existing product lines. Indeed a significant number of acquisitions would be housed in Google X, created in 2010 as a research lab to kindle future initiations. In spite of a supposed new focus for acquisitions, few seemed to question that Google X-related deals were an essential element of Google's corporate development strategy.

Yet, an emphasis on M&A to support existing Google divisions was evident. And clusters of acquisitions supporting Google's current core products were common. In 2011, for example, three acquisitions that supported Google's push into the social space were completed: Fridge, Social Grapple, and Katango. Four acquisitions directly supported Google's commerce initiative: Daily Deal, Spark Buy, Talk Bin, and The DealMap. (Google later sold Daily Deal back to its founders.)

The bottom line on Apple versus Google in acquisitions? Although Apple was expanding its use of M&A (becoming more *Googley*), Google was attempting to directly attach its acquisitions to specific products and services (becoming more *Appley*).

In Chapter 13, we'll expand upon Google's heighted attention to attaching most of its acquisitions to specific product/service areas. And we'll see how this prism for future acquisitions was important in refining how the company executed the vital area of M&A integration.

Watch the Video

www.wiley.com/go/semiorganicgrowth

To view videos relating to the content of this chapter, refer to (1) *Contrasting Apple's Acquisition Strategy with Google's* and (2) *Acquisition Cascades,* which accompany this book as a supplemental resource.

Notes

1. See, for example, Hugh McIntyre, "Beats by Dr. Dre Is Worth $3.2 Billion, Especially to Apple," *Forbes* (May 16, 2014).
2. "Google Acquisitions and Integrations—A Tale of Two Cities," *Beyond the Deal* blog (May 30, 2012).

CHAPTER 4

M&A Market Modeling

I n a classic essay, Nobel laureate Herbert Simon argued that both scientists and executives must gather a large number of "chunks of knowledge" to make world-class contributions. "In neither science nor business does the professional look for a fair bet. Rather, the creative professional has superior knowledge that comes from persistence in acquiring more chunks than others."[1]

M&A market modeling fundamentally involves chunk building—accumulating meaningful pieces of information about market segments/sub-segments, companies, and deals. A robust market model can only be built with persistent effort. An organization must put in place a system that actively supports the continual building of M&A deal knowledge. Over time, as information chunks are accumulated, a market modeling resource grows increasingly valuable in supporting a corporate development program.[2]

Almost all functional areas within a company deploy digital systems to capture and analyze information. Accountants have financial information systems. Human resource managers have payroll and other human capital systems. Operations planners deploy supply chain management systems. Sales executives have customer experience applications.

However, all too few corporate business development professionals have at their disposal a systems capability relating to M&A activities that has an adequate view of outside market dynamics. Yet this is exactly the type of thinking that is necessary to create corporate business development as a strategic resource.

Some two decades ago, organization theorist Peter Drucker lamented that information technology had barely impacted how top management develops business strategy. He predicted that systematically collecting outside information would become the next frontier for information technology.[3] Most companies still have quite a ways to go in conquering this frontier.

To successfully build M&A as a core organizational capability, system designers must couple internal operations to the external world of *dynamic market* sectors, competitors, and deals. Deal analysis and execution should not be a discrete, unitary action, but rather a continuous process involving information gathering and analysis relating to hundreds, if not thousands, of companies and deals.

M&A market modeling involves the visual, dynamic representation of industry sectors and sub-sectors so as to understand past corporate business development patterns and suggest future directions for acquisition activity. To take M&A success to the next level, organizations must develop a market modeling system.

In this chapter, we will illustrate the market modeling process by building a sample market model for Google. Given the extremely broad reach of Google's ambitions, our market model will reach across three major market sectors: media/advertising, Internet software and services, and technology platform.

Although our focus will be on Google, corporate development success for any company can be dramatically enhanced by utilizing the insight that derives from systematically developing market knowledge chunks. Marketing modeling is applicable to all companies across all industries.

An MIT Market Model for Google

We begin by classifying Google's activities into a dynamic category tree that includes a detailed breakdown of the sectors in which Google participates now or possibly in the future. The word *dynamic* is of particular importance in that we intend to make real-time updates to this tree as new sectors of importance emerge.

Figure 4.1 shows a high-level view of a preliminary category tree for Google. (This tree will be enhanced in later chapters.)

First of all, let's focus on the *market segment* column of the tree. As already mentioned, for Google there are three main sectors in this tree: (1) media, (2) Internet software/services, and (3) technology platform. (Any activity that does not fit into one of these categories is placed in the *other* sector.) We'll use the acronym MIT (media/Internet/technology) to represent these main sectors:

- The *media* sector includes subsectors such as advertising, movies and entertainment, online media, and publishing.
- The *Internet* sector includes subsectors such as broadband services, cloud services, Internet retail, social networking, search engine software, and Web analytics.
- The *technology platform* sector includes subsectors such as application software, artificial intelligence, robotics/drones, semiconductors, smart home, and wearables.

Categories

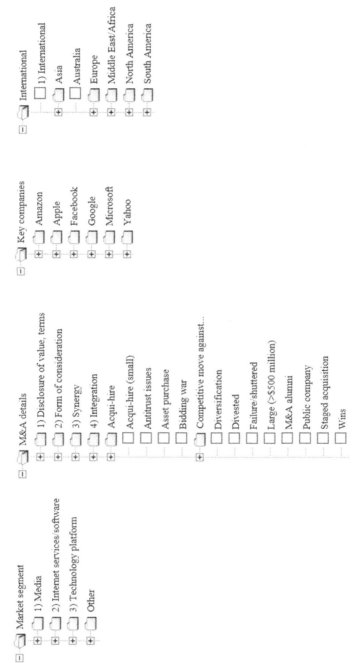

FIGURE 4.1 High-level category tree

47

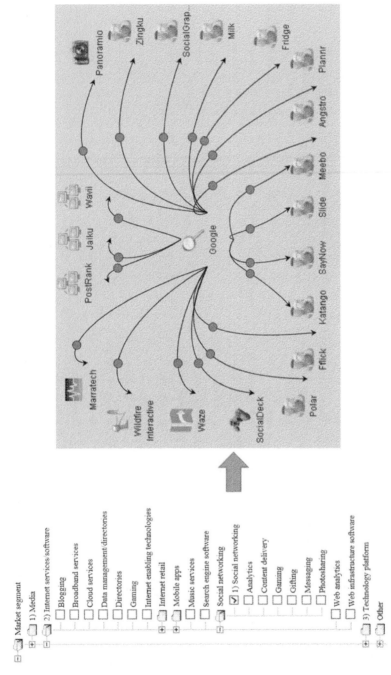

FIGURE 4.2 Using a category tree to display acquisitions in social networking

Unlike traditional industrial classification schemes such as SIC (Standard Industrial Classification) or NAICS (North American Industry Classification System), a marketing modeling classification must be designed to accommodate very recent industry subsectors relevant to the company or market being modeled.

To illustrate how this sector classifications scheme can provide insight into a company's business activity, examine Figure 4.2. In this figure, we have selected the social networking checkbox, searched a database of deals, and found the resultant infographic of Google acquisitions relevant to the social networking space.

Several nodes of the category tree are expanded in Figure 4.2 as compared to Figure 4.1, as we want to search for and depict acquisitions that specifically relate to social networking. (Even though there are social networking–related acquisitions by other companies in our database of companies/deals, only Google's deals are being displayed in this constellation.)

In this infographic, each company is assigned an icon that represents the *primary* sector to which the company belongs. For example, there is a grouping of companies from Zingku (a mobile social networking service) to Kantango (technology to segment one's social network) that directly belong to the social networking sector. However, there are other companies more *indirectly* related to social networking that are assigned a different primary icon, such as Social Deck (a social gaming company) and Waze (a crowd-sourced mapping service).

Companies in other primary sectors such as advertising (Wildfire) and photography (Panoramio) are also indirectly associated with social networking, and thus appear in this infographic. Companies directly or indirectly related to social networking are displayed, thereby providing a rich context to understand M&A activity that Google is doing in the entire social networking domain.

One can then obtain specific information about the company or deal by clicking on the company icon or deal node. For example, clicking on the node associated with the Waze acquisition yields (in part) the following information:[4]

Google buys Waze (real-time traffic)

Companies in Relationship

Google, Waze

Deal Facts

Initial Announcement Date: 6/13

Consideration: $966M cash + retention bonuses; (Sources: Google 10Q & Google interviews); $847M attributed to goodwill; Google also assumed $69M in liabilities

Google purchases Waze, an Israeli crowd-sourced mapping and navigation company, for $966 million in cash. (Retention bonuses may increase this amount as Waze has confirmed that 100 employees stand to receive $120 million from the deal to be earned over four years after closing.) Google will use the technology to enhance its Google Maps service with Waze's real-time traffic.

Waze has raised $67 million through three rounds of financing. Investors include Kleiner Perkins Caufield and Byers, Horizons Ventures, Magma Venture Partners, BlueRun Venture Capital, and Vertex Venture Capital.

A key term of the acquisition included the ability of Waze to continue to operate independently for a period of three years and that employees were not required to relocate from Israel.

Once again, keep in mind that the categories in this market model must be dynamic. Both incumbent and insurgent companies will generate novel products and services, which, if significant, must be accommodated. New enabling technologies quickly give rise to innovative subsectors. To effectively support corporate development, a market model must deal with such rapidly changing activities.

Of course, there are many alternative systems by which market modeling can be performed. However, the key idea we're stressing here is that this modeling should be able to access and represent company and deal information with a level of granularity that provides insights about past and possible future M&A moves of companies of importance to a given corporate development manager. The model can focus on one company or a group of companies, as we will shortly see.

Additional Market Model Dimensions

In addition to classifying M&A transactions by dynamic market sectors, Figure 4.1 also shows other major dimensions by which deals might be categorized and filtered. As depicted in this figure, some additional dimensions might include *M&A details, key companies,* and *international.*

What core structural dimensions should be included in a deal database? Meaningful market modeling requires building a database that can be searched or filtered to answer specific strategic questions. A manager must be able to identify a set of deals and/or companies that is neither too broad nor too restrictive for the particular corporate development issue being addressed. Using too broad a filter is like painting a portrait with a four-inch brush—necessary details can't be discerned. Using too restrictive a filter is like painting the portrait with a palette lacking a primary color—vital elements are missing. A deal database must be set to a level of granularity that supports meaningful corporate development analysis.

Let's provide examples of each of the sample dimensions mentioned above (refer again to Figure 4.1).

The *M&A details* dimension provides a means of analyzing deals by categories such as: (1) whether the value or terms of a deal were disclosed; (2) what form of consideration was provided (cash, stock, and so on), (3) whether the deal was an acqui-hire; (4) whether the acquisition should be considered a failure; and (5) whether it was a large transaction. As shown in the figure, many other M&A details are also categorized.

Let's illustrate how the M&A details dimension might be used. Assume we are interested in depicting the acquisitions for which Google directly disclosed that it used its stock in the transaction as consideration. Figure 4.3 shows this analysis.

Four deals in which Google used stock as full or partial consideration are displayed. (Almost all of Google's acquisitions do not involve stock—more on this in Chapter 10.) From Chapter 2, we're already quite familiar with

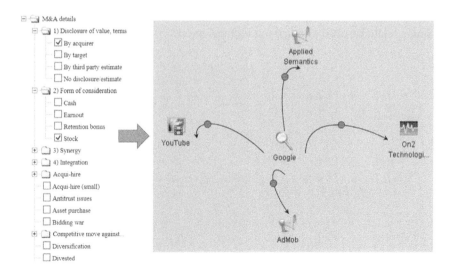

FIGURE 4.3 Deals using stock as consideration

the Applied Semantics transaction, so let's examine another deal, YouTube. Clicking on the node associated with the YouTube acquisition would provide details such as:

▪ Consideration: $1.65 billion stock-for-stock transaction that included $21 million in cash payments (*Source:* Google 10-K). Google announced that it has agreed to acquire YouTube, a consumer media company that displays a wide variety of video content as well as amateur content, for $1.65 billion in a stock-for-stock transaction.

The level of categorization that is available in this *M&A details* dimension should allow a corporate development professional to filter by any dimension deemed to be important. Although not likely to be as dynamic as the *market segment* dimension, this M&A details dimension will still need to be updated to support any new areas of interest.

The *key companies* dimension provides a categorization of major companies (typically competitors) that are of high interest in a given M&A market model. For example, Figure 4.4 lists six companies (Amazon, Apple, Facebook, Google, Microsoft, and Yahoo) in our sample market model. Note by examining the entry for Apple that a sample of Apple products or services are broken out as subcategories. (Subcategories for the other companies are not currently displayed.)

The infographic in Figure 4.4 shows Apple's acquisitions that relate to the company's mapping initiatives. Note that most, but not all of these companies relate directly to mapping technologies. For example, in 2013 Apple

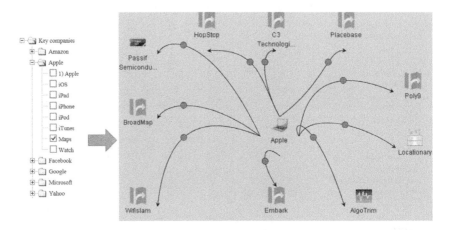

FIGURE 4.4 Apple's M&A activity in mapping

acquired Locationary, a database software company that provided mobile and Web solutions to manage local business place information. Apple would likely use Locationary's technology to improve and enhance its *mapping* capability (as well as possibly in other application areas).

The *key companies* dimension demonstrates that in building an M&A market model for one company (say Google), it is often vital to be able to understand the deal activity of other significant players in Google's market spaces. A robust market model extends *at least* to a company's major competitors and possibly beyond.

The *international* dimension provides an understanding of M&A activity by geographic focus. International acquisitions may be made by a company as a mode of entry into that region. Other times, these acquisitions are made to obtain distinctive talent or technology or possibly establish a beachhead for future acquisitions in the region.

Suppose a corporate development manager would like to view known acquisitions made by Apple, Facebook, or Google in the country of Israel. The manager starts by selecting these three companies as from the *key companies* dimension and then selecting Israel from the *international* dimension. The result is shown in Figure 4.5.

At first glance, we might conclude that Apple is acquiring semiconductor companies (PrimeSense and Anobit) in the region, while Facebook is acquiring mobile applications (Onavo and Snaptu) and Google is buying mapping companies (Quiksee and Waze). Of course, the company/deal results from this (or any) search will depend on when the query is made.

Other major dimensions can be included in an M&A market model. For example, customer segmentation is often an important element to use in searching or filtering a deal database. A company and its products or services can be classified by the customers that it targets—including race, gender, age, price sensitivity, product preferences, and so on.

Simultaneously Analyzing Model Dimensions

A robust M&A market model will allow for deals to be analyzed across multiple, simultaneous dimensions. For example, the model should be able to depict transactions in a given sector within an international region such as we've seen in Figure 4.5, where the M&A constellation consists of Apple, Facebook, and Google deals in Israel.

For another example, see Figure 4.6 for a depiction of Google's transactions that have been identified as deals where Google is selected as the *key company*, and Facebook is selected as the company against which a competitive response is being made. Clicking on the deal node for Google/Titan would reveal that in 2014, Google purchased Titan Aerospace, a developer

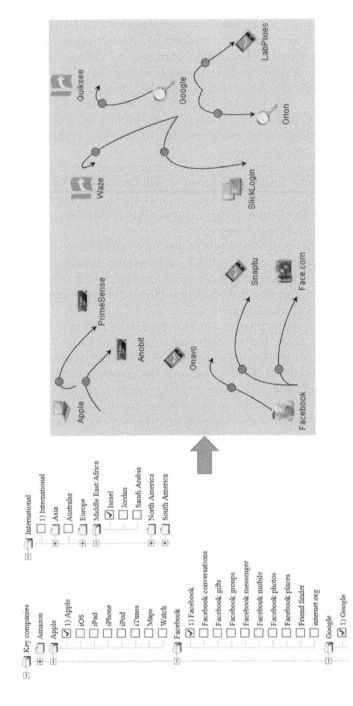

FIGURE 4.5 Acquisitions by Apple, Facebook, or Google in Israel

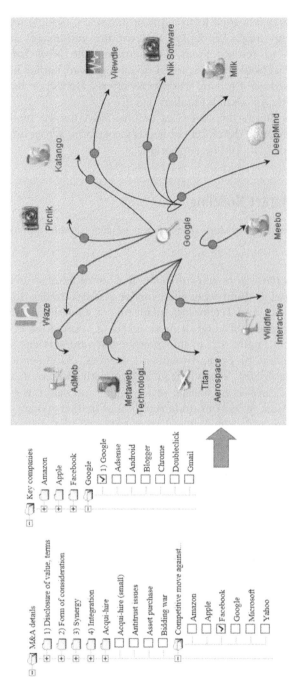

FIGURE 4.6 Google deals in response to key competitors

55

of jet-sized drones designed to fly nonstop for years. Google reported that Titan's technology might be deployed to capture geo-images and provide Internet access to remote areas. Furthermore, the *Wall Street Journal* reported that Facebook had explored acquiring Titan earlier in 2014, but Google promised to top any Facebook offer.[5] Hence, a head-to-head competitive battle for Titan had taken place.

Once again, here's the core idea behind M&A market modeling. Any analysis that corporate development needs to perform, across any combination of dimensions, should be supported.

Key Steps in Market Modeling

Here is a summary of key steps that are necessary to develop an M&A market model:

1. *Categorize the sectors and subsectors* that are of interest. In our sample Google model, there were three major sectors: Media, Internet software/services, and Technology platform. As categories under each of these sectors identify one or more levels of subsectors. For example, as shown in Figure 4.2, in the Internet software/services sector, subsectors such as blogging, broadband services, cloud services, and so on are established. You will find that your initial pass at categorizing sectors and subsectors will be revised time and again as market conditions change or as your understanding of market space is enhanced. As we've stressed through this chapter, to be effective, market modeling can't be constrained by a static view of market categories. To support real-world thinking, this system must be dynamic.
2. *Start building a company database* by *identifying key companies.* The first step in building a company database is to identify a select set of companies considered central to your analysis. In our sample Google MIT market model, in addition to Google, central companies included Amazon, Apple, Facebook, Microsoft, and Yahoo!.
3. *Build a deal database for key companies.* This should consist of known historical deals for each company. Three of the major fields that will typically be found in a deal database are: (a) deal facts, (b) strategic implications, and (c) current status. Earlier in this chapter we provided a sample entry for the Google/Waze deal. Making an entry in your deal database will require adding the target to your company database.
4. *Enhance the major dimensions of market model.* As shown in Figure 4.1, major dimensions could include: (a) M&A classification

categories (ranging from whether or not deal terms were disclosed to whether or not the deal is viewed as a "win;" (b) key companies, including subcategories detailing each company's products/services; (c) international. As previously mentioned, other dimensions central to supporting a company's corporate development analysis needs should be added.

5. *Expand your company database to include potential targets.* We now move from the historical to the future. By including companies that you have identified as potential targets, your M&A market model can support current and future deal analysis within the context of a timeline. (We'll illustrate timeline analysis in the next section.) At a minimum, for each entry you will want to include a company description as well as classify the company into the appropriate sector/subsectors. Figure 4.7 shows a sample entry for Wonder Workshop, an ed-tech robotics company. Note that in addition to developing a company description, Wonder Workshop is classified as both an education systems application and a robotics company.

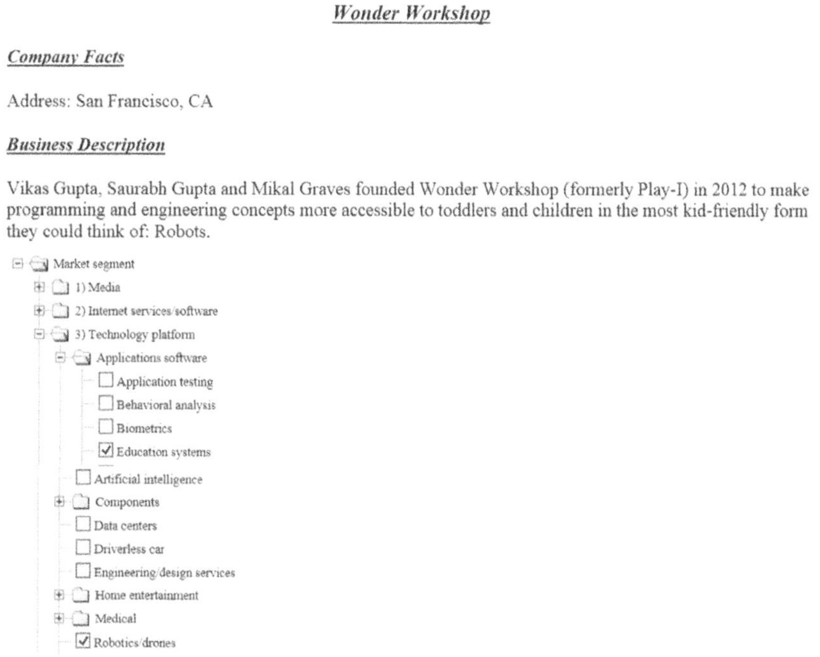
Wonder Workshop

Company Facts

Address: San Francisco, CA

Business Description

Vikas Gupta, Saurabh Gupta and Mikal Graves founded Wonder Workshop (formerly Play-I) in 2012 to make programming and engineering concepts more accessible to toddlers and children in the most kid-friendly form they could think of: Robots.

Market segment
1) Media
2) Internet services/software
3) Technology platform
Applications software
☐ Application testing
☐ Behavioral analysis
☐ Biometrics
☑ Education systems
☐ Artificial intelligence
Components
☐ Data centers
☐ Driverless car
☐ Engineering/design services
Home entertainment
Medical
☑ Robotics/drones

FIGURE 4.7 Description and classification of sample target

The number of deals and companies in your market model can ulti-mately consist of hundreds or even thousands of entries. But don't let the potential size of the effort be daunting. When first getting started, the initial set of companies/deals will be much smaller and typically include prominent players and their key deals. As market modeling continues, systematically adding companies and deals will refine the model, and it will become better and better in supporting the creative process of deal making. The effort will pay dividends, as a well-designed and up-to-date market model enables an executive to cut through confusion and respond quickly and more confi-dently to M&A opportunities.

Using Marketing Modeling

In a large company such as Google, the idea for an M&A transaction can orig-inate from any of a number of sources, including an internal strategy group, a product manager, a sales unit, or top management. In smaller compa-nies, senior management tends to drive deal origination. Wherever the deal originates, the rationale for the transaction needs to be communicated to concerned parties throughout an organization. Assessing both strategic fit and organizational fit are critical first steps in the M&A process.[6]

Building a market modeling system such as we've described in this chapter provides an excellent means of communicating a context for your company's moves going forward. Markets are complex entities, consisting of dozens if not hundreds of companies and relationships. Robust corporate development requires a system for visualizing both past and future potential M&A activity undertaken by a company and its competitors.

We conclude this chapter by developing a scenario that illustrates the use of market modeling to establish a historical context as well as support the identification of potential M&A targets.

Identifying a Target in Historical Context

Here's the scenario. It's May 2014, and your strategy group within Apple has been called on to make a presentation on Google's mapping capabilities in light of a rumored acquisition of Skybox Imaging, a designer of small, relatively inexpensive satellites that gather daily photos and video of the Earth. You want to provide a historical context for both Google's and Apple's acquisition activity in the critical mapping sector.

Since you have built an M&A market model with dynamic category fil-tering, gathering this information is straightforward. You select mapping in the *market segments* category and Apple and Google in the *key companies*

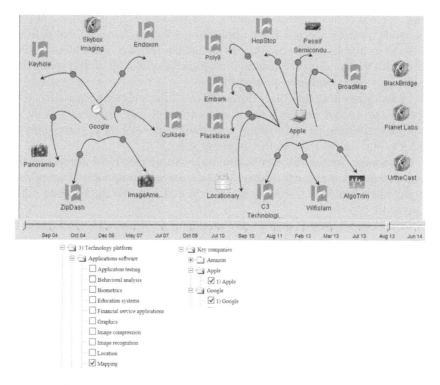

FIGURE 4.8 Apple/Google mapping-related acquisitions

category. You search your market modeling database and the company/deal constellation shown in Figure 4.8 is generated.

The infographic shown in Figure 4.8 is similar to earlier ones we've seen earlier in the chapter, with two notable embellishments:

1. In addition to historical acquisitions and related deal links that appear for both Apple and Google, companies that are potential targets in the mapping space also appear. These companies are Skybox Imaging, Google's rumored target, as well as BlackBridge, Planet Labs, and Urthecast, other competitive satellite-mapping players.
2. A timeline appears at the bottom of the infographic. Dragging the markers on this timeline will provide a time-series portrayal of all transactions, thereby adding perspective to the historical unfolding of these deals.

You note that starting with the 2004 acquisition of Keyhole, Google has long held the belief that satellite imagery and aerial photography is a core element of its mapping technology. (Keyhole's technology was used in the wildly popular Google Earth application.) You further note that Google is likely to accelerate its capabilities in satellite photos and videos of the earth with the pending acquisition of Skybox. (Google did, in fact, purchase Skybox for $500 million in June 2014.)

You further note that BlackBridge, Planet Labs, and Urthecast also compete in the satellite imaging space and comment that Apple may want to explore establishing a relationship with one or more of these companies in order to stay competitive in the mapping space.

Of course, setting this simulation aside, Apple may have already established contact with these (or other) satellite-imaging companies, If so, details of any talks could be stored as data associated with the appropriate company icon.

The central point is that market modeling must move beyond tracking the historical and also include a system that supports thinking about future deals. The ultimate timeline slider would be to pull the slider to the future to forecast likely deals yet to occur in a market sector!

Broad Appeal of Market Modeling

Market modeling is not just for large companies such as Google or Apple. All companies need to identify the sectors and subsectors important in stimulating their growth. For corporate business development moves and for competitive intelligence, the model needs to be supported with information relating to companies and deals that will provide a vibrant picture of historical transactions as well as suggest future development opportunities.

As we noted at the start of this chapter, virtually all other functional areas in the organization, from accounting to human resources, have vital systems in place. So should the corporate development group. We've described the framework for one such system in this chapter. Your company can build on this framework or create one of its own.

Watch the Video

www.wiley.com/go/semiorganicgrowth

To view a demo of the type of market modeling described in this chapter, refer to the video *M&A Market Modeling for Target Acquisitions*, which accompanies this book as a supplemental resource.

Notes

1. Herbert Simon, "What We Know about the Creative Process," *Frontiers in Creative and Innovative Management* (Cambridge, MA: Ballinger, 1985).
2. See Geis and Geis (2001), Chapter 2, for a discussion of the concept of market modeling that extends beyond M&A transactions.
3. Peter F. Drucker, "The Next Information Revolution," *Forbes ASAP* (August 1998), pp. 47–58.
4. See, for example, http://www.trivergence.com/link.asp?LinkID=901193.
5. Alistair Barr and Reed Albergotti, "Google to Buy Titan Aerospace as Web Giants Battle for Air Superiority," *Wall Street Journal* (April 14, 2014).
6. For a holistic view of the M&A process, starting with assessing strategic and organizational fit, see Gomes et al. (2013).

CHAPTER 5

Google Media Deals

G oogle's mission statement reads: "to organize the world's information and make it universally accessible and useful." Although knowledge organization enriched by search technology was the core value proposition behind Google's founding and growth, it was advertising that paid the bills and also generated huge investor returns.

We documented in Chapter 2 how the acquisition of Applied Semantics was instrumental in dramatically expanding Google's advertising reach beyond its own search page to millions of Web content publishers. In this chapter, we'll explore the critical role that M&A continued to play in building Google into an advertising giant.

Our media journey will take us to several major M&A stops along the way, including *digital video* and YouTube, *display advertising* placement and DoubleClick, and *mobile advertising* and AdMob. There will also be other significant M&A initiatives that support each of these major initiatives.

We'll also examine Google's M&A activity in other media domains, such as entertainment and publishing-related content. The M&A imprinting from Applied Semantics has expressed itself scores of times as Google's media/advertising canvas continues to expand.

Media Deal Categories

Both advertising and media content have dramatically changed in the digital technology era. For example, the rapidly growing Internet advertising segment is poised to challenge traditional television advertising as the largest media advertising sector. According to a PricewaterhouseCoopers (PwC) study, in 2013, total Internet advertising revenue was $117.2 billion. This figure was projected to reach $194.5 billion in 2018, reflecting a 10.7 percent CAGR over the period. In 2009, total Internet advertising revenue was only $58.7 billion.[1]

Some subsegments of Internet advertising were particularly hot. Market research company eMarketer expected that mobile advertising would make up nearly 10 percent of the U.S. ad market by the end of 2014, surpassing newspapers, magazines, and radio. eMarketer estimated that some $18 billion would be spent on mobile and tablet advertising in 2014, an 83 percent increase over 2013.[2]

The PwC study asserted that Internet video advertising would see the sharpest growth in the near future, predicting a 23.8 percent CAGR to 2018. YouTube had perfected its pre-roll ad format, and YouTube's TrueView ads were deployed widely across many new consumer devices. (TrueView video ads provided viewers with significant choice and control over which ad they watch and an advertiser is charged only when a viewer chooses to watch its ad.)

Given the ever-changing advertising and digital media landscape, categorization of the media segment in a market model is almost as *dynamic* as the frenetic Internet and technology platform segments. Traditional segmentation no longer suffices. Media and advertising market breakdown need to continually reflect the major segment and subsegment transformation forces such as mobilization and digital video.

So the segmentation presented in Figure 5.1 must not be viewed as carved in stone. As we stress throughout this book, any successful market modeling system must be able to respond to rapid sector changes. Static classification schemes subject themselves to decreasing utility. Nevertheless, Figure 5.1 presents a reasonably good high-level segmentation of the media world, together with a more detailed advertising segmentation circa 2015 from the perspective of Google and its corporate development activity.

Note that Internet advertising has subsectors that include Google's core search advertising, as well as semantic advertising (reflected in the Applied Semantics acquisition). In addition, advertising-related acquisitions in areas such as display, online video, social media, smart home appliance advertising, and video games can also be modeled. Note further that mobile advertising has been broken out as a major category (with its own subsectors) in our market model. Dignifying mobile advertising with its own high-level place in our category tree reflects the growing importance of this advertising sector.

Using this market model, we'll now explore Google's M&A activity within a number of these subsectors.

Online Video Advertising Deals

In February 2005, YouTube was created as a video-sharing website by three former PayPal employees, Chad Hurley, Steve Chen, and Jawed Karim. It is

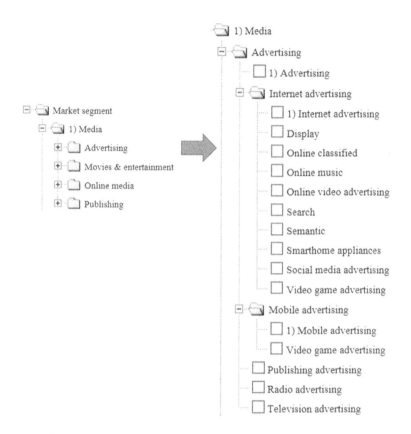

FIGURE 5.1 Media (overview) + Advertising segmentation

often stated that inspiration for YouTube came after Janet Jackson's 2004 Super Bowl incident. Jawed Karim was seeking to view the incident, but had difficulty finding a clip online.

At the time, Google had its own dedicated team working on a competitive product called Google Video, but YouTube's traction was blowing Google Video out of the water. Google Video was building its business by working cooperatively with major content producers to protect their intellectual property, attempting to avoid piracy of their movies, television shows, and music videos. As a result, content on Google Video largely consisted of home videos. YouTube was taking a much more aggressive approach, not overly concerned about monitoring user-posted content to control for piracy. YouTube was becoming a destination for exploring high-production video content such as music videos, television clips, and other pieces of professional work. YouTube's popularity enabled it to achieve strong network effects resulting from coupling content generating "suppliers" with content consumers.

In October 2006, Google concluded it could not effectively complete with YouTube and agreed to acquire YouTube for $1.65 billion in a stock-for-stock transaction. Following the acquisition, YouTube would operate independently, retaining its brand and all their employees, including co-founders Chad Hurley and Steve Chen.

Unlike other earlier Google targets, YouTube was allowed to run completely autonomously. Eric Schmidt was proactive in defending the company's autonomy. Google had witnessed other companies absorb smaller companies and ruin their product innovation and agile culture. A former Google Group Product Manager knowledgeable about the transition stated: "YouTube was growing so well that they were afraid to mess it up like big companies sometimes do when they acquire smaller ones." To that end, YouTube maintained its San Bruno office location rather than moving to the Google company headquarters. As late as 2014, there was no overt Google branding visible at YouTube's offices.

Google purchased YouTube because it was witnessing YouTube's explosive growth as a video destination site. This network had such a strong groundswell that Google Video was deemed unable to catch up. Additionally, Google acquired YouTube as a defensive tactic to prevent another player such as Yahoo! from sweeping up the company.

YouTube helped provide Google with an entrée into brand marketing. Previously, its products had focused on direct response ads, but YouTube allowed it to present opportunities to ad agencies that related to general branding. The 2008 presidential debate hosted on YouTube between John McCain and Barack Obama was an example of how Google sought to demonstrate the brand-marketing efficacy of the platform.

However, Google would find no "silver bullet" associated with the YouTube acquisition as it had benefited from with the Applied Semantics purchase and AdSense.[3] No rapid high-margin revenue bump would occur. Instead, as Google attempted to expand its advertising reach to online videos, it would need to tweak and re-tweak the YouTube platform. Acquisitions would play a major role in doing so.

Figure 5.2 shows a number of *semi-organic* acquisitions that would help complement YouTube's talent and technology and stimulate its growth during the five-year period after Google's acquisition of the company. (Additional M&A activity related to YouTube would continue after this five-year period.)

In October 2008, Google acquired Omnisio, a provider of online video services, for an estimated $15 million. Omnisio technology would allow

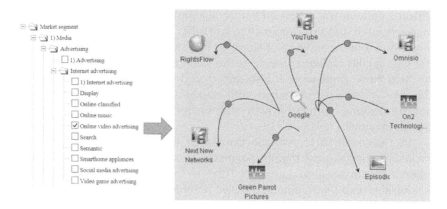

FIGURE 5.2 YouTube and some YouTube-related acquisitions

users to annotate videos, mash up clips into compilations, and synchronize Slideshare presentations to videos. Omnisio employees joined the YouTube team.

In October 2009, Google agreed to acquire On2 Technologies, a publicly held company, for $123 million in stock and cash. On2's platform and video compression/decompression software delivered video over proprietary networks and the Internet. A corollary purchase to YouTube, the On2 acquisition proved crucial in moving Google's video efforts forward. Google open-sourced On2's VP8 video codec as a piece of its video format, WebM. YouTube began converting new and existing videos to that format. On2's talent also advanced other Google products and services. For example, in 2013 Matt Frost, former On2 CEO, became head of Strategy and Media for Google's Chrome team.

In April 2010, Google acquired Episodic, which provided a platform that enabled publishers, marketers, and businesses to stream, analyze, and monetize video content through computers, mobile devices, and IPTV devices. Episodic also offered content management and provided an ad server to let its customers insert ads. The deal was aimed at boosting YouTube's analytical and monetization capabilities. The Episodic team joined YouTube.

In March 2011, Google bought Green Parrot Pictures, a developer of tools that made it easier to manipulate digital video and images. YouTube would integrate Green Parrot's technology to help users make better-quality videos, particularly for videos taken with mobile phones.

Also in March 2011, Google purchased Next New Networks, Next New was one of the early efforts into curating professional quality online content in order to make it more attractive to advertisers. All Next New affiliated content was screened before distribution, setting it apart from the user-generated content dominating YouTube at that time. The Next New acquisition represented one of Google's first attempts to cultivate and package high-quality online content. At the same time that Google announced the Next New acquisition, it also announced the YouTube Next initiative. This was a "new team tasked with supercharging creator development and accelerating partner growth and success."—clearly, a *semi-organic* growth initiative.

In December 2011, Google purchased RightsFlow, a company that tracked and processed royalty payments to songwriters and music publishers. The acquisition gave YouTube technology to help manage its relationship with the fragmented music publishing industry.

After 2011, Google remained intent on adding technology and talent to YouTube via acquisition. However, the company would be frustrated in at least one highly publicized deal. In 2014 Google attempted to acquire Twitch for a reported $1 billion. Twitch was the most popular e-sports streaming site on the Web. Twitch claimed to have some 55 million monthly users, with more than one million members who uploaded videos each month. But it was Amazon that would purchase Twitch in a signal that Google and Amazon would be facing off in the media/advertising space (more on the Google/Amazon dynamic in Chapter 14 where we discuss competitive deal constellations).

Display Advertising Deals

In 2007, Google extended its ad-tech reach beyond core search, contextual ads (AdSense), and video (YouTube) by acquiring DoubleClick. In what was its largest acquisition to date, Google acquired DoubleClick from Hellman & Friedman, JMI Equity, and company management for $3.2 billion in cash. DoubleClick had emerged as a real-time exchange marketplace for buying and selling advertising. It provided a market for advertisers to bid on *display advertising* across the Internet.

DoubleClick employed "cookies" (tiny bits of code placed on a hard drive that track a user's browser history) so that relevant display ads could be shown when the user arrived at a particular webpage.

Since 2007, Google has enhanced DoubleClick capabilities with a number of M&A transactions. Figure 5.3 shows some of the DoubleClick-related acquisitions that Google has made.

In November 2009, Google signed a definitive agreement to acquire Teracent, a developer of data-driven advertising optimization technology. Teracent technology was integrated into Google's ad network and DoubleClick offerings. Teracent's technology could create display ads customized for

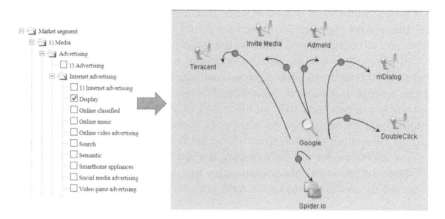

FIGURE 5.3 DoubleClick and DoubleClick-related M&A deals

a particular customer, with algorithms automatically selecting display ad images, colors, and text as determined by elements such as geographic location, language, the time of day, or the past performance of ads.

In August 2010, Google acquired Invite Media, a company that developed a demand-side platform (DSP) to facilitate navigation of high-volume display advertising exchanges for buyers. (A DSP is used by advertisers and agencies to help them buy display, video, mobile, and search ads.) Although Invite would operate as an independent brand and product in the short-run, the company was ultimately integrated into DoubleClick. Google's acquisition of Invite Media signaled Google's interest in strengthening ties with advertising agencies.

In June 2011, Google agreed to acquire Admeld, a provider of advertising network optimization technology for online publishers, for an estimated $400 million. The acquisition was aimed at assembling an end-to-end solution in online display advertising. The transaction rounded out Google's presence in the display ad value chain, which starts with a demand-side platform, then goes on to the ad exchange (DoubleClick), leading on to a supply-side platform such as Admeld. By tightly integrating Admeld's platform with DoubleClick's DART for Publishers product, Google attracted more volume into its exchange.

In February 2014, Google acquired Spider.io, a developer of technology to identify and weed out fraudulent clicks relating to online ads. The technology also helped detect attacks originating from devices infected by malware. Spider.io's seven employees, including founder Douglas de Jager, would join Google. Three of these seven employees held PhDs. In announcing the deal, Google blogged: " ... [a] vibrant ecosystem only flourishes if marketers can buy media online with the confidence that their ads are reaching real people, that results they see are based on actual interest. To grow the pie for everyone, we need to take head on the issue of online fraud."

In June 2014, Google bought mDialog, which developed technology that allowed large media companies to manage and deliver video advertising across a range of products, including iPhones and iPads, Android devices, and streaming products such as Xbox and Roku. In the short run, mDialog would continue to operate its service. However, Google would eventually fold the company's technology into DoubleClick, which now was serving as a major exchange for not only display ads but also video ads.

This portfolio of deals demonstrates that DoubleClick would continue to accelerate its development via *semi-organic* acquisitions.

Advertising Deals in Other Sectors

As Google continued to expand its advertising canvas to additional forums and formats, as usual, M&A activity played a prominent role in these growth initiatives.

Figure 5.4 depicts some of Google's deal activity in advertising formats that include social media, video games, and mobile. We'll analyze these

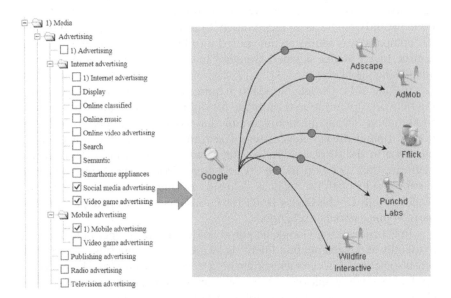

FIGURE 5.4 Advertising deals in additional formats

transactions in time order of their occurrence, identifying the advertising subsector to which each deal belongs.

- *Video-game advertising.* In March 2007, Google acquired Adscape, a video-game advertising company, for an estimated $23 million. Adscape's AdverPlay product let developers place dynamic ads right inside a game. In part, the Adscape acquisition was a *cascade response* to Microsoft's $200 million acquisition in 2006 of Massive, another in-game advertisement company.
- *Mobile advertising.* In November 2009, Google announced plans to acquire AdMob, an emerging player in mobile advertising that Apple had been courting, for $681 million in stock and cash. (After a six-month investigation, the Federal Trade Commission approved the Google/AdMob deal.) AdMob sold ads that appeared on websites geared for smartphones. The company was a first-mover in delivering ads on Apple's iPhone, as well as on devices that used Google's Android mobile operating system. The AdMob acquisition proved to be a critical component of Google's impressive run rate in mobile revenue growth in 2011, which more than doubled over 2010. A major part of this growth came from mobile ad revenue ($2.5 billion in 2011) on Android-powered phones.
- *Social media advertising.* In January 2011, Google acquired Fflick, which operated a service that featured movie trailers, reviews, and ratings, for an estimated $10 million. After signing in with a Twitter account, a user was shown a list of top-ranking movies, and a set of relevant tweets from the people the user followed appearing next to each film. Fflick was launched in August 2010 by Kurt Wilms and three other ex-Digg employees. The team/talent was assigned to YouTube, working on projects that built on Fflick technology—clearly an *acqui-hire* for growth acceleration.
- *Mobile advertising.* In July 2011, Google acquired Punchd Labs, a provider of offers-related advertising services. Punchd developed digital versions of loyalty cards on a customer's mobile phone. Although Google had invested in mobile payment applications such as its Google Wallet, the company had not gained traction in this area. Industry analysts contended that existing payment solutions (such as credit cards) were simply too effective. In 2013, Punchd was shut down, and the team "dedicated its time and energy into integrations with other Google products."
- *Social media advertising.* In July 2012, Google acquired social marketing software developer Wildfire Interactive for an estimated $350 million in cash plus another $100 million in earn-outs/retention bonuses.

(The large contingent consideration was apparently intended to motivate Wildfire founders Victoria Ransom and Alain Chuard to continue
leading the company's 400 employee team.) Wildfire allowed companies
to serve marketing and ad campaigns on Facebook, Google+, Twitter,
Pinterest, YouTube, and LinkedIn. Ransom led the integration of Wildfire into Google and was responsible for setting the social strategy for
Google's Display division. For example, DoubleClick would now be able
to use Facebook Ad Exchange (FBX) to sell advertising through the
DoubleClick Bid Manager. DoubleClick advertisers were able to target
Facebook users based on their visits to webpages outside of Facebook.
In 2014, Wildfire was discontinued as a standalone entity. The company
would no longer sign up new customers, and its offering was integrated
into Google's general adtech platform.

In analyzing the constellation of deals found in Figure 5.4, here are some
significant takeaways:

- The *deal cascading* phenomenon (blow-for-blow M&A combat) discussed in Chapter 3 in our discussion of Apple versus Google was
  evident in subsectors that included mobile advertising and video-game
  advertising. Adscape and AdMob are clear examples.
- Small company *acqui-hires* (such as Fflick and Punchd) were actively
  being used to experiment in new product areas and to accelerate growth
  for Google's existing products and services.
- Acquisitions were playing a significant role in obtaining a foothold and
  in attempting to stimulate *semi-organic growth* for Google in emerging
  advertising venues (social, mobile, and video games).
- *Mobile advertising* had emerged as a major category leader, and Google's
  M&A activity was helping to position the company to compete in this
  hotly contested space. We'll see in Chapters 6 and 7 that Google was also
  acquiring numerous other Internet and technology-platform companies
  that would have an indirect, but not inconsequential, impact on Google's
  mobile advertising prowess.

Media Content Deals

Although we've already discussed the acquisition of YouTube as a keystone
element of Google's *online video advertising* deal constellation, YouTube
must also be included as a central aspect of a media content–related constellation of acquisitions (see Figure 5.5).

Since being acquired by Google in 2006, YouTube has experimented
with many ways of enhancing original user-generated content. Indeed,

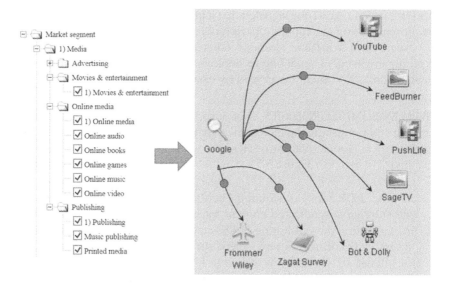

FIGURE 5.5 Sample media content–related acquisitions

as mentioned earlier, the Next New acquisition was one of Google's early attempts to cultivate high-quality online content. The YouTube Next initiative was designed to supercharge creator development and accelerate partner success.

YouTube, unlike companies such as Netflix with break-out internal programming such as *House of Cards*, had largely refrained from directly developing its own original programming. But YouTube was making every effort to directly support partners as they developed distinctive media content.

Instead of handing creative partners hundreds of millions of dollars to create digital content, YouTube was providing modest funding and production services for partners through creator spaces in London, Los Angeles, Tokyo, and New York. This approach was viewed as providing YouTube with flexibility as it experimented to find the best creators to support.

Video Game High School (VGHS) was a production set in an environment where teenagers go to school to study video games—a Hogwarts for video gamers. *VGHS* was one example of the way YouTube wanted to support the creation of content that could attract major ad dollars. After initial commercial-free episodes, *VGHS* content migrated to TV-length 30-minute episodes that were sponsored by A-level advertisers such as Dodge.

Media creation was destined to play an ever-increasing role in YouTube's future as the company competed in the emerging world of Internet TV.

And late in 2014, YouTube signaled that it intended to re-open its checkbook in support of original content development.

Apart from YouTube, Google's other media-related M&A transactions typically involved: (1) enabling technologies that facilitate the publishing of digital media; 2) content developed by established publishers.

MEDIA ENABLING TECHNOLOGIES   Not surprisingly, Google wanted to make crafting and publishing digital media as easy as possible for content creators, especially on Google platforms. Here are some acquisitions that supported this initiative (refer to Figure 5.5):

- In June 2007, Google acquired FeedBurner, a distributor of RSS (rich site summary) syndicated content for blogs and other media websites. In stimulating the publishing of RSS content, Google gave its advertisers access to FeedBurner's news feeds. In 2014, FeedBurner continued to be offered by Google, but was not actively being enhanced. RSS had become less vital with the advent of services such as Twitter, which ironically was being run by former FeedBurner founder Dick Costolo.
- In April 2011, Google acquired PushLife for an estimated $25 million. PushLife enabled a user to port iTunes and Windows Media player libraries to non-Apple phones such as Android. The PushLife team joined Google's offices in Kitchener, Canada. In 2012, Google Play Music launched its music-streaming service in the United States.
- In June 2011, Google brought SageTV, which developed digital entertainment and placeshifting solutions. It allowed users to create and operate media centers from an existing PC. In 2012, Google modified and updated SageTV to work with its Google Fiber TV service. SageTV v8 was being used for the Google Fiber Storage Box (DVR) and TV Box (Client).
- In 2013, Google acquired Bot & Dolly, which used robot arms for "cinematic automation." The company's technology was used in the blockbuster film *Gravity*.

PUBLISHED CONTENT   Google has dabbled in buying some established publishers, but not without some major challenges. Figure 5.5 depicts some examples.

- In September 2011, Google acquired Zagat Survey for approximately $151 million in cash. Zagat published reviews for restaurants worldwide. The company's offerings included printed guides, website information, and mobile products. Tim Zagat and Nina Zagat, founders of Zagat Survey, would continue to work as co-chairs. In acquiring Zagat, Google was supporting its move into the rapidly growing local commerce market. However, the integration of Zagat into Google did not go smoothly. Zagat employees, designated as temps without Googler benefits, were informed in late 2012 that their contracts would not be extended. See more on this deal in Chapter 12 in our detailed discussion of M&A integration.

- In August 2012, Google brought the travel assets of John Wiley & Sons Inc. for $22 million in cash. The assets included all of interests in the Frommer's brand and WhatsonWhen brands. Shortly thereafter, in April 2013, Google reversed course and sold the Frommer brand to its founder, Arthur Frommer. However, Google kept Frommer's social media accounts.

The Frommer's deal reflected Google's schizophrenia in acquiring establish media properties, especially in industries such as travel. Let's examine this double-mindedness by analyzing a Google Internet software acquisition that created conflicts with its media strategy.

Google's Media Schizophrenia

In a highly controversial 2011 transaction, Google purchased ITA Software. ITA offered Internet-based software to the airline industry. The company's products included an airfare pricing management system for airlines and travel distributors as well as a passenger reservation management and departure control system. The deal raised questions regarding how far Google would attempt to go into the online travel business.

Later in 2011, Google launched Flight Search, the first product resulting from its purchase of ITA. Also, Google continued to improve its hotel listing service by including virtual tours as well as pricing information.

However, according to some estimates, a significant amount of Google's advertising revenue (some 5 percent) was coming from online travel agents such as Expedia and Priceline. In 2014, online travel agents were spending some $4 billion in digital advertising.[4] Therefore, Google appeared to be conflicted on how aggressively to compete in this space.

Google perhaps was pondering a lesson from the AOL/Time Warner merger, in which AOL struggled (often unsuccessfully) to harmonize the conflicts that emerged with its advertising partners after it owned competing media and other content as a result of the Time Warner deal.

As we saw in Chapter 1 when examining a potential Apple acquisition of Universal Music in the early days of iTunes, M&A can present a company with major channel/partner conflict. Google appeared to be wrestling with two minds about exactly how it should position itself in the online travel service business. And some media content deals (such as Frommer's) were being whipsawed by this debate.

Watch the Video

www.wiley.com/go/semiorganicgrowth
    To view a video relating to the content of this chapter, refer to *M&A's Role in Building an Ecosystem,* which accompanies this book as a supplemental resource.

Notes

1. PricewaterhouseCoopers, *Global Media and Entertainment Outlook 2014-2018,* http://www.pwc.com/gx/en/global-entertainment-media -outlook/territory-segments-digital-forecast-overview.jhtml.
2. Steven Perlberg, "Rivals Wary of Comcast's Mobile-Ad Prowess," *Wall Street Journal* (July 7, 2014).
3. Levy (2011), p. 262.
4. "Sun, Sea and Surfing," *The Economist* (June 21, 2014), p. 65.

CHAPTER 6

Google Internet Deals

G oogle has used M&A to both strengthen its position in search as well as extend its reach into an expanding array of Internet products and services. In this chapter, we'll build a market model that supports the analysis of Google's Internet-related acquisitions and explore deal rationales for these transactions. We will also identify three major types of post-closure M&A activity at Google that relates to acquired technology and talent.

Internet Services/Software Market Model

Figure 6.1 depicts a market model that we will use to analyze Google's M&A activity in the Internet services and software segments. Recall that market models are dynamic, so structures such as the one in Figure 6.1 must be revisited and updated regularly.

While Google has done M&A transactions in each area of this market model category tree, in this chapter we will focus on and illustrate Google's deals relating to four subsectors of this model:

1. Blogging
2. Internet retail
3. Mobile apps
4. Social networking

Note that we designate some of these sub-sectors such as *mobile apps* as a major heading (with its own folder) of Internet services and software. In fact, one might argue that mobile is becoming so significant that it deserves an even higher-level place in this market model (at the same level as media, Internet services and software, and technology platform). There is surely more than one way to build a market model classification scheme. And we've stressed that these schemes certainly must change with market conditions.

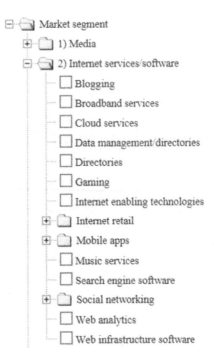

FIGURE 6.1 Internet services/software market model

They must also be able to respond to shifting perceptions that corporate development managers have of strategic opportunities and related acquisition plans.

Blogging

The importance of supporting *blogging* became clear to Google very early in its history. One of Google's first acquisitions was Pyra Labs in 2003, Pyra's Blogger had some one million users at the time, and early speculation was that after the acquisition, Google would charge an annual membership fee for the Blogger Pro service.

However, it soon became clear that Google's game plan would not involve Blogger subscription fees. Blogging would be all about creating another content distribution vehicle for the company to place contextually relevant ads.

Curiously, in 2007 Evan Williams, creator of Blogger, later became co-founder of Twitter. Williams provided a significant amount of Twitter's early

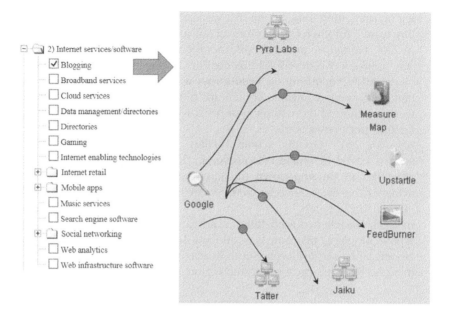

FIGURE 6.2 Blogging-related M&A activity

funding and served as the company's first chairman. Williams is featured in Chapter 13, where we will identify Google's prominent M&A alumni. (M&A alumni are entrepreneurs who sold their companies to Google and then over time went on to other significant activities.)

Over the years, Google continued to use M&A as a means of adding to its blogging technologies and offerings. See Figure 6.2 for a constellation of blogging-related deals.

- In 2006, Google acquired Measure Map, technology that enabled publishers to analyze the amount of traffic their blogs were receiving. Later that year, Measure Map technology was used in the redesign of Google Analytics, a service that generates detailed statistics about a website's traffic as well as measuring marketing data such as sales conversions—clearly a *semi-organic* deal.
- Also in 2006, Google acquired Upstartle, which developed a Web-based application (Writely) that enabled users to access and edit documents from the Internet. The company also offered blog posting and other Internet publishing services. In joining Google Upstartle, co-founder Claudia Carpenter posted: "Coming to Google will eventually give us a

leg up on getting things done that we just haven't been able to with our tiny team." Another *semi-organic* acquisition for talent and technology.

- In 2007, Google acquired FeedBurner for an estimated $100 million plus stay bonuses. We described this deal in Chapter 5 in our discussion of media-related acquisitions. FeedBurner was an RSS (rich site summary) that distributed syndicated content for blogs and other media websites. Google acquired the company in order to give its advertisers access to FeedBurner's news feeds.
- Also, in 2007, Google acquired Jaiku, a microblogging/Twitter-like service based in Finland. However in 2011, Google announced that it would be shutting down the Jaiku services. Not all M&A activity achieves the deal's success metrics. (We'll chronicle some of Google's failures in Chapter 8.)
- In 2008, Google acquired Tatter, a Korean blogging-software company, whose blogging platform was dubbed Textcube. This reportedly was Google's first acquisition in South Korea, and represented an attempt to increase Google's presence in the region.

Overall, we conclude that blogging was persisting as a significant content distribution vehicle and advertising outlet that Google has continued to accelerate and enrich through targeted M&A activity.

Internet Retail

The *e-commerce* market in the United States has become massive and was estimated to be around $300 billion in 2014. Although Amazon, and not Google, is the first company name that comes to mind when one mentions Internet retail, Google would like to change this. The attempt to do so has not been easy.

Amazon and Google are locked in fierce battle to be the search box of choice for users when they make purchases online. If more Internet users search for items on Amazon, Google loses advertising opportunities.[1]

Most analysts feel Google faces significant obstacles as it attempts to compete with Amazon in online retail product search. Amazon is certainly ahead in providing shoppers with an end-to-end experience that features efficient search, extensive customer reviews and product information, extremely broad selection, favorable pricing, easy ordering and rapid delivery. And we've not even talked about Amazon's back-office capabilities that include cutting-edge inventory and fulfillment capabilities.

When you type "coffee" into Amazon's search box, it's naturally assumed that you want to make a purchase, and search results are tuned to your shopping goals. When you type "coffee" into Google's traditional search box, the first result is likely to be a Wikipedia article on coffee, following by news stories about coffee.

Google has created vertical search platforms for online shopping, starting with Froogle (a coupling of *frugal* with Google), but this branding was a little too cutesy. Google later rebranded its commerce initiative to Google Shopping. But as late as 2015, many shoppers did not know where to find Google Shopping even if they happened to know it existed.

According to Forrester Research, in 2012 almost a third of Internet shoppers started research for an online purchase on Amazon, with only 13 percent beginning with a search engine like Google's. Even more importantly, product searches on Amazon were enjoying significant annual increases, while searches on Google Shopping had been essentially been flat.[2]

Unlike Amazon, Google was not making Zappos-like acquisitions in the Internet retail. (Zappos is an online shoe and clothing store purchased by Amazon for more than $1.1 billion in stock and stock options in 2009 and was known for its exceptional customer service.) Google did reportedly approach online "deal-of-the day service" Groupon in 2010, offering some $6 billion to purchase the company, but was rebuffed. The fallout may have been fortunate for Google, as Groupon lost its high-flyer status shortly thereafter.

Nevertheless, Google was moving inch-by-inch to improve Google Shopping, first introducing product pictures and pricing as a result of a search in addition to plain-vanilla text results. And in 2014, Google Shopping improved its product listing ad technology, enabling retailers to obtain premium visibility on a PPC (pay-per-click) basis. Google Express was also competing with Amazon Prime on same-day delivery in certain locales. Google's prime objective was to create a major revenue stream through product search advertising.

Furthermore, Google had made a series of acquisitions to improve its positioning in the Internet retail space. Not all of these acquisitions were successful, but ever the experimenter, Google was using M&A to test possible value-added services to its e-commerce initiatives.

Figure 6.3 depicts a number of Google acquisitions related to Internet retailing. These deals provide an indication of how Google intended to advance its efforts in this space. Let's describe *some* of these transactions, starting at the lower left of the figure and working our way across the bottom:

▪ *Digital loyalty coupons.* In 2011, Google acquired Zave Networks. Zave operated an online incentive program platform that supported in-store redemption of offers distributed via digital media. In early 2013, Google introduced Zavers by Google, which gave retailers and manufacturers the

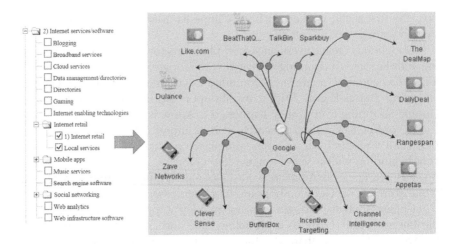

FIGURE 6.3 Google's M&A activity in Internet retailing

ability to reward loyal customers with digital coupons. In 2014, Zavers was being closed down, with Google apparently unsatisfied with the growth of the offering. In addition, later in 2012 Google acquired Incentive Marketing, also pictured in the infographic shown in Figure 6.3. Incentive was a developer of targeted shopper promotion systems.

- *Personalized venue recommendations.* In 2011, Google purchased Clever Sense, a maker of mobile apps for personalized recommendations for nearby restaurants, bars, and other venues using machine-learning algorithms. Yet, just as with Zave, Google closed down Alfred, the Clever Sense recommendations app, in 2012. Google wanted to consolidate its offerings into fewer products, and recommendations were now appearing in Google Maps. It was not clear how much of Clever Sense technology had been redeployed.
- *E-commerce kiosks.* In 2012, Google acquired BufferBox, which delivered e-commerce goods to physical kiosks in grocery and convenience stores in Canada. BufferBox's services were similar to those of Amazon Lockers. The BufferBox acquisition supported the narrative that Google was considering expanding its Internet retail offerings towards an end-to-end consumer experience.
- *Product search enhancements.* In 2013, Google acquired Channel Intelligence for $125 million. Channel Intelligence supported retailers in promoting products across the Web by helping manage their product listings on comparison shopping sites that included Google Shopping. As mentioned earlier, estimates were that about one-third of shoppers start

searches on Amazon, compared to only 13 percent on a search engine. Google hoped the Channel Intelligence deal would help change these statistics.

- *Restaurant vertical.* In 2014, Google acquired Appetas, including technology that restaurants could use to build their own websites, adding services such as OpenTable for delivery services and reservations. Google planned to shut down the service and apparently would integrate it with Google's location-based services and with restaurant content obtained from the Zagat acquisition. Google wanted to enhance its relationship with local businesses, especially the restaurant sector, in order to complete better against services such as Yelp.
- *Back-end e-commerce support.* Also in 2014, Google acquired Rangespan, a UK-based online shopping retailer. The company was founded in 2011 by two former Amazon executives. Rangespan provided back-office services to companies that included Tesco. Rangespan's technology included real-time analytics to support retailers in dynamically determining product offerings.

In examining these deals, it's clear that Google was using M&A to help it edge into Internet retail, but not without both failure and caution. A number of targets had been shuttered and related initiatives abandoned. And as we saw earlier with online travel services, Google was trying to avoid major conflict and was carefully dancing to avoid being perceived as competitive with major advertisers.

Nevertheless, the company continued to square off with Amazon in its goal of becoming the search option of choice for goods and services, Google was placing major M&A bets in improving its product search technology. We'll expand on the Amazon/Google faceoff and related acquisition activity in Chapter 14.

Mobile Apps

Google has acquired a very large number of companies in order to stimulate the vitality of its Android mobile operating system. We identified some of these transactions in the previous chapter in discussing media-related apps.

In this section, we'll illustrate Google's diversity of acquisitions in the mobile app sector. As we explore these deals, consider the significance of these transactions in fostering *semi-organic* growth at Google.

Figure 6.4 shows a selection of M&A transactions that relate to mobile apps. We'll briefly describe these acquisitions starting at the top left of the infographic.

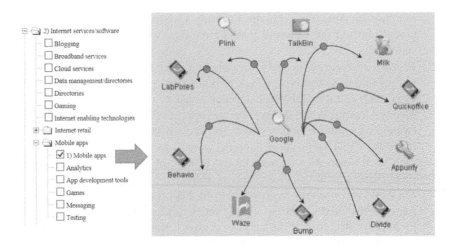

FIGURE 6.4 Google's M&A activity in mobile apps

- *Mobile app gadgets.* In 2010, Google acquired LabPixies for an estimated $25 million. LabPixies published Web and mobile applications such as personalized calendars, to-do lists, news feeds, games, and other entertainment. LabPixies team joined the iGoogle team and operated out of Google Israel's Research and Development Center. LabPixies represented Google's first acquisition in Israel and would be followed by a string of other deals in the region. In 2013, iGoogle was discontinued as Google stated: "With modern apps that run on platforms like Chrome and Android, the need for something like iGoogle has eroded over time." LabPixie founders stayed at Google for three years helping accelerate app technology and then left Google to establish ubimo, a mobile location based-ad platform.

- *Visual search.* Also in 2010, Google acquired Plink, a visual search engine developer. Plink's first product was PlinkArt, an art recognition application for the Android mobile phone. The application focused on identifying artwork through photographs submitted by users. Plink's founders, Mark Cummins and James Philbin, would both join Google to work on Google Goggles, a mobile search application that shared some PlinkArt functionality. Until May 2013, Mark Cummings (PhD, Oxford), was a senior software engineer at Google working on computer vision issues. The systems he worked on were used in products such as Google Goggles, Translate, Drive, and Google+.

- *Customer service feedback.* In 2011, Google acquired TalkBin, which provided a platform that allowed customers to give immediate feedback to local businesses by submitting opinions and critiques via mobile applications. Businesses could respond to customer comments via a Web app. However, Google later reported: "TalkBin usage has dwindled over the past two years, and we have decided to shut down the service on July 31st, 2014." This local commerce experiment apparently had failed.

Pure talent. In 2012, Google purchased Milk, a mobile app incubator established by Digg founder Kevin Rose. Google *acqui-hired* Rose and members of Milk's product development team reportedly to work on projects related to Google+. Shortly thereafter, Rose became a general partner at Google Ventures, the company's corporate venture capital arm.

More pure talent. In 2013, Google acquires Bump, a mobile application that allowed two smartphones to connect wirelessly to send contact information, photos, and files between devices. Almost immediately, Bump announced that its team would be focused on new projects within Google. This deal was apparently more of an *acqui-hire* of Bump's talent than a technology-acquisition deal. An online technology journal was speculating that David Lieb (Bump co-founder) might be working on Google's self-driving car project, working to adapt Bump's technology to short-range communication between vehicles, thereby avoiding "bumps."[3]

Office functionality. In 2012, Google acquired Quickoffice. The company provided office software solutions for mobile phones/smartphones and tablets. Quickoffice allowed users to create and edit Microsoft Word, Excel, and PowerPoint documents on their mobile devices. Later, Quickoffice functionality was integrated into the Google Docs, Sheets, and Slides apps, a clear *semi-organic* move that blended existing Google technology with that of the target.

Predictive analytics. In 2013, Google bought Behavio, a developer of software for mobile devices to sense context and predict human behavior, such as the next place someone was likely to visit. The company was founded by Nadav Aharony, Cody Sumter, and Alan Gardner at the MIT Media Lab while the three were students at the school. All three founders became Googlers.

Mapping. In 2013, Google purchased Waze, an Israeli crowd-sourced mapping and navigation company, for $966 million in cash. (Retention bonuses could increase this amount, as Waze confirmed that 100 employees stood to receive $120 million after deal closing.) Google would use the technology to enhance its Google Maps service with Waze's real-time traffic. Later in 2013, Google Maps introduced Waze's real-time incident reports to Android and iOS applications. Indications were that Google would not immediately absorb Waze into Maps, but enable Waze to continue developing separately as a product feeder.

▪ *Mobile application management.* In 2014, Google acquired Divide, which developed technology to support companies in managing the growing diversity of mobile devices used by employees. Divide helped corporate IT departments keep employee smartphones and tablets secure in the enterprise. Divide allowed Google to position its Apps For Business as a safer, more enterprise-friendly product, which it could later use in attempting to migrate companies over from Microsoft Office to Google Apps. In addition, Divide's network of technology and channel partnerships with companies like Box, IBM, Dell, Verizon, and Vodafone promised to give Google a stronger foothold in the enterprise space. Divide's founders, who had worked in Morgan Stanley's IT team, had a deep understanding of the financial industry's needs.

▪ *Mobile app development.* Also in 2014, Google acquired Appurify, which offered technology to automate the testing and optimization of mobile apps and websites for developers. Appurify's 20+ employees would join Google. Google Ventures had led an investment round in Appurify, so the deal represented a *staged acquisition*. Application testing and optimization had become a major issue for Android. Tim Cook (Apple CEO) had highlighted Android's fragmentation problem, glibly quoting others who have called Android a "toxic hellstew of vulnerabilities."

By no means have we covered all of Google's acquisitions in the mobile application space. But this deal sample clearly illustrates that *semi-organic* growth that coupled a target's talent and technology with Google's products and services was a major force in Google's growth strategy for mobile.

Social Networking

In 2014, debate was intense over the future of Google+, Google's social networking offering. Google+ was continuing to be thrashed by Facebook, and some pundits were asserting that Google+ should be placed among the "walking dead." Yet others were arguing that not all was lost in that Google had evolved Google+ into social plumbing infrastructure for application environments such as Hangouts and YouTube. Doing so could allow the company to pull together data about a user's likes, interests, and background to use in targeted ads in multiple platforms.[4]

In this section, we'll examine a number of Google's acquisitions in the social networking space (both successes and failures) to obtain insight about where Google has attempted to go with its social initiatives. As already implied, gaining traction in social has been one of Google's greatest challenges.

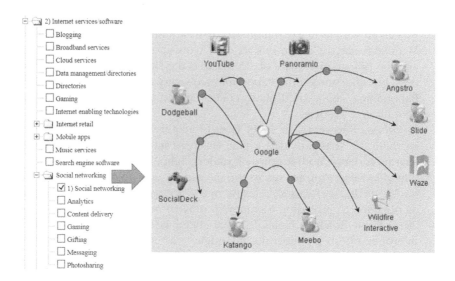

FIGURE 6.5 Select Google M&A's in social networking

Figure 6.5 depicts 10 of the acquisitions Google has made in the social space.

- *Early exploration.* In 2005, Google acquired Dodgeball, whose technology allowed people to text friends, as well as friends of friends within a 10-block radius. Photos could be sent with the text. The service targeted users wanting a convenient way to organize a meeting at a local bar or other venue. The company was co-founded by Dennis Crowley and Alex Rainert, graduates of NYU's Interactive Telecommunications Program. In 2009, Dennis Crowley co-founded FourSquare after leaving Google, feeling Dodgeball had been neglected. FourSquare became a prominent meet-up application with functionality similar to Dodgeball, but sported an improved mobile Web user interface.
- *Video social mega-deal.* We've already discussed Google's $1.65 billion acquisition of YouTube in 2006, but this deal can't be omitted in our discussion of Google's significant *social media* deals. YouTube was the leading video sharing site on the Web. In 2015, YouTube continued to progress as a platform for growing Google's ad revenue beyond core search. YouTube has been allowed to run largely as an autonomous unit.
- *Social photo mapping.* In 2007, Google bought Panoramio, a community website that allowed people to "map" photos on Google Earth/Google

Maps. The technology linked the exact geographical spot where a photo was taken with its map location. In 2010, Panoramio co-founder Eduardo Manchón exited Google but stated: "Acquisitions can be complicated, and the private nightmare of a founder is the site not surviving the process, but after some time Panoramio feels very comfortable at Google." Panoramio's geo-located photo collection had grown from 2 million to 20 million at Google.

- *Social business news.* In 2010, Google acquired Angstro, a social networking site that provided online business information discovery and sharing services. Both Angstro's founders, Salim Ismail and Rohit Kohare, joined Google. Angstro (as in the measuring unit angstrom) attempted to deliver "highly focused, relevant news" across a user's social network, as opposed to providing a scattered array of random search results. In 2014, Rohit Kohare's LinkedIn page stated he was working on open, interoperable social networks at Google.
- *Social apps.* Also in 2010, Google acquired Slide for approximately $180 million. According to TechCrunch, Google agreed to pay an additional $46M in employee retention bonuses.[5] Slide developed online applications for social networking websites, including slideshow, image and video personalization, guestbook, and virtual gift applications. However, only a year later in 2011, Google announced it would dissolve Slide and focus its social networking efforts on Google+. Slide founder Max Levchin would leave Google and later join Yahoo's board. Many other Slide employees joined the YouTube team.
- *Social games.* Google's social M&A spree continued in 2010 when it bought social games start-up SocialDeck, a gaming company that developed titles for Facebook, as well as for other platforms. By 2014, the Google Play Games service was growing rapidly, activating over 100 million users during a six-month period.
- *Social network segmentation.* In 2011, Google acquired Katango, which developed technology to analyze friend lists to generate related people so that users could better segment social networks. Katango's application was capable of sorting and organizing social contacts by life stage or activity using Facebook data. The Katango team would be assigned to Google+. Curiously, Katango was an early investment of the sFund, a $250 million venture fund to back innovation in social media. This fund was managed by Kleiner Perkins, but Facebook provided guidance to the fund and was an investor. Hence, in buying Katango, Google acquired a company with ties to Facebook! This would not be the last time this type of acquisition would occur.
- *Instant message chat.* In 2012, Google acquired Meebo for an estimated $100 million. With Meebo, users could chat with each other across

different instant message services. Meebo's core offerings were shut down so that talent from the acquired team could focus on technology tightly tied to Google+.

- *Social advertising.* Also in 2012, Google acquired social marketing software developer Wildfire Interactive for an estimated $350 million plus retention bonuses for employees that included co-founder Victoria Ransom, CEO. Wildfire enabled companies to serve marketing and ad campaigns on social sites. Wildfire was one of few remaining independent social marketing players with an enterprise client list. And, once again, Facebook had been an investor in the company through the Kleiner Perkins sFund. In 2014, Wildfire stopped signing up new customers as Victoria Ransom stated that Wildfire technology would be integrated into the core Google adtech platform. Wildfire's tenure as a "preserved" entity would come to an end.
- *Social traffic information.* As mentioned in our discussion of mobile app transaction, in 2013 Google purchased Waze, an Israeli crowd-sourced mapping and navigation company, for $966 million in cash. Google would use the technology to enhance its Google Maps service with Waze's real-time social traffic information.

Post-Closure Deal Analysis

In analyzing our sample of social networking transactions, we can identify three major categories of post-closure M&A activity at Google.

1. Acquisitions whose products continue within Google after transaction close, meeting at least some major deal success metrics. Examples include YouTube, Panoramio, and Waze. ***Three deals total***.
2. Acquisitions whose products are shuttered after missing major success metrics. Examples include Dodgeball. Slide, and possibly Wildfire. (Some Wildfire technology was deployed in Google's general adtech platform.) ***Three deals total***.
3. Classic *acqui-hires* where target products were quickly shuttered in order that acquired talent/technology could be deployed to other Google teams: Angstro, SocialDeck, Katango, and Meebo. ***Four deals total***.

Classifying deals into these post-closure categories is not always clear cut and certainly can ignore organization subtlety involved in post-merger integration. Nevertheless this tri-partite scheme will provide a beginning point for our deeper discussion of M&A integration that we will undertake in Chapters 12 and 13.

Watch the Video

www.wiley.com/go/semiorganicgrowth
To view a video relating to the content of this chapter, refer to *Contrasting Amazon's Acquisition Strategy with Google's,* which accompanies this book as a supplemental resource.

Notes

1. Rolfe Winkler, "Amazon vs. Google: It's a War for the Shopping Search," *Wall Street Journal* (December 20, 2013).
2. Claire Cane Miller and Stephanie Clifford, "Google Struggles to Unseat Amazon as the Web's Most Popular Mall," *New York Times* (September 9, 2012).
3. Michael del Castillo, "Now that Google's Bump Is Dead, Are Self-Driving Cars on the Horizon?" *Upstart Business Journal* (January 4, 2014).
4. Ryan Tate, "Why Google+ Should Give up Its Battle against Facebook," *Wired* (April 25, 2014).
5. Sarah Lacy, "Google Buys Slide for $182 Million, Getting More Serious about Social Games," *TechCrunch* (August 4, 2010).

CHAPTER 7

Google Technology Platform Deals

Although Google's main roots have grown in the media/advertising and Internet/search soil, the company is exploring and expanding into an ever-widening range of segments that are best classified under the *technology platform* heading.

Figure 7.1 depicts a high-level schema of a sample market model relevant to Google's reach into the technology platform sector.

In this chapter, we will explore M&A activity in three subsectors within this technology platform that are significant for Google's strategic direction:

1. Smartphones
2. Smart home
3. Robotics (and AI)

Although some of the acquisitions in these subsectors have appeared in our earlier discussions of Google's M&A activity, it will be important to revisit these deals within the context of Google's goals for expanding the range and effectiveness of its technology initiatives.

Smartphones

When one thinks of Google in connection with the *smartphone* market, Android naturally comes to mind. In 2005, Google acquired Android for an estimated $50 million. Android was a small startup based in Palo Alto that made operating system software for mobile phones. This purchase triggered rumors that Google was entering the mobile phone market, although it was unclear at the time exactly how the company would play in this space.

In 2007, Android emerged from being a stealth project as Google spearheaded the unveiling of the Open Handset Alliance (OHA) and introduced Android as an open source mobile operating system for smartphone devices. Over time, the Android operating system became the dominant platform for

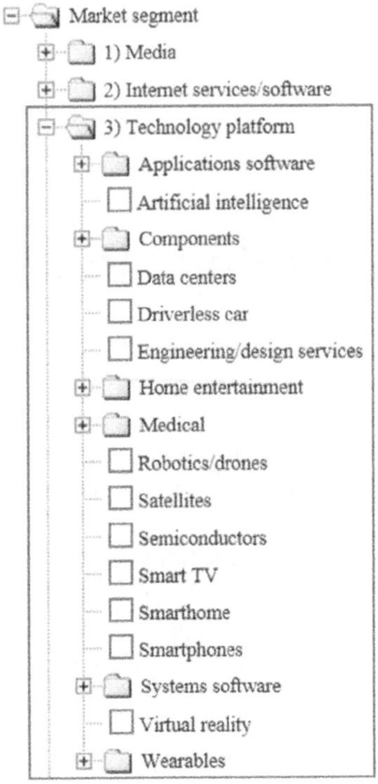

FIGURE 7.1 Technology platform market model

mobile phones. By 2014, Android was powering over 1 billion smartphones and tablets around the world.

As early as 2010, David Lawee, then vice president of M&A at Google, remarked at the Stanford Accel Symposium that the Android acquisition was Google's "best deal ever." Lawee noted that initially he was skeptical about the acquisition, and after seeing founder Andy Rubin hanging around Google for several years recalls saying: "I hope this guy does something." On the other hand, seeing Rubin around for years after the acquisition did inspire some hope, as Lawee added that when a deal isn't working "the people leave."[1]

Figure 7.2 provides an infographic of Google's acquisition of Android and some other smartphone-related transactions.

Mobile Operating Systems

As mentioned above, the 2005 acquisition of Android has been regarded by some as Google's best deal ever. Although Google did not charge a

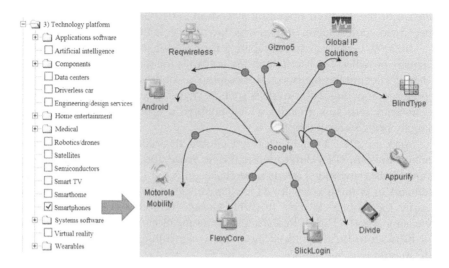

FIGURE 7.2 Android and related acquisitions

licensing fee for the operating system itself, the company has greatly profited from mobile ads displayed on Android phones as well as from revenues earned in the Google Play store. The strategy to open source Android drove rapid adoption of the platform, which augured well for Google's ad-based business model.

Google made additional acquisitions in the direct support of Android. For example, in 2013 Google acquired FlexyCore, a developer of system solutions for mobile applications. FlexyCore was best known for Droid-Booster, which improved the performance of Android, both for speed and battery life. The FlexyCore team was integrated with Google's Android team. Reportedly, the acquisition of this French company was a year in the making, and was considered a long courtship for an *acqui-hire* type transaction.

Mobile Web Browsing and Voice over IP

Shortly after acquiring Android, in 2006 Google purchased Reqwireless, which made Web browser and rich e-mail software for use on wireless devices. By making this acquisition, Google would establish a wireless technology beachhead in the Waterloo region of Canada, in the very backyard of BlackBerry. Google stated that it acquired Reqwireless "because of the talented engineers and great technology." In addition to buying Reqwireless, Google actively recruited software engineers and developers in Waterloo in anticipation of its major move into wireless technology spearheaded by the release of the Android operating system in 2007. Google had gone into a mecca for wireless talent to *semi-organically* accelerate its mobile capability.

In 2009, Google acquired Gizmo5 for an estimated $30 million in cash. Gizmo5 provided Internet telephony software for mobile phones and PCs. Gizmo5's technology supported incoming or outbound voice calls to real phones, competing with products such as Skype. Google integrated Gizmo5 technology into Gmail/Gtalk, which enabled a user to make phone calls directly from a Gmail inbox.

Also, in 2010, Google acquired Global IP Solutions (GIPS) for $68.2 million in cash. GIPS developed real-time voice and video processing software for IP networks. Google's purchase reflected its belief in heightened demand in coming years for video conversations over IP networks, principally for mobile devices. In 2011, Google utilized GIPS technology in releasing WebRTC (Web Real Time Communications), a proposed standard for browser-to-browser applications for voice calling, video chat, and P2P file sharing without plugins.

Smartphone Keyboards

One of the major challenges in the use of smartphones involved input limitations. In 2010, Google acquired BlindType, a developer of virtual keyboards. BlindType allowed users to type on touch screens without having to look at the screen. The software enabled a user to type anywhere on a screen, and then BlindType predicted the words one wanted to type based on the vicinity of the letters one typed. In 2011, the keyboard of Android 4.0 (Ice Cream Sandwich) was apparently built using BlindType technology.

Major Move into Smartphones

In 2011, Google made its largest acquisition to date when it bought Motorola Mobility for $40 per share in cash, or a total of about $12.5 billion. This price tag reflected a premium of 63 percent over the previous closing price of the target's shares. The acquisition of Motorola Mobility substantially augmented Google's thin patent portfolio of about 2,000 patents, increasing it to approximately 20,000. With another 7,500 Motorola patents awaiting approval, the acquisition would enable Google to better defend itself against more fundamental IP attacks, and gain additional leverage in global patent negotiations and litigation. The transaction allowed (for a while) Google to enter the handset business in a big way, possibly tightening hardware/software integration, which had so long been a key competitive advantage for Apple. Nevertheless, the deal was controversial, with major concerns arising on the impact of the transaction on existing Android OEMs such as Samsung, who might now view Google as a competitor. In 2014, Google announced plans to sell Motorola Mobility to Lenovo, ending its role as a major handset manufacturer. Much more about this deal is covered in Chapter 8, where we will discuss *shuttered* deals.

Smartphones for Authentication

In 2014, Google acquired SlickLogin, which had developed technology allowing users to authenticate password-protected accounts by placing a smartphone near a computer or tablet. SlickLogin was attractive to Google, given its philosophy that security should be simple and that "logging in should be easy instead of frustrating, and authentication should be effective without getting in the way." SlickLogin's founders were formerly with the cybersecurity unit of the Israeli Defense Force. The three-person team would join Google as a small *acqui-hire* working with Android in semi-organically growing mobile.

Mobile Device Management

In 2014, Google acquired Divide, which developed technology to support companies in managing the growing diversity of mobile devices used by employees. In contrast to Apple, Google had traditionally controlled apps in its Play store less tightly, thereby making Android apps more susceptible to malware. Google hoped the Divide acquisition would help Android achieve more penetration in the enterprise market, allowing Google to position its Apps For Business as a safer, more enterprise-friendly product. Divide's founders, who worked in Morgan Stanley's IT team, would also bring a useful understanding of the financial industry's needs.

Mobile Application Testing

Also in 2014, Google acquired Appurify, whose technology automated the testing and optimization of mobile apps and websites for developers. Appurify was founded in 2012 and had 20+ employees who would join Google. Appurify would continue to offer its freemium cross-platform service, but was likely to enjoy major adoption acceleration as it is integrated into the Google developer tool stack. Application testing and optimization was a big deal for Android. Tim Cook (Apple CEO) had highlighted Android's fragmentation problem, glibly quoting others who have dubbed Android a "toxic hellstew of vulnerabilities."

Overall, by 2014, not only was Android providing a platform that promised to fuel a rapidly growing mobile advertising market, but it also was the underpinning of a frenetic market associated with the Google Play app store, which was now challenging Apple's highly successful App Store.

The Android acquisition and *semi-organic* acquisitions related to Android were spawning revenue sources far beyond Google's imagination when it began its mobile platform initiatives. Android, if not Google's best acquisition, had certainly earned its place on the medal platform for deals.

The Smart Home

The $3.2 billion cash acquisition of Nest Labs in 2014 represented Google's second largest purchase to date, surpassed only by the Motorola Mobility deal. Nest was a leading player in the Internet of Things (IoT), which involved enabling everyday objects with communications technology to become more efficient and convenient. The company's initial products included smart thermostats and smoke alarms for homes.

The Nest deal reflected a major Google diversification effort beyond its core advertising business into the *smart home* space. Google asserted that Nest would continue to operate under its own brand, sell its products, and provide support to existing and future customers. It was unclear what, if any, customer data Nest would share with Google.

Although Nest was *the* transformative deal for Google in the smart home market, the company was also making other acquisitions relating to this segment. Figure 7.3 depicts some of these deals.

Smart Home Anchor Deal

The acquisition of Nest Labs put a major stake in the ground for Google, as it signaled its intent to be a major player in the smart home space.

Nest was founded in 2010 by Tony Fadell and Matt Rogers. Nest's founders stated that its goal was to create a "conscious home" where devices interact with one another and the home's inhabitants in order to make the home smarter and improve the performance of devices. The IoT space was receiving substantial attention and investment as the tech industry competed to deliver responsive devices that would operate interactively.

The first product released by Nest was a smart thermostat that could learn what temperature one preferred at different times and also save energy. The product was touted as "what Apple would have done" if it had released a thermostat. It was visually simple and appealing. Nest intended to reinvent unloved but important devices in the home.

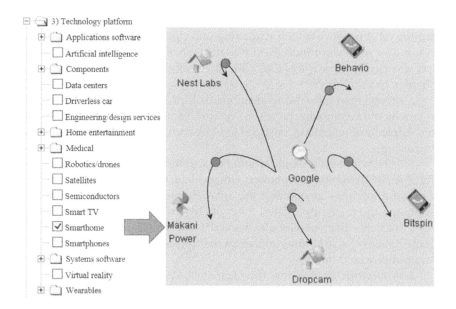

FIGURE 7.3 Google's smart home–related acquisitions

With Nest asserting it was shipping some 40,000 thermostats a month, the smart thermostat was hailed as a success both financially and as an innovation in a slow-moving and heavily regulated sector. The company's second product, a smart smoke and CO_2 detector, was launched in fall 2013. It was unclear how well the product would perform. In 2014, a defect in the motion sensor that could turn the alarm off accidentally led to a halt in sales. Nevertheless, the feedback had been positive overall, and the fact that the two products could communicate indicated a larger scale opportunity.

Nest products were built around an operating system that allowed interaction with the gadget directly or via a user's mobile device. Given that products were connected to the Internet, software updates would automatically be downloaded to fix bugs, improve performance, and add features.

Nest products would learn a user's habits over time and adjust temperature (for example) accordingly. Human behavior could be profiled and user needs could be anticipated.

Google acquired Nest for reasons that included: (1) talent, (2) to fend off a possible acquisition offer from Apple and, perhaps most importantly, (3) the opportunity to get ahead of the Internet of Things revolution with a proven product.

In terms of talent, founders Fadell and Rogers were both former Apple employees. Fadell's skill was particularly appealing as he was known as "one of the fathers of the iPod," and had deep experience in design, engineering, and product launch marketing and operations. He would stay on to run Nest post-acquisition. Nest was not a small *acqui-hire*, but nevertheless was clearly an *ACQUI-HIRE*. (We discuss four forms of "acqui-hires" in Chapter 13.)

A second reason for the acquisition involved a rumored offer from Apple to purchase the company. As we've seen in Chapter 3, over the years Google and Apple have repeatedly engaged in M&A competition and in *dyadic M&A cascading*.

Finally, with Nest, Google would move to the front of the pack in bringing a smart thermostat to market. Google had made numerous less-than-successful attempts at entering the smart home market, and Nest would overcome the company's failed attempts by making a distinctively strong entry into this market. Google wanted to revitalize its Android for the home initiative, a 2011 announcement that promised a home connected by Android-powered devices.

Semi-organic growth was the clear goal. As Nest stated, "Google will help us fully realize our vision of the conscious home and allow us to change the world faster than we ever could if we continued to go it alone."

Behavioral Analysis

In 2013, Google bought Behavio, a developer of software for mobile devices to sense context and predict human behavior, such as the next place someone was likely to visit. The company was founded by Nadav Aharony, Cody Sumter, and Alan Gardner at the MIT Media Lab while the three were students at the school. Behavio was a classic acqui-hire, as all three founders would become Googlers.

Although the talent and technology acquired in the Behavio deal could be applied to many Google products and services, consider some possible links to the smart home and to Nest. Google could utilize the data gathering capabilities of Behavio to optimize performance and make the smart home "smarter." For example, a thermostat could be alerted that a user is on her way home early and automatically change settings. In turn, Behavio's technology might access Nest product data and integrate that into the pattern of data it collected relating to a user.

Green Energy for the Smart Home

In 2013, Google acquired Makani Power, a green energy startup that was building airborne wind turbines (AWTs). Google had previously invested

$15 million in the company. Makani would be nurtured within the Google X skunkworks.

Makani (Hawaiian for wind) was developing technology that combined kites with turbines flying in large vertical loops to capture a stronger, more consistent wind with on-board power generation traveling down a tether to a grid. Since AWTs promised to be more aerodynamically effective than conventional turbines, they could produce more power at any given wind speed. AWTs operated between 80 to 350 meters, an altitude that enabled them to generate wind power economically in more locations. For example, in the United States, AWTs could generate wind power economically in about two-thirds of the landmass, considerably larger than the area available to conventional wind.

Could it emerge in Google's grand vision of the Internet of Things? Makani's AMTs and Nest's portfolio of products regulating and automating the home might become two "smart" nodes of the same network. Still in the experimental stage, only time will tell if the Makani technology would pan out for commercial use.

Home Security

In 2014, Google announced plans to acquire Dropcam, which developed Wi-Fi–connected video cameras and services that streamed live video to mobile apps. The service sent alerts based on activity sensed by Dropcam cameras and allowed users to communicate with people in their homes (such as children) while the user was away. The company's products and services were often used as a home-security system.

With the Dropcam deal, Google/Nest was continuing to add products and services in its push to become the dominant home operating system for a widening variety of connected devices.

Smart Home Apps

Also in 2014, Google acquired Bitspin, a developer of the elegant Smart Rise alarm app based on sleep-cycle theory. The stylish app ran on the Android operating system for mobile devices and was available on Google Play. Bitspin's Timely could be used to synchronize alarms across multiple devices owned by a user. Elegant design in apps continued to be highly valued by Google as it ramped up its offerings with Apple competition clearly in mind.

Google, through Nest Labs and related acquisitions, was moving to become the hub for the smart home. In June 2014, Nest launched a developer program that allowed other apps and devices access to what Nest detected through its sensors. These services would be able to talk to one another via Nest as the hub. Opening up to other services was viewed as "integral to Nest's reinvention of the humble thermostat, which was paralleling the way Apple reinvented the mobile phone as an app-centric device."[2] The unassuming thermostat might be destined to develop into an *operating system platform* for life in the home.

Robotics and Artificial Intelligence

Google X is widely known as Google's factory for moonshots. It was the romantic vision of the self-driving car that in 2005 triggered the conception of this research lab. At an obstacle course in the Mojave Desert, Larry Page witnessed a team led by Stanford computer scientist Sebastian Thrun win the DARPA Grand Challenge, taking home a $2 million prize as the robotic car "Stanley" outperformed all comers.

Page and Thrun discovered a common interest in *robotics* and *artificial intelligence*. In 2007, Thrun and several of his students joined Google's Street View mapping project. In 2009, Thrun initiated the self-driving car project. Within 15 months, Google's driverless car was successfully navigating Los Angeles and Silicon Valley streets.[3]

In this section, we will examine a cluster of acquisitions that supported Google's thrust into robotics and artificial intelligence, especially featuring mapping technology and the driverless car. As behavioral economist and data scientist Colin Lewis argued:

"Maps are clearly at the core of Google's development strategy, from driverless cars, online shopping and search, to wearable technology. Many of the recent robot acquisitions will enhance Google's mobile strategy and improve its delivery services, hardware capabilities, and above all localization experiences. Google's geographic data may become its most valuable asset. Not solely because of this data alone, but because location data makes everything else Google does and knows more valuable."[4]

Figure 7.4 presents an infographic depicting some Google acquisitions that are highly relevant to the company's robotics, artificial intelligence (AI), and driverless car initiatives.

Early Mapping Technology

Google's interest in mapping began quite early in its corporate history. In 2004, Google acquired ZipDash, which developed technology to reduce frustration in daily commuting, with the goal of giving drivers a sense of control over when to leave and which routes to take. ZipDash gathered

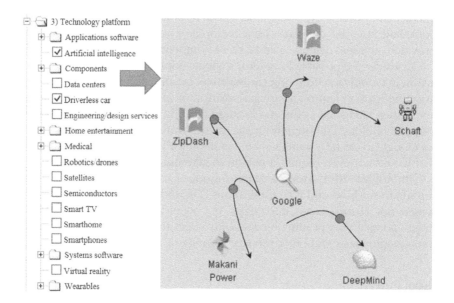

FIGURE 7.4 Robotics, AI, and driverless car-related acquisitions

"location information of individual cell-phone users, data from taxi and trucking fleets, and captures highway sensor data to provide a map of traffic speeds as green, yellow and red arrows." In 2007, ZipDash technology appeared in Google Traffic, a feature of Google Maps that displayed real-time traffic conditions on major roads and highways. ZipDash engineers also helped develop another technology that became "My Location," which enabled users to search relative to their current locations.

Crowd-Sourced Traffic Information

Google's commitment to mapping rose to an even higher level when it acquired Waze for $966 million plus retention bonuses in 2013. Founded in 2008 in Israel, Waze Mobile was a crowdsourced traffic application set out to "help people create local driving communities that work together to improve the quality of everyone's daily driving." Waze accomplished this by enabling "drivers to build and use live maps, real-time traffic updates, and turn-by-turn navigation for an optimal commute, as well as report to the community on traffic, accidents, police traps, and blocked roads."

Waze's scale not only extended the reach of Google Maps but also added another dimension of consumer engagement. Waze's mission of "contributing to the common good out there on the road" empowered its users to interact and provide the content beneficial to other drivers. Apple and Facebook had also bid on Waze; hence, Google's acquisition of the company provided strategic defense against these competitors.

Consider the possible long-term strategic implications of the Waze transaction in Google's self-driving car initiative. Imagine a fully integrated offering in which you request a car via a smartphone and a self-driven car arrives and is then navigated to the end location utilizing Google Maps powered by Waze technology. Although futuristic, pieces were starting to come together for Google to create a seamlessly integrated pickup and delivery mechanism that would not even require a person to take out a wallet or keychain.

In August 2013, Google Maps introduced Waze's real-time incident reports to Android and iOS applications. The indications were that Google would not absorb Waze into Maps, but would allow Waze to maintain independence as a product feeder, with select functionality being brought into Google Maps and other service offerings.

Robot Drivers

In Chapter 2, we illustrated a cluster of eight robotics acquisitions Google made in 2013. We will feature one of these deals in the context of our driverless cars discussion. One of the robotics companies Google purchased in 2013 was Schaft, a designer of humanoid robots using a water-cooled, capacitor-powered motor system. Schaft's technology was designed to make its robots stronger while keeping them compact.

In late 2013, Schaft's robot dominated competition in the DARPA Robotics Challenge. The Pentagon had set up a robot boot camp, which included eight challenges such as turning off a valve, opening a set of doors, cleaning up debris, and driving an all-terrain vehicle. A robot that could do all of this certainly seemed capable of evolving to use Google Maps to drive a delivery vehicle and carry a package a customer's front door.

Vehicle Green Power

Remember Makani Power, the green energy startup acquired by Google described in our earlier discussion of smart home–related acquisitions? Would it become possible to use Makani's airborne wind turbines to power driverless car charging stations?

AI Talent

Recall Google's talent grab when it purchased DeepMind in 2014. DeepMind was an artificial intelligence company that built learning algorithms that could be used in a wide range of applications to tackle contextually sensitive and complex situations requiring substantial data mining. For example, using DeepMind algorithms, Google Now could crawl your Gmail Inbox, and proactively inform you the time when a specific package is likely to arrive.

Additionally, DeepMind algorithms might serve as an ongoing driver's education instructor for Google's self-driving cars, making the vehicles ever more sensitive to route subtleties on specific roads at specific times.

Technology Platform Scope and Endgame

As Figure 7.1 shows, we have far from exhausted the extensive reach of Google's technology platform and the acquisitions that support this platform. However, in exploring three major sectors (smartphones, the smart home, and robotics/AI), we can appreciate the extent to which M&A activity has and will continue to support Google's *semi-organic* growth relating to its technology platform. Although future market victory is far from uncertain in these arenas, the acquisition of key talent and technology certainly seem to improve Google's odds of success.

And from a broad strategy perspective, these Google initiatives are designed to reduce menial tasks for users, whether such tasks involve mobile, home, or automobile activity. Doing so could well enable users to spend more time watching digital video or doing other things they enjoy online, where Google can continue to advance its historic core—high-margin advertising revenue.

Notes

1. Owen Thomas, "Google Exec: Android Was 'Best Deal Ever,'" *Venture-Beat* (October 27, 2010).
2. Pammy Olsen, "Google's Nest Moves to Become Master of the Smart Home, by Talking to Other Devices," *Forbes* (June 24, 2014).
3. Brad Stone, "Inside Google's Secret Lab," *Bloomberg Businessweek* (May 22, 2913).
4. Colon Lewis, "Google's Robot and Artificial Intelligence Acquisitions Are Anything but Scary," *Robohub* (February 12, 2014).

CHAPTER 8

Failed or Shuttered Deals

A s stated in Chapter 1, Google has enjoyed an enviable success rate in its M&A transactions, asserting in recent years that some two-thirds of its deals are viewed as having achieved the major goals established by the company. Broadly speaking, Google regards a deal as a failure if: (1) it doesn't incorporate the target's technology into a Google product; (2) Google shutters a product that it intended to continue; (3) a team leaves earlier than Google desires.[1]

Google's M&A track record is arguably the best in Silicon Valley history.[2] And we have touted the dramatic semi-organic growth that deals such as Applied Semantics and Android have brought. But Google has also experienced dozens of failed acquisitions.

Not wanting to gild the deal lily, in this chapter we feature some of Google's significant M&A failures and suggest why these deals did not attain Google's success metrics.

Success Metrics

Before M&A failure can be identified, we need to determine what constitutes success in a deal. Establishing predetermined success metrics and measuring results against these metrics at regular intervals after acquisition close is an essential dimension of a sound M&A program. For example, consider what such metrics might look like for two Google acquisitions, Makani Power in 2013 and Nest Labs in 2014.

Makani Power was a green energy startup building an Airborne Wind Turbine (AWT) that combined kites with turbines flying in vertical loops to capture on-board power generation that traveled down a tether to a grid. In 2013, Google acquired Makani for an estimated $30 million.

What type of success metrics might Google set for Makani? Because of the "moonshot" nature of this technology, Makani's AWT was not yet generating revenue, so the typical financial metrics would not do, at least in the short run.

However, here are some metrics that could be established in evaluating the Makani acquisition:

- Patents obtained
- Initial model build time
- Integration milestones with other Google products (including the smarthome offerings from Nest Labs)
- Time to complete first commercially viable prototype
- Manufacturing cost curves
- Power generation capacity

And then there was an actual, rather unconventional metric established by Larry Page as a condition for approving the acquisition. According to Astro Teller, a Google X director, Page insisted: " ... that we had to make sure to crash at least five of the devices in the near future."[3] More about the rationale behind such *crash and burn* metrics later.

Next consider Nest Labs. Recall that in 2013, Google purchased Nest for $3.2 billion in cash. Nest designed, manufactured, and distributed sensor-driven, Wi-Fi–enabled, self-learning, programmable thermostats, smoke detectors, and other devices with the mission to reinvent "unloved but important devices in the home."

Here are some metrics that could be established in measuring the success of the Nest acquisition:

- Product unit sales, which could serve as an indicator of the number of homes Nest technology has reached
- Progress in large-scale partnerships with utility companies designed to accelerate adoption
- Number of states reached in the United States
- Number of new international markets entered
- Documented average energy savings costs per household
- Development of a Nest hub, serving as the core device for the Android operating system in the home
- Retention of key Nest management, designers, and engineers

Once deal success metrics are established, actual results should be measured against these goals at regular (for example, six month) intervals. The goal posts should not be moved, unless there is a compelling rationale to do so. And even if success metrics are adjusted, the original set of metrics should not be forgotten as these metrics provide insight as to management's skill in the initial analysis of a deal.

In any case, after metrics are established for a given deal, the stage is set for tracking acquisition success or failure.

Goodwill Write-Downs and Deal Failure

Goodwill is a big number on the balance sheets of many technology companies. For example, in 2013 Google had $10.5 billion of goodwill, Microsoft $14.7 billion, Cisco $17.0 billion, and Hewlett-Packard $30.9 billion.

How does this asset arise? Contrary to how it sounds, goodwill is not booked as a result of strong brands, excellent customer relations, or talented management admired by shareholders. As much as a corporation might like to claim its favor with customers or other stakeholders as an asset, it can't be done for financial reporting purposes.

Goodwill results from acquisitions and acquisitions only. Goodwill arises when an acquirer pays more than the fair market value of acquired net identifiable assets. For example, when Google bought YouTube in 2006 for $1.65 billion, it allocated over $1.1 billion to goodwill, far more than, for example, the $0.1 billion allocated to trademarks and customer contracts.

For a number of technology companies goodwill is much larger than other major balance sheet items such as property, plant, and equipment (PP&E). In 2013, Cisco's goodwill was about 500 percent of its PP&E; Hewlett-Packard's was 265 percent; Microsoft's was 169 percent.

For other tech companies, goodwill has been a relatively minor asset. In 2013, historically low-acquisitive Apple, goodwill was only 9 percent of PP&E. And Samsung's goodwill is less than 1 percent of its PP&E. (As both companies became more acquisitive starting in 2014, this percentage was destined to rise.)

Goodwill must be tested for impairment at least once per year, and any impairment charge reduces operating income. For example, in 2012 HP announced it was taking a $5 billion goodwill impairment charge related to its Autonomy acquisition. Also in 2012, Microsoft announced it was taking a $6.2 billion charge to write down goodwill relating its aQuantive online-advertising acquisition.

Google, although extremely acquisitive as we've seen, as of 2014 had never taken a charge for M&A goodwill impairment. (Google has taken impairment charges relating to acquired assets, such as a patent impairment charge taken in 2014 relating to the Motorola deal.) This hardly means that all Google acquisitions have been successful. Goodwill impairment is typically analyzed at the operating segment level, and success can continue to occur within a segment even if some deals within that segment have failed. Indeed, dozens of Google deals have been classified as failures.

Failure and the Spirit of Experimentation

We noted earlier the pervasive spirit of experimentation that is part of Google's culture. The proclivity for experimentation is clearly present in Google's M&A activity. Of course, an acquisition such FlexyCore, which provided an application for improving the performance of Android, involves a much lower level of experimentation than moonshot acquisitions such as Makani Power.

Failure is inherently associated with experimentation and risk. In fact, we've seen, somewhat paradoxically with acquisitions such as Makani, that planned failure can be viewed as a success metric. With such acquisitions, Google feels it must not move too cautiously into the unknown.

Given Google's experimentation mentality, one would expect that some M&A activity would be likely to miscarry. In addition, Google's use of M&A to expand its market reach increases the level of risk as the company attempts to move farther away from its core competency.

So some of Google's M&A miscarriage can be attributed to the company's *failure is a feature* mentality. Even before the company had huge financial resources, Google's founders exhibited a proclivity for making bets with the potential to change the way the world works. According to Ramsey Allington, a Director of M&A Integration at Google: "Larry and Sergey are scientists and they believe in allowing people to fail. Yes, it costs time and money, but that kind of exploration is what makes us who we are."[4]

However, there are Google M&A failures that do not have primary roots in scientific exploration. We now examine some of these deals.

Some Shuttered Transactions

Figure 8.1 presents an infographic displaying some Google acquisitions that could be considered failures. We'll explore each one of these details to identify the root causes of these deal disappointments.

Unresolvable Execution Differences

In 2006, Google acquired dMarc Broadcasting, a company that worked with radio advertisers in the sales, scheduling, delivery, and reporting of radio ads. According a 10-Q statement, Google paid $97.6 million in cash plus up

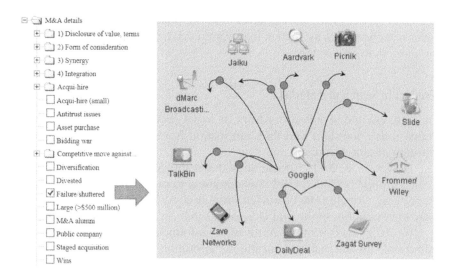

FIGURE 8.1 Some Google acquisition failures

to $1.136 billion in cash contingent payments for dMarc. Note that so-called earn-outs (cash contingent payments) reflected over 90 percent of the potential consideration!

In 2007, Chad and Ryan Steelberg, dMarc's founders, left Google in an apparent conflict over the extent to which the radio ad process should be automated. Evidently, the dMarc founders wanted more salespeople than Google and were concerned about lower-than-expected revenue growth.[5] The Steelbergs asserted that Google owed them more money, given the earn-out associated with the sale. (As we'll see later in Chapter 11, failed deals such as dMarc had a major impact on Google's reliance on earn-outs as contingent consideration.)

Then in 2009, Google pulled the plug on its Google Audio Ads and Adsense for Audio products, intending to sell off its Google Radio Automation software business. The campaign to transform the radio advertising market had failed. Building the technology to auction and track radio ads was not working. And getting stations to allocate a portion of their advertising slots to auction was much more challenging than expected.[6]

Inability to Compete against Incumbent

In 2007, Google acquired Jaiku, a microblogging/Twitter-like service based in Finland. However, in 2011 Google announced it would be shutting down the Jaiku service. The offering never took off, unable to compete effectively against services such as Twitter. It appeared that few people wanted to tweet on more than one service.

Product in Search of a Market

In 2010, Google acquired Aardvark, a social search solution that allowed users to ask questions and find information from people in their network through instant messaging and email.

However, in 2011, Google shut down the Aardvark initiative, as the search group concluded Q&A was not going to play a major role in search. Reportedly, Google's M&A team felt strongly about the role social Q&A could play in search, but in the end Google's search organization didn't concur.

In 2013, Max Ventilla, Aardvark's co-founder, left Google to found AltSchool, an alternative educational institution that based learning on specific child's needs and challenges rather than a fixed curriculum based on standardized test results (more on Max later when we discuss a number of Google's M&A alumni in Chapter 13).

More Wood behind Fewer Arrows

In 2010, Google acquired Picnik, an online photo editing and sharing service that worked across platforms such as Facebook, Photobucket, Flickr, and Picassa.

In 2012, Google announced plans to shutter Picnik. Although the rationale for the closure was not completely clear, most likely the move was motivated by Google's goal of putting "more wood behind fewer arrows." The Picnik website stated: "Picnik is moving its easy yet powerful photo editing tools to Google+." Google apparently concluded that the Picnik service, although quite popular, was more a feature than stand-alone destination.

Departure of Highly Regarded Founder/Entrepreneur

In 2010, Google acquired Slide for $179 million plus the possibility of an estimated additional $46 million in employee retention bonuses. Slide was a social entertainment company that developed online applications for social networking websites. Slide offered slideshow, image and video personalization, guestbook, and virtual gift applications for networks such as Facebook, MySpace, and Friendster.

In 2011, Google dissolved Slide saying it would focus its social networking efforts on Google+. Slide founder Max Levchin (who also was a founder of PayPal) would leave the company. Apparently, Levchin found himself on the fringes of Google+. Levchin had other significant opportunities and in 2012 joined the board of directors of Yahoo!.

Dwindling Usage

In 2011, Google acquired TalkBin, which provided a platform that allowed customers to give immediate feedback to local businesses by submitting opinions via mobile applications. Google acquired the company less than five months after it was founded. However, in 2014, Google reported that "TalkBin usage has dwindled over the past 2 years, and we have decided to shut down the service...."

Also in 2011, Google acquired Zave Networks, which operated an online incentive program platform for the exchange of non-cash values across retail verticals. The company's platform supported in-store redemption of offers distributed via digital media. Yet, as was the case with TalkBin, Zavers by Google was being closed down in 2014, with Google apparently unsatisfied with the growth of this offering.

Rebound Romance That Failed

In 2011, Google purchased DailyDeal for $114 million. The company offered daily coupon promotion deals in Germany, Austria, and Switzerland and had been characterized as a Groupon clone. In 2013, the Heilemann brothers (founders of DailyDeal) bought back their company from Google. Daily-Deal was intended to support Google Offers international expansion after Google's bid for Groupon was turned down at a time when the daily deal market was red hot. Google apparently felt this space was now turning colder.

Integration Mess

In 2011, Google acquired Zagat Survey for approximately $151 million in cash. Zagat published reviews for restaurants worldwide. The company's offerings included printed guides, website information, and mobile products. Tim and Nina Zagat, founders of Zagat Survey, would continue to serve as co-chairs of the company.

In acquiring Zagat, Google was supporting its move into the rapidly growing local commerce market. The deal underscored Google's mobile initiatives as well. Zagat was a significant add-on to Google Places, and would help it compete with companies like Yelp in popular searches for restaurants and hotels.

However, in 2012, the integration of Zagat into ran into major snarls. Marissa Mayer, the senior executive championing the acquisition, was demoted and eventually left Google to become CEO at Yahoo!. Zagat employees, designated as temps without Googler benefits, were informed that their contracts would not be extended. While Google gained highly useful restaurant-related data with the Zagat acquisition, Google certainly did not enhance its M&A integration reputation with the badwill that arose out of this deal.

Competing with Ad Customers

In 2012, Google acquired the travel assets of John Wiley & Sons for $22 million in cash, $3.3 million of which was held in escrow. The assets included all of interests in the Frommer's brand and WhatsOnWhen brands. Frommer's published travel information including frommers.com, which provides an online travel excursion guidebook.

In 2013, Google reversed course and sold the Frommer's brand to its founder, Arthur Frommer. Google would retain Frommer's social media accounts. As we observed in Chapter 5, a significant amount of Google's advertising revenue (some 5 percent) was coming from online travel agents such as Expedia and Priceline. Google appeared reluctant to become too aggressive in competing with some of its key advertising customers. It was attempting to execute a Goldilocks strategy of being neither too hot nor too cold in the online travel space. The jury was out as to how strongly Google would compete in online travel, but in the meantime Frommer's was gone.

Other Less-than-Successful Deals

There are numerous other Google acquisitions not appearing in Figure 8.1 that could be characterized as less than successful. For example, Google's 2012 acquisition of Wildfire, a social marketing software developer, was shuttered in 2014 after apparently making less than hoped-for progress in functionality. Wildfire allowed companies serve ad campaigns on Facebook, Google+, Twitter, Pinterest, YouTube, and LinkedIn. Google's absorption of Wildfire's technology into its DoubleClick platform appeared to be an admission that Wildfire's growth as an innovative service was not developing as planned.

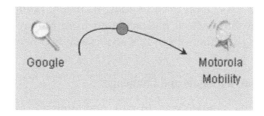

FIGURE 8.2 Google buys Motorola Mobility

However, perhaps the most controversial acquisition in Google's history had also been its largest to date. We now discuss this acquisition: the convoluted Motorola Mobility deal.

An Acquisition and Rapid Exit

Recall that in 2011, Google announced an agreement to acquire Motorola Mobility for $40 per share in cash, a total of $12.5 billion. This purchase price represented a premium of 63 percent over the previous closing price of Motorola Mobility shares. Motorola's product portfolio included mobile devices such as smartphones and tablets, wireless accessories, end-to-end video and data delivery, and management solutions, including set-tops and data-access devices. See Figure 8.2.

The acquisition of Motorola Mobility, a dedicated partner with Google within the Android ecosystem, would substantially expand Google's mobile patent portfolio. The acquisition would enable Google to better defend itself against IP attacks, and gain additional leverage in global patent negotiations and litigation.

The transaction allowed Google to enter the handset business in a big way and attempt to experiment with tighter hardware/software integration, which had become a key competitive advantage for Apple.

Concerns loomed on the impact of the transaction on existing Android OEMs, who might now view Google as a competitor and therefore opt toward another operating system such as Windows Mobile or perhaps develop their own software strategies, thereby disrupting the Android ecosystem.

The acquisition of Motorola Mobility, which was the largest set-top box manufacturer in the world, was viewed as possibly helping Google's initiatives relating to Google TV, which had not gotten off to a strong start.

However, by 2014, apart from building its patent portfolio, Google had largely unwound the assets it had acquired from Motorola Mobility. And debate was raging whether or not this acquisition had been successful.

Vertical Integration: Rationale and Challenge

In buying Motorola, Google was, in part, acquiring an option to vertically integrate the Android platform should alliances with key smartphone partners become problematic. In particular, Google executives were becoming concerned that Samsung was dominating the Android smartphone market and that Samsung might attempt to renegotiate its partnership to Google's detriment, asking for a larger share of mobile advertising revenue.[7]

If Google's alliance with Samsung went south, Google's Android could establish a special relationship with Motorola's device unit, mimicking how Apple's hardware and software dovetailed together. Motorola's Android smartphones could emerge as a superior offering, given the tight integration advantages. But this vertical integration play (bring additional pieces of the value chain in-house) would face significant challenges.

As we observed in Chapter 1, using M&A to move up or down a value chain is fraught with peril. For example, recall our discussion of the conflict Apple was likely to face if it had purchased Universal Music (upstream vertical integration) as it was launching the iTunes/iPod platform. Other suppliers of music would be far less likely to want to cooperate with a company that had become their competitor.

Research findings indicate that executives must often make tough choices when determining the degree of vertical integration versus the extent of strategic partnership/outsourcing. Pursuing either vertical integration or strategic outsourcing in isolation may well be suboptimal. An executive must address questions relating to the boundaries of the firm at an aggregate level as opposed to doing an isolated analysis.[8] Doing so can involve some of the toughest strategic choices faced by a company.

Google was confronted with such choices when it decided to acquire Motorola Mobility and continued to be faced with vertical integration challenges in the aftermath of the deal closure.

Aftermath of Motorola Mobility

In 2012, Google appointed Dennis Woodside as CEO of Motorola Mobility. Woodside had worked at McKinsey as well as served in a variety of management roles at Google. Woodside wasted no time in restructuring Motorola.

Later in 2012, Google sold Motorola Mobility's home division (which included television set-top box products) to Arris for $2.35 billion. Google had originally stated two main benefits of the Motorola acquisition:

- "Google and Motorola Mobility together will accelerate innovation and choice in mobile computing. Consumers will get better phones at lower prices.
- "Motorola Mobility's patent portfolio will help protect the Android ecosystem. Android, which is open-source software, is vital to competition in the mobile device space, ensuring hardware manufacturers, mobile phone carriers, applications developers, and consumers all have choice."[9]

If it wasn't crystal clear from the start that Google had little interest in Motorola's set-top box offerings, it became so after the divestiture to Arris.

But uncertainty remained as to how aggressive Google would be in the first benefit stated above. How far would Google go in attempting to replicate Apple's strategy of integrating software and hardware in order to "accelerate innovation and choice in mobile computing?" Or did Google have other goals primarily in mind?

One other possible goal was to whip Samsung back in line. Samsung had been a dominant power behind Android's rapid growth, enjoying about 80 percent of the Android smartphone market. But Samsung was doing more than selling Android smartphones and tablets. It was also doctoring up Android with TouchWiz, a Samsung skin that made Android appear more *Samsungy* than *Googley*. In addition, Samsung was developing Tizen, its own operating system that closely resembled the TouchWiz interface.[10]

By acquiring Motorola, Google was signaling that it could ramp up its own smartphone offerings through vertical integration and launch what could possibly be a death knell to Samsung's hegemony.

In January 2014, Google and Samsung signed a patent deal that would last 10 years. Included in the agreement was a provision that Samsung would concentrate on core Android and deemphasize TouchWiz. A few days later, Google announced plans to sell Motorola Mobility to Lenovo.[11]

Indeed, in late January 2014, Google said it would sell Motorola Mobility to Lenovo for $2.9 billion. Google would receive $660 million in cash, $750 million in Lenovo shares, and a three-year note worth $1.5 billion. Google would retain key patents acquired in the original deal. With this semi-graceful exit, Google would receive a boost to its bottom line (given operating income losses at Motorola) and achieve improved relationships with hardware partners such as Samsung.

Overall Assessment of the Motorola Deal

There have been many assessments of Google's rapid foray into and exit out of smartphone manufacturing. Some criticize Google for brashly attempting a vertical integration play that could have done vast damage to its Android ecosystem. Others have a much more favorable view of the adventure, asserting that it: (1) dramatically beefed up Google's mobile IP; (2) slapped an overly assertive partner (Samsung) back in line; (3) was not economically damaging—at least not in a major way; and (4) created in Lenovo an excellent smartphone partner going forward.

With respect to Motorola's mobile IP, Google most certainly fortified itself against the likes of Apple and Microsoft. For example, in the 2014 court battle between Samsung and Apple over mobile intellectual property, it emerged that Google would "defend and indemnify" Samsung, assuming some defense costs, as well as a share of the damages in the event of a loss. In fact, Apple obtained only a pyrrhic victory in a May 2014 ruling.

With respect to the immensely symbiotic, yet tension-filled, relationship between Google and Samsung, it's clear that as a result of the patent agreement between the two companies, Samsung would move back into pure Android territory, at least for the immediate future.

Then there's the economics of the Motorola Mobility adventure. One source[12] analyzed the financial outcome as follows:

Google paid:

- **$12.5 billion** (total consideration for Motorola Mobility)

Google received:

- $2.9 billion (Motorola cash)
- $5.5 billion (amortized value of patents that Google is retaining)
- $2.35 billion (total consideration from Arris for Motorola Home)
- $2.91 billion (total consideration from Lenovo for Motorola Mobility)
- Total value received = **$13.66 billion**

Of course, as this same source points out, these calculations do not include the operating loss (estimated at some $2 billion) that Google realized while owning Motorola. (This estimated operating loss "cost" does not include tax-loss benefits that accrued to Google.) The overall takeaway from this analysis is that in analyzing direct economic costs, Google did not get hurt in any major way and may have essentially broke even.

But we must also consider opportunity costs and benefits associated with the Motorola deal. We've already discussed the benefit that Google may have in bringing Samsung back into the Android fold. In exiting the Motorola handset business, Google had reduced the risk that Samsung or other smartphone manufacturers would develop an alternative mobile operating system.

There's also considerable upside in developing a closer relationship with Lenovo. "In Lenovo, Google gains another partner with grand ambitions to penetrate the global smartphone market with low-cost phones, a segment Apple has ignored."[13]

So here's our bottom line on the Google/Motorola mobility acquisition:

- Google took on major risk in potentially alienating its Android hardware ecosystem.
- Google receives kudos for moving quickly to restructure the assets acquired, retaining a patent portfolio that has upped its defensive capabilities in mobile markets.
- Google did not add or subtract any significant value, at least from analyzing the transaction from a direct economic perspective.
- Google did receive indirect strategic benefits in realigning its relationship with Samsung and creating a new Android-centric relationship with Lenovo.

The Motorola deal was shuttered, but had not necessarily failed. Nimble moves and perhaps some opportunistic luck enabled Google to scramble in the backfield, avoid being sacked for a major loss of yardage, and ultimately connect with a receiver for what could produce a nice gain.

Watch the Video

www.wiley.com/go/semiorganicgrowth

To view a video relating to the content of this chapter, refer to *M&A Financial Accounting Considerations,* which accompanies this book as a supplemental resource.

Notes

1. Matt Lynley, "Google's M&A Boss: with Larry Page in Charge, Only a Third of Our Acquisitions Are Busts," *Business Insider* (March 6, 2012).
2. Mark Rogowsky, "Apple's Beats Deal Is Tech's Worst Acquisition, Except for All the Others," *Forbes* (May 10, 2014).

3. Brad Stone, "Inside Google's Secret Lab," *Bloomberg Businessweek* (May 22, 2013).
4. Ben Popper, "Failure Is a Feature: How Google Stays Sharp Gobbling up Startups," *The Verge* (September 17, 2012).
5. Miguel Helft, "Google Encounters Hurdles in Selling Radio Advertising," *New York Times* (February 10, 2007).
6. Jessica E. Vascellaro, "Radio Tunes out Google in Rare Miss for Web Titan," *Wall Street Journal* (May 12, 2009).
7. Emir Efrati, "Samsung Sparks Anxiety at Google," *Wall Street Journal* (February 25, 2013).
8. See Rothaermel, Hitt, and Jobe (2006).
9. https://www.google.com/press/motorola.
10. Gorden Kelly, "How Google Used Motorola to Smack down Samsung—Twice," *Forbes* (February 10, 2014).
11. Ibid.
12. Larry Dignan, "Google's Motorola Mobility Detour: Running the Numbers," *Between the Lines* (January 30, 2014).
13. Rolfe Winkler, "How Google's Costly Motorola Maneuver May Pay Off," *Wall Street Journal* (January 30, 2014).

CHAPTER 9

Disclosure versus Secrecy

In late February 2014, Apple CEO Tim Cook announced at the company's annual shareholders' meeting that Apple had acquired 23 companies over the past 16 months. The announcement sent analysts and the media scurrying off on a treasure hunt to see how many of these companies could be identified.

Apple was notoriously secretive about its M&A activity, often making a cryptic boilerplate comment only after a deal had been reported in the media: "Apple buys smaller technology companies from time to time, and we generally do not discuss our purpose or plans."

When must a publicly traded company announce an acquisition? When must the company disclose the valuation and terms of the transaction? Does an acquirer ever allow the target or a third party to reveal such information? How commonly does an acquirer forbid such disclosure?

Why might a company such as Google feel that the important news is not the transaction per se and therefore deemphasize a deal announcement? When and why might Google keep an acquisition secret? And how does Google's *M&A disclosure* approach compare to other companies such as that of Apple?

In this chapter, we'll discuss these and related questions by exploring the extent to which M&A activities are put out in the open or held close to the chest.

SEC Guidelines for Disclosure

In the United States, the Securities and Exchange Commission (SEC) and Financial Accounting Standards Board (FASB) rules state that an acquisition/merger must be disclosed in the next annual 10-K or quarterly 10-Q filing (or in extraordinary circumstances, an interim 8-K) *if it is material.* In addition, the rules outline which terms of the transaction (such as transaction size) must be disclosed, also based on materiality.

Materiality is not precisely defined in the rules by an exact formula, but is usually determined by the public companies' lawyers and outside accountants. Case law describes public company information as material if "there is a substantial likelihood that a reasonable shareholder would consider it important in making an investment decision." FASB Statement of Concepts #2 states:

> *The omission or misstatement of an item in a financial report is material if, in the light of surrounding circumstances, the magnitude of the item is such that it is probable that the judgment of a reasonable person relying upon the report would have been changed or influenced by the inclusion or correction of the item.*

In general, the aggregate consideration for all acquisitions in any given year is disclosed since the sum of the deal prices flows through the financial statements. If only one acquisition took place during an accounting period, the acquisition price can be obtained from the statement of cash flows (if a cash purchase) or the statement of shareholders equity (if an equity purchase).[1]

However, if a company such as Google makes multiple (even dozens) of acquisitions during a given year, it becomes impossible to determine from the financial statements the purchase price for any one transaction unless it is specifically disclosed.

Whether or not there is a disclosure about a specific transaction (including its price and form of consideration) in the notes accompanying a company's financial statements will depend on the size of the acquisition relative to the size of the company and whether or not the acquisition is considered material.

A company's corporate lawyers and/or external auditors typically set a materiality threshold based on the company's market capitalization, revenue, assets, or net income. Given that companies such as Google or Apple enjoy market capitalizations in the hundreds of billions of dollars, these companies can make acquisitions in the tens or even hundreds of millions of dollars without disclosing details.

Here is an abstract from Google's Form 10-K for the year ending December 31, 2013, illustrating the company's disclosures relating to M&A as found in the notes to its financial statements:[2]

> *In June 2013, we completed our acquisition of Waze Limited (Waze), a provider of a mobile map application which provides turn-by-turn navigation and real-time traffic updates powered by incidents and route information submitted by a community of users, for a total cash consideration of $969 million .... Of the total purchase price, $841 million*

was attributed to goodwill and $193 million was attributed to intangible assets, offset by $65 million of other net liabilities assumed. The goodwill of $841 million is primarily attributable to the synergies expected to arise after the acquisition. Goodwill is not expected to be deductible for tax purposes.

During the year ended December 31, 2013, we completed other acquisitions and purchases of intangible assets for a total cash consideration of approximately $489 million, of which $268 million was attributed to intangible assets, $238 million to goodwill, and $17 million to net liabilities assumed. These acquisitions generally enhance the breadth and depth of our expertise in engineering and other functional areas, our technologies, and our product offerings. The amount of goodwill expected to be deductible for tax purposes is approximately $38 million.

Note that:

- Google disclosed the specific consideration and allocation of the purchase price for only one of its acquisitions: Waze. The Waze acquisition valuation amounted to approximately $1 billion.
- All other acquisitions and purchases of intangible assets are not separately disclosed or valued in the 10-K. The aggregate purchase price (in cash) for all other acquisitions and purchases of intangible assets is provided ($489 billion). Given that Google made some two dozen acquisitions alone during this year, it is not possible to determine from this information the purchase price of any one of these acquisitions.

Now consider Apple's 10-K disclosure relating to M&A as found in the notes to its financial statements for the fiscal year ending September 28, 2013:

During 2013 and 2012, the Company completed various business acquisitions. In 2013, the aggregate cash consideration, net of cash acquired, was $496 million, of which $419 million was allocated to goodwill, $179 million to acquired intangible assets and $102 million to net liabilities assumed. In 2012, the aggregate cash consideration, net of cash acquired, was $350 million, of which $245 million was allocated to goodwill, $113 million to acquired intangible assets and $8 million to net liabilities assumed.

Note that:

- All the consideration that Apple gave in its M&A transactions is lumped together. There is no transaction that is called out separately for disclosure.

- As we'll observe later, for a period of time lasting longer than 10 years, Apple did not disclose the specific purchase price information for any one of its acquisitions in its annual 10-Ks. This would change only with Apple's $3 billion purchase of Beats in 2014.

Company Secrecy/Disclosure Motives

Apart from any mandated disclosure of acquisition purchase price and terms by companies such as Google and Apple, technology companies are driven by a number of factors in deciding whether or not to disclose basic information about an M&A transaction. Such basic information includes even whether or not to publicly announce the acquisition.

Why Not Disclose

Here are some factors that argue for *minimum or no disclosure* of the purchase of a private company:

- Provides no valuation metrics that other potential targets could use to their benefit in future acquisition negotiations.
- Signals little or no information that could help determine a company's future strategic moves by a competitor.
- Delays a competitor's response to a short-term product innovation likely to result from the transaction.
- Generates excitement when new products or services are announced (which could be months or even years after the acquisition).

In addition to requiring founders and employees of the target to not disclose valuation, terms, or even the occurrence of an acquisition, it is also common for investment bankers or outside lawyers to be asked to sign NDAs relating to the transaction event. An acquisition agreement can state the valuation and terms must be kept secret by the target and others involved in the transaction *permanently*, essentially treating such information as a trade secret.

As mentioned earlier, Apple has tended to take an extreme position in its nondisclosure of M&A activities. Even when Apple has acquired a public company, it traditionally has done so with as little fanfare as possible.

For example, in 2012 Apple acquired AuthenTec, a Nasdaq publicly traded company that developed fingerprint sensor technology for $356 million in cash. Apple did not issue a news release or conduct an analyst call about the event. Furthermore, AuthenTec, a company with a proclivity to issue press releases about almost anything, did virtually nothing to publicize the deal. All AuthenTec did was file required documentation with the Securities and Exchange Commission.[4]

The AuthenTec deal demonstrates the "sound of silence" that Apple values and may consequently impose on a target and other third parties when acquiring a company. In contrast, Tim Cook later in 2014 characterized Touch ID, resulting from the acquisition of AuthenTec, as "incredibly well received." Touch ID was viewed as supporting Apple's goal of maintaining a premium on the iPhone's ASP (average selling price).

Of course, a primal drive by a company to keep an acquisition quiet may be frustrated by a media scurry to find someone who is willing to talk about the deal off the record. And as we'll see, many third-party estimates about deal occurrence, valuation, and terms do, in fact, emerge.

Why Disclose

Given disclosure requirements, a public company often is not able to guarantee to a private target that an M&A transaction can be kept confidential. Consequently, in the definitive agreement relating to the acquisition, the need to disclose is often one of the carve-outs to the confidentiality provisions of the transaction. Some private company owners might object to the announcement or details surrounding their liquidity event, but such owners need to be aware that disclosure may be mandated or desired by the acquirer.[5]

Apart from mandated disclosure, here are some reasons why a technology company such as Google or Apple may choose to disclose more specific information about its M&A activity:

- Demonstrating to the market that the company is embarking upon or continuing a series of acquisitions as a core strategic initiative
- Signaling to a competitor that the acquirer is serious about entering or enhancing its position in a given space
- Building a deal flow by motivating other entrepreneurs and/or venture capitalists to consider the company as an attractive exit opportunity
- Convincing investors that the company is not merely sitting on its cash hoard, but actively pursuing new opportunities via M&A

The latter consideration (not being perceived as sitting on a cash cache) has perhaps even motivated secretive Apple to become more forthcoming about at least the number of M&A transactions the company is closing. As mentioned earlier, at Apple's annual shareholders' meeting in 2014, Tim Cook touted that his company had acquired 23 companies in the previous

16 months. Cook may have injected this fact into his comments attempting to convince investors that Apple was not hunkering down on its pile of cash, but allocating capital to support future growth. (Apple was also instituting huge share buybacks and dividend distributions.)

Unlike Apple, Google has typically announced (or encouraged targets or third parties to announce) most of its acquisitions. According to internal estimates, some 95 percent of Google acquisitions are announced in press releases or blog postings.

For example, here is a 2014 announcement made by Bitspin, which had developed a rather elegant alarm app based on sleep-cycle theory: "We're thrilled to announce that Bitspin is joining Google, where we'll continue to do what we love: building great products that are delightful to use. For new and existing users, Timely … a beautiful wake-up experience will continue to work as it always has."

In spite of its proclivity to announce (or encourage the target to announce) an acquisition, Google did not view most M&A's as highly newsworthy events. In contrast, a product announcement (often months later) associated with a given transaction was considered much more significant.

Disclosing Value and Terms

Let's now examine M&A transactions for which Google and Apple did disclose deal valuation and select terms.

Google Deals

Figure 9.1 presents an infographic depicting acquisitions from Google's inception through June 2014, for which Google disclosed purchase price, together with some of the terms associated with the deals. Publicly traded companies as well as private companies are included. Not surprisingly, we have seen a number of these companies in our earlier discussions of Google's acquisition strategy. But the focus here is on valuation disclosure.

Note that 18 companies are displayed in Figure 9.1. Given that Google had made over 160 acquisitions during this time period, it follows that Google disclosed specific purchase price for about 10 percent of its transactions.

Here is a summary of purchase price and select terms for each of these disclosed transactions:

- In 2003, as described extensively in Chapter 2, Google bought Applied Semantics, a developer of semantic text processing and online advertising technology.

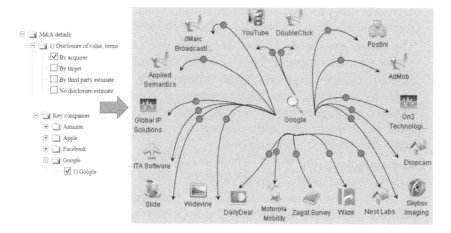

FIGURE 9.1 Acquisitions for which Google has disclosed purchase price/terms

The consideration: $102.4 million, consisting of $41.5 million in cash, and stock and stock options valued at $60.9M; $84.2 million of the transaction was allocated to goodwill (source: Google S-1). This acquisition was made prior to Google's public offering, and this disclosure was made in Google's initial public offering registration statement.

- In 2006, Google purchased dMarc Broadcasting, a company that worked with radio advertisers in the sales, scheduling, delivery, and reporting of radio ads.

The consideration: $97.6 million in cash plus up to $1.136 billion in cash contingent payments (source: Google 10-Q). As noted in Chapter 8, contingent consideration in the form of earn-outs reflected a whopping 92 percent of the potential consideration! And subsequent conflict between Google and dMarc's founders on post-merger execution caused to Google to rethink how it would use earn-outs going forward. More on this in Chapter 11.

- In 2006, Google acquired YouTube, a consumer media company that displayed a wide variety of online video offerings including amateur content.

The consideration: $1.65 billion in a stock-for-stock transaction (source: Google 10-K). Immediately following the acquisition, YouTube would continue to operate independently, retaining its brand and all their employees, including co-founders Chad Hurley and Steve Chen.

- In 2007, Google announced it would purchase DoubleClick from Hellman & Friedman, JMI Equity, and management. DoubleClick was an exchange that provided services and products for advertising agencies, marketers, and Web publishers to support marketing programs.

The consideration: $3.2 billion in cash (source: Google 10-K). The deal was subject to approval by US antitrust regulators.

- In 2007, Google acquired Postini, a provider of on-demand communications security and compliance solutions. Postini's offerings, which included message security, archiving, encryption, and policy enforcement, were used to protect a company's email, instant messaging, and other Web-based communications.

The consideration: $545.7 million in cash plus $44.8 million in retention bonuses (source: Google 10-K).

- In 2009, Google announced plans to purchase mobile advertising start-up AdMob. AdMob sold ads that appeared on websites geared for smartphones. The company was a first-mover in developing technology to deliver ads on Apple's iPhone as well as on devices that used Google's Android.

The consideration: $681 million, consisting of 1.2 million Class A common shares plus $26 million in cash (source: Google 10-K). After a six-month investigation, the Federal Trade Commission approved Google's acquisition of AdMob.

- In 2009, Google signed a definitive agreement to acquire On2 Technologies, a publicly held company. On2 developed video compression software and offered related video services to deliver content over proprietary networks and the Internet.

The consideration: $123 million, consisting of 174,000 shares of Class A common stock valued at $95 million at deal closing plus $28 million in cash (source: Google 10-Q). If the merger was terminated by On2, the company would pay a break-up fee of $2 million. No more than one of three specified employees of On2 could rescind or terminate their offers of employment from Google.

- In 2010, Google announced plans to acquire Global IP Solutions (GIPS). GIPS was a developer of real-time voice and video processing software for IP networks. The company provided high definition and super wideband voice.

The consideration: $68.2 million in cash (source: Google press release). The offer price reflected a 142 percent premium over the closing share price of GIPS stock on January 11, 2010, the last trading day prior to GIPS making a public announcement of strategic interest from a potential buyer. (The offer price reflected a premium of 27.5 percent compared to the closing share price immediately before Google announced the acquisition.) Google would delist the company (from the Oslo Stock Exchange) after the acquisition was completed.

- In 2010, Google signed a definitive agreement to acquire ITA Software. ITA offered Internet-based software to the airline industry.

  The consideration: $676 million in cash (source: Google 10-Q). In April 2011, Google received antitrust clearance on its acquisition of ITA. However a number of conditions were imposed by the Department of Justice, limiting how Google could use the company's technology. These conditions, which were to last until 2016, required Google to continue licensing the software to other companies, to develop ITA products and offer them to competitors, and to erect a firewall so it could not see sensitive information from competitors.

- In 2010, Google acquired Slide, an entertainment company that developed online applications for social networking websites.

  The consideration: $179 million cash (source: Google 10-K). Tech-Crunch reported an additional $46 million in retention bonuses were part of the deal.

- In 2010, Google acquired Widevine, a developer of digital rights management software for Web-connected TVs and other devices that protected video content from unauthorized use.

  The consideration: $158 million in cash (source: Google 10-K).

- In 2011, Google bought DailyDeal. The company offered daily coupon promotion deals in Germany, Austria, and Switzerland and was considered a Groupon clone.

  The consideration: $114 million cash (source: Google 10-Q).

- In 2011, Google announced an agreement to acquire Motorola Mobility.

  The consideration: $12.4 billion in cash; the preliminary valuation for acquired assets included allocations of $2.9 billion to cash, $5.5 billion to patents/developed technology, $0.7 billion to customer relationships, $0.8 billion to other net assets, and $2.5 billion to goodwill (source: Google 10-K). The deal reflected a premium of 63 percent over the previous closing price of Motorola Mobility shares. In 2012, Google won EU and US antitrust approval to purchase the company.

- In 2011, Google acquired Zagat Survey, a publisher of restaurant reviews worldwide.

  The consideration: $151 million in cash; $37 million attributable to Zagat brand; $102 million to goodwill (source: Google 10-Q).

- In 2013, Google purchased Waze, an Israeli crowd-sourced mapping and navigation company.

The consideration: $966 million in cash plus retention bonuses (sources: Google 10-Q and Google interviews). $847 million was attributed to goodwill. Google also assumed $69 million in liabilities. Retention bonuses might increase this amount, as Waze confirmed that 100 employees stood to receive $120 million from the deal to be earned over four years after closing.

- In 2014, Google acquired Nest Labs. Nest made smart thermostats and smoke alarms for homes.

   The consideration: $3.2 billion in cash (source: Google press release). According to a Google 10-Q, $2.35 billion was allocated to goodwill.

- In 2014, Google acquired Skybox Imaging. Skybox designed small, relatively inexpensive satellites that gathered daily photos and video of the Earth.

   The consideration: $500 million in cash (source: Google press release).

- In 2014, Google acquired Dropcam, which developed and marketed Wi-Fi–connected video cameras and services that streamed live video to mobile apps. The service sent alerts based on activity sensed by Dropcam cameras.

   The consideration: $555 million in cash, subject to adjustment (source: Google/Nest press release).

In analyzing the disclosures from these 18 transactions, here are some additional comments and key takeaways:

- To reemphasize what is stated above, Google disclosed valuation on only about 10 percent of the acquisitions it had made.
- No purchase price information for private companies had been revealed by Google for acquisitions where the total consideration was valued at less than $100 million.
- Unless there were other drivers for disclosure (such as the target being a public company), the lower limit for Google to disclose the consideration for an acquisition, appeared to be approaching $500 million. (Of course, other factors may be used in deeming a transaction as *material*.)
- At times, Google apparently provided early details regarding an M&A transaction to a media outlet in an attempt to manage a story that would need be disclosed later given its size. For example, when Google purchased Waze, knowledgeable sources provided valuation details regarding the deal to a select media provider.
- Although Google did not disclose valuation for most of its acquisitions, third parties were scrambling to provide *estimates* for many (over 25 percent) of Google's other deals

Apple Deals

Figure 9.2 presents an infographic depicting acquisitions from the beginning of 2000 through June 2014, for which Apple has disclosed a specific purchase price, together with some of the terms associated with the deal in its annual 10-Ks. Some extremely interesting trends emerge.

Note that only five companies are displayed in Figure 9.2. Given that Apple had made an estimated 70 acquisitions during this time period, it follows that Google disclosed purchase price for less than 10 percent of its transactions. Of particular note is that since 2002, the only purchase price disclosure Apple made was its acquisition of Beats in 2014!

Here is a summary of purchase price and select terms for each of these disclosed transactions:

- In 2001, Apple acquired PowerSchool. PowerSchool provided student information management, reporting, and analysis solutions for the K-12 student industry.

  The consideration: $62 million in stock and stock options (source: Apple 10-K).

- Also in 2001, Apple acquired Spruce Technologies. Spruce Technologies was a provider of DVD and WebDVD authoring software.

  The consideration: $14.9 million in cash (source: Apple 10-K).

- In 2002, Apple acquired Nothing Real, which developed and marketed high-performance tools designed for the digital image creation market.

  The consideration: $15 million purchase price; $7 million allocated to acquired technology; $8 million identified as contingent consideration,

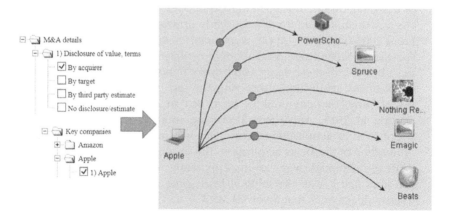

FIGURE 9.2 Acquisitions for which Apple has disclosed purchase price/terms

allocated to future compensation expense in appropriate periods over the next three years (source: Apple 10-K).

- Also in 2002, Apple acquired Emagic, which developed professional software solutions for computer-based music production.

  The consideration: $30 million in cash, $26 million of which was paid at closing and $4 million of which was held back for future payment contingent on continued employment by certain employees allocated to future compensation expense over the next three years (source: Apple 10-K).

- The next M&A purchase price Apple disclosed was in 2014 when the company acquired Beats, which developed and marketed consumer headphones, earphones, and speakers, as well as audio software technology and a streaming music subscription service.

  The consideration: $2.6 billion in cash and $400 million in Apple stock to vest over an unspecified time period (source: Apple press release).

Here are some key takeaways relating to these transactions, as well as overall Apple disclosure practices:

- During the early years of the period analyzed, Apple disclosed the purchase price of very small acquisitions. For example, consider the 2002 acquisition of Spruce Technologies, a privately held company for a mere $14.9 million.
- We can discern that Apple spent hundreds of millions of dollars on cash for business acquisitions in fiscal years such as 2011 through 2013, by examining the company's cash flow statements. For example, Apple reported "payments made in connection with business acquisitions, net" of $244 million in 2011, $350 million in 2012, and $496 million in 2013. (As noted earlier, the trend was clearly upward.)
- From 2003 until 2014, Apple went *notoriously dark* with respect to the specifics of what it disclosed about its acquisition activity. Although during a number of these years Apple spent hundreds of millions of dollars on business acquisitions, the company did not disclose the purchase price of any company until the Beats deal in 2014.
- Starting in 2014, Apple was becoming more forthcoming about the specifics of its acquisition activity. This was in part due to the *material magnitude* of the Beats acquisition. But also in revealing the number of deals the company was closing, apparently Apple wanted to signal to investors that it was allocating at least some of its mega-cash balances to growth activities that involved M&A.

Materiality Revisited

Some scholars have argued that the SEC's current rules do not always ensure the disclosure of material information regarding M&A activity. For example, Rodrigues and Stegemoller showed that "acquisitions of privately held targets classified as 'insignificant' by the SEC can appreciably affect market prices, and therefore are material by the SEC's definition. The authors argued empirically that some 80 percent of the acquisitions of privately held firms that the SEC classifies as insignificant are nonetheless economically important to acquirer shareholders."[6]

The SEC rules state that acquirers disclose financial information on private targets that will become "significant" subsidiaries of the acquirer. At present, the SEC's rules used to determine whether or not an acquirer's subsidiary is considered significant can be summarized as follows:[7]

1. *Investment test*: The company's (including any of its subsidiaries') investments in and advances to the subsidiary as of the end of the last fiscal year exceed 10 percent of the company's total assets.
2. *Asset test*: The company's (including any of its subsidiaries') proportionate share of the total assets of the subsidiary exceed 10 percent of the company's total assets.
3. *Income test*: The company's (including any of its subsidiaries') share of the subsidiary's income exceeds 10 percent of the company's total income.

There is a higher threshold (one of the above 10 percent metrics has to be above 20 percent) for an acquiring company being required to disclose the actual financial statements of the target.

In practical terms, these tests establish a very high threshold at which Google (or Apple) must disclose the purchase price of a private company. For example, given Google's total assets of approximately $122 billion on June 30, 2014, an acquisition would have to exceed $12.2 billion to be considered significant under test (1) shown above.

As Rodrigues and Stegemoller argue: " ... the SEC's definition of a 'significant' acquisition relies solely on the relative size of the target to the acquirer. Although the SEC's disclosure framework captures the most material takeovers, ... it misses targets that are economically important to acquiring stockholders."[8]

The bottom line? Companies such as Google and Apple have considerable degrees of freedom in determining exactly when and what to disclose in M&A transactions. Decisions on what to reveal depend not only on SEC guidelines but also on a company's motivations, as described in this chapter.

Watch the Video

www.wiley.com/go/semiorganicgrowth
    To view a video relating to the content of this chapter, refer to *M&A Financial Disclosure Practices*, which accompanies this book as a supplemental resource.

Notes

1. See comments at http://www.quora.com/Mergers-and-Acquisitions-M-A/ For-a-public-company-when-does-the-size-of-an-acquisition-have-to-be -disclosed-publicly for an excellent discussion of significant acquisition disclosure issues.
2. Google Form 10-K for the period ending December 31, 2013, p. 70.
3. Apple Form 10-K for the period ending September 28, 2013, p. 63.
4. Steven M. Davidoff, "Apple's Quiet Deal for AuthenTec," *New York Times* (August 1, 2012).
5. See Note 1.
6. Rodrigues and Stegemoller (2007) provide an excellent overview and analysis of SEC disclosure requirements with respect to M&A activity.
7. 17 C.F.R. § 210.1-02(w).
8. Rodrigues and Stegemoller.

CHAPTER **10**

Forms of Consideration

A buyer can pay for an acquisition in ways that include deploying accumulated free cash flow, using cash raised by issuing new debt or stock, exchanging shares of its stock for the shares of the target, as well as combinations of these methods. For the acquisitions of any given company, the *form of consideration* used by the acquirer may vary from deal to deal.[1]

In this chapter, we explore several consideration questions: How often has Google used stock in an acquisition? How often has the company used cash or a combination of cash and stock? How does Google's consideration patterns in M&A transactions compare to that of other major technology companies such as Apple or Facebook?

What special lessons can be learned from deals that are largely stock-for-stock deals, such as Google's purchase of YouTube or Facebook's purchase of Instagram? What are the varied motives for a company to use cash or stock as payment for an M&A transaction?

What additional consideration beyond payment in cash and/or equity at deal closing can be part of a transaction? And what role does such delayed or contingent consideration play in stimulating *semi-organic growth*? Although we'll introduce contingent consideration as a form of potential additional payment, this topic will explored in depth in Chapter 11.

Stock versus Cash as Consideration

In Chapter 1, we cited studies concluding that publicly traded acquirers using cash for M&A transactions tend to do better long term than those that use stock. One argument supporting this conclusion is that companies are more prone to use stock when they believe their own shares are overvalued. So it appears reasonable that share price would tend to drop after the acquisition. The descent in AOL's shares after its stock-for-stock merger with Time Warner is often used as a classic illustration of this dynamic.

However, as also indicated in Chapter 1, the performance of cash versus equity-financed acquisitions may be more nuanced. Indeed there are numerous studies that suggest that acquirer returns on equity-financed acquisitions of private firms (or subsidiaries of public firms) often outperform deals that are largely cash based.[2]

Here's one reason why such *stock deals* may do well. An acquirer and the target may consider the buyer's stock to be an attractive currency, and the acquirer may use the appeal of its shares to woo a target and close a transaction. Google's stock-for-stock acquisition of YouTube or Facebook's largely stock-for-stock acquisition of Instagram might be viewed as illustrations of the attractive acquirer currency hypothesis. (In fact, Google's share currency significantly appreciated one year after the YouTube deal, while Facebook's share price languished for a year after the Instagram deal and then shortly thereafter rapidly increased.)

The motives for using equity or cash in an M&A transaction vary across acquirers and likely vary as well as across transactions for any given company. So far, we've discussed two such motives: (1) equity might be used when the purchaser feels its currency is overvalued; or (2) equity might be used to close a critically important deal by being willing to use a tender that the target believes has substantial potential for appreciation.

We'll see there are also additional motivations present in making the decision to structure a transaction with equity or cash consideration. And some of these motives are very important in the process of engendering semi-organic growth.

Google's Use of Stock Consideration

The number of M&A transactions where Google has used stock as the primary source of consideration is very small. In a sense, Google has mirrored the position (cited in Chapter 1) once stated by Warren Buffett of Berkshire Hathaway: "Charlie [Munger] and I like using stock about as much as preparing for a colonoscopy." Buffett also clarified, however, that although he preferred buying a company for cash, he was not opposed to a stock transaction where Berkshire would receive as much intrinsic value as it gave.

Figure 10.1 provides an infographic of four (yes, only four!) M&A transactions where Google has *specifically disclosed* in its S-1 or 10-Ks that it used stock as primary consideration in the acquisition.

1. *Applied Semantics.* This company was featured in Chapter 2. Recall that in 2003 Google bought Applied Semantics, which developed semantic text processing and related online advertising technology.

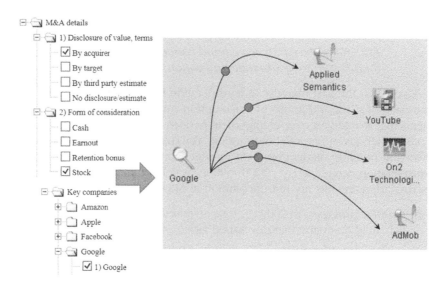

FIGURE 10.1 Google's use of stock in acquisitions

The consideration: $102.4 million, consisting of $41.5 million in cash plus stock and stock options valued at $60.9 million (source: Google S-1).

The Applied Semantics transaction is the only one of these four acquisitions that occurred before Google went public.

2. *YouTube*. This company was featured in Chapter 5. In 2006, Google bought YouTube, the consumer media company.

The consideration: Originally reported by Google in a press release to be a $1.65 billion stock-for stock transaction, the transaction was disclosed in a later Google 10-K as follows:

> *The purchase price was $1.194 billion and consisted of cash payments of $21.2 million, … the net issuance of 2,427,708 shares of our Class A common stock and 30,171 fully vested options to purchase our Class A common shares valued at $1.173 billion. In addition, we issued unvested options, restricted stock units and warrants to purchase 1,189,524 shares of Class A common stock valued at $564.5 million which will be recognized as stock-based compensation as the awards vest over the related vesting periods of 20 to 41 months. These unvested awards are earned primarily*

contingent upon each individual's continued employment with us. Also, under the terms of the agreement, twelve and one-half percent (12.5%) of the equity issued and issuable will be subject to escrow for one year to secure indemnification claims.

Note that the vast majority of consideration in the YouTube transaction consisted of stock and grants of stock options or other stock-related instruments that would vest over employment periods of roughly 1.5 to 3.5 years. Note further, given potential outstanding YouTube liabilities (most certainly involving possible media copyright infringement), one-eighth of all equity consideration, valued at over $200 million, was held back in escrow. (Such escrow arrangements are not uncommon in M&A transactions.)

3. *On2 Technologies.* In 2009, Google acquired On2 Technologies, a publicly held company that developed video compression technology.

   The consideration: $123 million, consisting of 174,000 shares of Class A common stock valued at $95 million at deal closing plus $28 million in cash. Each share of On2 common stock was converted into $0.60 worth of Google class A common stock. Google also acquired On2 options valued at $1.1 million (source: Google 10-Q).

On2 was one of the few public companies acquired by Google, with Motorola Mobility, of course, being another. Motorola, however, was not a stock-for-stock transaction.

4. *AdMob.* Also in 2009, Google acquired AdMob, which sold ads running on mobile phones.

   The consideration: $681 million, consisting of 1.2 million Class A common shares plus $26 million in cash (source: Google 10-K).

Apple had also pursued AdMob in 2009, but reportedly was outbid by Google.

Here are some significant takeaways regarding Google's use of stock in M&A transactions.

- Three of these four acquisitions can be identified as *highly significant.* These include: (1) Applied Semantics, a *cornerstone semi-organic* deal that enabled Google to move beyond search-based advertising; (2) YouTube, a *watershed* acquisition that propelled Google into online video advertising; (3) AdMob, a *pivotal* acquisition in Google's move into mobile advertising.
- It is highly likely that Google's attractive stock currency was used to help close all transactions, except possibly in the case of Applied Semantics, the only pre-IPO deal.

- Google stock-for-stock acquisition of the public company On2 increased the attractiveness of the deal to On2's shareholders by providing the option to defer capital gains tax on the transaction.
- Google's reluctance to use its stock for consideration in M&A transactions can be demonstrated by the number of large transactions that have used cash as consideration. These include targets such as DeepMind, Dropcam, ITA, Motorola Mobility, Nest, Postini, Skybox, and Waze.
- Between 2010 and 2014, Google did not disclose any M&A transaction that used its stock as consideration. However, in 2014, Google split its shares and issued a new nonvoting class of stock. These nonvoting shares provided the option of doing future acquisitions with a currency that would not dilute the voting rights of current shareholders.
- While it is possible that Google did not disclose that it used stock as consideration in other acquisitions, it is clear that Google viewed its share currency as precious.

Apple's Use of Stock Consideration

If Google's use of its stock as consideration in M&A transactions has been scant, Apple's has been rare. Figure 10.2 depicts *two* disclosed acquisitions since 2000 where Apple has use stock as consideration in whole or as a significant part.

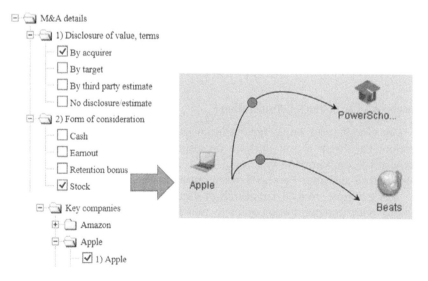

FIGURE 10.2 Apple's use of stock in acquisitions

1. *PowerSchool*. In 2001, Apple agreed to acquire PowerSchool, which provided student information management, reporting, and analysis solutions for the K-12 student industry.

   The consideration: $62 million in stock and stock options (source: Apple 10-K).

2. *Beats Electronics (Beats)*. As noted earlier, in 2014 Apple acquired Beats, which developed headphones and Beats Music streaming music service.

   The consideration: $2.6 billion in cash and $400 million in Apple stock vesting over an unspecified time period (source: Apple press release).

Here are some significant takeaways regarding Apple's use of stock versus cash in M&A transactions:

- The relatively tiny PowerSchool acquisition was Apple's only disclosed 100 percent stock-for-stock acquisition made after 2000, and this deal was done back in 2001.
- The Beats deal was essentially a cash deal, although a sizable stock consideration was included in the transaction as a retention incentive for key talent from Beats. There was a clear, *semi-organic growth* dimension to the Beats deal.
- By 2014, Apple had accumulated a huge cash hoard (exceeding $160 billion), Never before in corporate history had a company massed so large a cash balance primarily derived from cash flow from operations. There was increasing pressure to deploy this cash, and cash acquisitions was one way to do so.
- While it is possible that Apple used stock as consideration in other acquisitions that the company did not disclose, it is quite clear that Apple, like Google, viewed its share currency as precious.

Facebook's Use of Stock Consideration

If both Google and Apple have seldom used their shares as M&A consideration, Facebook was a study in opposites. Facebook was an extremely acquisitive company and was regularly using its stock in acquiring targets, both before and after Facebook went public in May 2012.

For example, in its S-1 registration statement, Facebook listed 16 transactions with unnamed companies in which it used its stock as consideration. Six of these transactions involved acquiring the targets' shares, nine involved acquiring assets from the companies, and one involved licensing a company's technology. The largest of these transactions involved about 11 million Facebook shares, while the smallest consisted of 40,000 shares.

Prior to Facebook's massive $19 billion purchase of WhatsApp in 2014, one source estimated that since 2007 Facebook had completed

51 acquisitions, many of which were *acqui-hires*.[3] As noted above, a significant number of these deals involved Facebook stock as consideration.

Immediately before Facebook's IPO and continuing thereafter, the company continued its pattern of using its stock as consideration in its M&A activity. Figure 10.3 depicts three such prominent acquisitions disclosed by Facebook for which the company's shares were used in the transaction.

> *Instagram.* In 2012, Facebook acquired Instagram, which developed a smartphone service that provided engaging functionality for users to share photos and short videos with family and friends.
>
> **The consideration**: A total purchase price of $521 million, consisting of approximately 12 million vested shares of Class B common stock to nonemployee stockholders of Instagram and $300 million in cash. Facebook also issued approximately 11 million unvested shares of Class B common stock to employee stockholders of Instagram on the closing date, with an aggregate fair value of $194 million, which was to be recognized as share-based compensation expense as the shares vested over a three-year service period.

Note that the value of the equity component of the purchase price was determined based on the fair value of common stock on the closing date of the transaction. On this closing date, Facebook stock had dropped from its

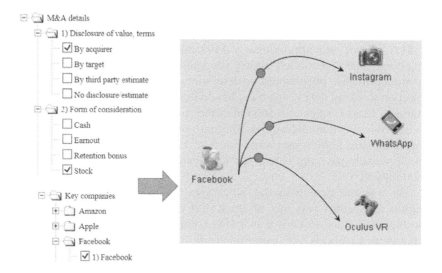

FIGURE 10.3 Facebook's use of stock in prominent acquisitions

IPO price. Consequently, the Instagram deal, which was initially announced as a $1 billion transaction ($700 million in stock and $300 million in cash), was now valued at a little more than one-half that amount. Note further that Class B shares with 10 times the voting rights of Class A were used in this transaction.

WhatsApp. In 2014, Facebook acquired WhatsApp, a highly popular mobile messaging company with some 500 million users.

The consideration: 183,865,778 shares of its Class A stock (initially valued at approximately $12 billion) and approximately $4 billion in cash. The transaction was subject to adjustments so that the cash paid would comprise at least 25% of the aggregate transaction consideration. Facebook would also issue 45,966,445 restricted stock units to WhatsApp employees (valued at approximately $3 billion) that would vest over four years.

Note that, as was the case in the Instagram deal, the consideration in the WhatsApp acquisition was a blend of stock and cash, but (as before) the majority of consideration was stock. This time, however, the equity consideration would be Class A shares with diminished voting rights.

Oculus. Also in 2014, about a month after the announcement of the WhatsApp deal, Facebook entered into an agreement to acquire Oculus, a developer of virtual reality technology. In announcing the acquisition, Facebook CEO Mark Zuckerberg speculated on how his company could apply Oculus technology beyond gaming: "After games, we're going to make Oculus a platform for many other experiences. Imagine enjoying a court side seat at a game, studying in a classroom of students and teachers all over the world or consulting with a doctor face-to-face—just by putting on goggles in your home."

The consideration: 23,071,377 shares of Class B stock (initially valued at $1.6 billion) and approximately $400 million in cash. As in the other Facebook deals mentioned above, the value of the equity component of the final purchase price would be determined based on the fair value of our common stock on the closing date. In addition, up to an additional 3,460,706 shares of Class B stock and $60 million in cash would be payable upon the completion of certain milestones. This earn-out portion would be payable to employee stockholders and was subject to continuous employment through the applicable payment dates. The total earn-out had a potential value of $300 million.

As was the case with the WhatsApp transaction, the direct consideration for Oculus was mix of stock and equity. However, with Oculus, the blend of stock to cash was 4:1 as compared to the 3:1 value ratio in WhatsApp. Facebook was using relatively more of its stock in the Oculus transaction.

And Facebook had established an earn-out based on performance milestones (beyond continuous employment only) as opposed to the retention bonus provided to WhatsApp employees. We will focus on the subtleties of contingent consideration in Chapter 11.

Here are some significant takeaways regarding Facebook's use of stock in M&A transactions:

- Prior to its 2012 IPO, Facebook was certainly not cash-poor. Indeed, the company listed about $4 billion in cash, cash equivalents and marketable securities in its S-1 registration statement. However, prior to the IPO Facebook made extensive use of equity in executing numerous relatively small deals. Although many companies experience difficulty using private stock as consideration to targets, the widely publicized forthcoming Facebook public offering made the company's stock an attractive currency.

- Starting with Instagram, the first of the three major Facebook acquisitions discussed above, Facebook used a blend of equity and cash as consideration. The equity-to-total consideration ratio was slightly increasing over this deal history: 70 percent for Instagram, 75 percent for WhatsApp, and 80 percent for Oculus.

- While Facebook used its Class B shares as partial consideration for the two smaller transactions (Instagram and Oculus), Facebook used its Class A shares (with one-tenth the voting rights of Class B) in the WhatsApp transaction.

- The purchase price at close for all three major acquisitions was subject to considerable risk, given the volatility in Facebook's share price. There was no collar (which, for example, could adjust the number of shares received in a transaction) reported for these transactions. The significant decline in purchase price valuation at deal close for Instagram clearly illustrates this risk.

- Facebook structured the consideration for all three major deals by including a significant part of consideration contingent upon target employees staying with the company and (in the case of Oculus) meeting performance milestones. As we'll see in the next chapter, such contingent consideration often plays a significant role in engendering *semi-organic growth*.

Motivations for Using Cash or Stock

In this chapter, we've explored patterns in the form of consideration used by Google as well as two additional prominent technology companies (Apple and Facebook) in acquiring targets. Given this background, let's delve more deeply into the motivations for using stock and/or cash in M&A transactions. Our goal here is not to discuss the use of cash or stock consideration in general, but within the context of these three companies.

Why Use Cash?

There are numerous reasons why companies such as Google, Apple, and Facebook opted to use cash as consideration in their M&A transactions:

- There was plenty of cash to deploy. Cash and near-cash assets were in abundant supply for Google, Apple, and Facebook. For example, during 2014 Google's such balances stood around $60 billion, $165 billion for Apple, and $14 billion for Facebook. While such cash can be allocated for other purposes such as internal R&D, share buybacks, and dividends, M&A activity for all three companies had become a strategically vital activity.
- However, substantial portions of this cash were outside the United States, and there could be considerable tax consequences if such cash was repatriated for use in a domestic deal. In 2014, Google disclosed in responding to SEC questions about the need for its $30 billion international cash stash by stating that $20 billion to $30 billion was earmarked for the acquisition of foreign companies and technology rights held outside the United States. Although Google did not provide a timetable for use of these international funds, the company argued that it needed these mega-cash balances to support its global M&A initiatives.[4]
- The value of cash was unambiguous. As we observed with Facebook's purchase of Instagram, where the majority of consideration was equity, a target can be subject to considerable risk in share price fluctuation associated with an acquirer's stock. As a result, the target may want to lock in the certainty of cash.
- Using cash may prevent the acquirer from giving away too much intrinsic value to the target. Recall Warren Buffett's acquisition maxim stating that the company prefers to use cash *unless* his company would receive as much intrinsic value as it gave. Buffett argued that when an entire company is sold, its purchase price approaches its intrinsic value. (For technology acquisitions in particular, intrinsic value may even be exceeded.) If the acquirer's stock is trading below its intrinsic value, in Buffett's language the acquirer is essentially exchanging "dollar bills for fifty-cent pieces." Undoubtedly, the concern about giving away too much intrinsic value has permeated Google's M&A philosophy. Indeed, during the first 10 years of being a public company, Google shares appreciated some 1,300 percent, proving the company stock was a currency that was best not distributed without compelling rationale.
- Cash can provide liquidity desired by the target. Immediate liquidity at the close of transaction, as opposed to being subject to a possible lock-up period for sale of stock, may be appealing to the target's shareholders. A lock-up period during which shares received by the target are not able

to be sold typically lasts for six months, but can extend even longer. (However, if a mega-cap company such as Google were to buy a small company using stock, it's unlikely that a lock-up holding period would be placed on the stock.)

- Using cash will not impact voting control. For Google's founders (Page and Brin) and Facebook's founder (Zuckerberg), maintaining voting control in order to be free to pursue long-term goals has been psychologically important. (On the other hand, after Steve Jobs returned to Apple in 1997, he would own less than 1 percent of the company.) Although creating a class of stock with super-voting rights can be used to maintain control, using cash in a deal is also a convenient way to avoid voting control dilatation.
- Using cash as consideration often provides less dilution in earnings per share than using stock, given that fewer shares will be outstanding.
- Cash can be used to pay stay (retention) bonuses in order to keep employees attached to the acquirer after the deal closes. Google almost always uses cash in paying out such stay bonuses. However, as discussed with deals such as Beats and WhatsApp, Apple and Facebook have used stock for retention incentives.

Why Use Stock?

On the other hand, Google, Apple, and Facebook at times may decide to use stock as consideration in an M&A deal.

- If a company's pre-IPO shares are viewed as a potentially attractive currency, using stock as consideration in an acquisition (or series of acquisitions) of strategic importance can overcome limited cash balances. Facebook's use of stock in its early M&A activity provides one example. Google's use of stock in its pre-IPO acquisition of Applied Semantics is another.
- Target shareholders may be able to avoid an immediate capital gains tax liability. For example, On2 shareholders could defer capital gains tax as a result of Google's purchase of this public company using stock as primary consideration. Receiving cash consideration would potentially bring with it an immediate capital gains liability.
- Being willing to acquire with stock perceived as an attractive currency can help sweeten or even close a deal. Google's acquisition of AdMob when bidding against Apple illustrates how the use of stock may be used to help seal a transaction. During the 1990s, Cisco frequently used its stock, which was considered highly desirable tender, to consummate M&A deals.

- Using stock with limited (or no) voting rights can enable founders to maintain control of a company. In 2014, Google split its shares, creating a new class of stock (Class C) with no voting rights. Doing so gave Google the option use this new class to acquire companies without diluting existing shareholders. Also, as we've seen, Facebook used its Class A shares (with one-tenth the voting rights of Class B) as the major component of consideration in its WhatsApp mega-deal.
- Stock can be used as consideration for stay (retention) bonuses in critical deals. As we noted with Apple's acquisition of Beats, $400 million of in-stock consideration would vest over time for key Beats employees, including Jimmy Iovine and Dr. Dre. Having the opportunity to accumulate a significant Apple share position as part of future compensation was intended to motivate long-term commitment to the company.

Why Use Cash and Stock?

For certain transactions, Google, Apple, and Facebook may deem it best to use a combination of cash and stock as consideration in completing an acquisition.

- Cash and stock blends are sometimes necessary to support a deal that would be difficult to close using all cash. Consider Facebook's acquisition of WhatsApp, where 75 percent of the closing consideration in the purchase price (a total of $16 billion) was in stock.
- Receiving cash as partial consideration does provide immediate liquidity and may be desired by some of the target's shareholders. When Google purchased Applied Semantics, many of the investors (believe it or not!) preferred cash payments. As illustrated in Chapter 2, Gil Elbaz and other Applied Semantics employees received their consideration in Google stock.

Consideration Beyond the Close

Whether stock, cash, or some combination of these two forms of consideration is used in closing a transaction, for Google it was quite common to include potential for additional consideration after the close of an acquisition. In this chapter, we've also seen such arrangements in deals made by other companies such as Apple's purchase of Beats or Facebook's acquisition of Oculus.

When Google purchased Waze for $966 million in cash, hefty retention bonuses were put in place such that 100 employees stood to receive additional consideration to be earned after closing.

Such contingent consideration is highly congruent with a philosophy of *semi-organic growth*. After all, it is almost always essential to keep founders, managers, engineers and other key talent involved after the deal closes if an acquirer is to effectively combine its own resources with those of the target.

Our next chapter is devoted to examining important subtleties that frame the design of consideration beyond deal close.

Watch the Video

www.wiley.com/go/semiorganicgrowth

To view a video relating to the content of this chapter, refer to *Contrasting Facebook's M&A consideration with Google's,* which accompanies this book as a supplemental resource.

Notes

1. Sudi Sudarsanam, "Value Creation and Value Appropriation in M&A Deals," Chapter 8 in Faulkner, Teerikangas, and Joseph (2012).
2. See Depamphilis (2014), pp. 30–32, for a summary of these studies.
3. "Facebook M&A Trends: 60% Raised Less than $5M, Sequoia Capital Invested in Five including WhatsApp & Instagram," *CB Insights* (February 20, 2014).
4. See Michael Liedtke, "Google Holding $30 Billion for Foreign Acquisitions," *San Jose Mercury News* (May 21, 2014).

CHAPTER 11

Contingent Consideration

I f *semi-organic growth* is to be successful, key talent associated with the acquired company must almost always stay around—at least for a while. New project milestones must be met, technologies must be blended, and business development initiatives must be executed.

Two key economic mechanisms for motivating founders and employees of an acquired company to remain with an acquirer are the: (1) *earn-out, contingent consideration* based on the successful attainment of post-closing objectives agreed to by the acquirer and target; and (2) *retention (stay) bonus*, also a form of contingent consideration, but based on the continued employment of founders and/or employees of the target.

In this chapter, we'll explore how both of these forms of contingent consideration have been used by Google and other leading technology and media companies, in isolation or in tandem. We'll see why Google commonly used earn-outs in its earlier deals, but essentially stopped doing so in later M&A transactions. We'll examine why stay bonuses came to play a more prominent role over time in Google's *semi-organic* deals.

The Earn-out

An *earn-out* has been defined as: "an arrangement under which a portion of the purchase price in an acquisition is contingent upon the achievement of financial or other performance targets after the deal closes."[1]

An earn-out can enable a buyer and seller to bridge a gap in differing valuation perspectives in order to complete a sale. In a typical earn-out scenario, the target has a more optimistic view of the future revenue and earnings potential of the business, whereas the acquirer may appreciate the seller's optimism, but is not as certain that the target's growth assumptions will materialize.

From the buyer's perspective, advantages of using an earn-out can include:[2]

- Conservation of cash
- Reduction of leverage (especially useful in a tight credit market)
- Incentive for the seller to make the transition in ownership a success
- Reduction in risk

From the target's perspective, an earn-out represents an opportunity to receive additional consideration (possibly substantial) should performance objectives be met or exceeded.

Earn-outs are typically used when the acquirer and target want to complete a deal, but need to close a valuation gap in situations that include the following:[3]

- Target is in the development or entrepreneurial stage with limited operating history.
- Target has introduced a new product line or developed a new technology that does not have a track record.
- Target is in a turnaround situation where the future existence of a business is in question.
- The target's sector has undergone expanding valuation multiples that may be peaking.
- Acquirer wants to motivate founders and/or employees of target to meet post-acquisition performance goals.
- Target's estimation of valuation is determined by revenue or gross margin projections more optimistic than the acquirer's projections.
- A *value buyer* is unwilling to purchase the company solely with upfront consideration.

Challenges in Structuring Earn-outs

Crafting an earn-out that bears fruit is not an easy task. Earn-outs can be based on a wide range of metrics from financial results such as revenue or EBITDA targets to nonfinancial project milestone goals. But whatever the choice of metrics, unplanned events and unintended consequences can upset one or both parties and derail the agreement.

It's easier to measure the earn-out performance of the acquired company if it is allowed to operate as a standalone entity for the duration of the agreement, as opposed to being tightly integrated or absorbed into the acquirer. Although not always possible or practical to do so, both buyer and seller may benefit from a standalone arrangement.

From the point of view of the buyer, it's important not only to establish performance metrics that will yield additional value, but also to structure the arrangement such that the target does not get a free-ride to the goal from efforts put forth mostly by the acquiring company. Once again, this is much easier to accomplish if the seller is able to operate essentially as an independent entity during the earn-out period.

From the point of view of the acquired company, a worst-case scenario is to be making demonstrable progress toward meeting earn-out performance goals, only to have the rug pulled out by the buyer. For example, the marketing budget may be gutted, funds to expand inventory might not be allocated, or any of a number of other growth-inhibiting moves could be made by the parent.

An earn-out must go beyond a mere legal document. It must involve a trusted relationship between acquirer and target. Deal metrics and payout schedules may define the borders of the earn-out, but a good-faith relationship is at the heart of the arrangement. Sincere commitment toward the goal of building company value must be the byword of both parties.

Earn-Out Valuation

Earn-outs closely resemble options and tend to be more valuable (*other things being equal*): (1) the longer the term of the instrument; and (2) the greater the uncertainty in the underlying performance.

Robert Bruner argued that the correct way to value an earn-out is to account for its optionality.[4] This implies that if a company simply discounts most-likely cash flows from the agreement, the earn-out will almost certainly be undervalued.

A more appropriate methodology for *earn-out valuation* involves developing probabilistic outcomes in order to determine the expected value and range of possible outcomes, together with the likelihoods of these outcomes. One commonly used method for doing so is Monte Carlo simulation. A Monte Carlo simulation can analyze thousands of possible scenarios to determine the most likely earn-out as well as the distribution of earn-out payments over all possible scenarios modeled. Additional simulations conducted in parallel can also be used to determine the expected value and range of value to be created for the acquirer via the earn-out agreement.[5]

Earn-Out Examples

Figure 11.1 presents some of the acquisitions we will examine throughout this chapter that included earn-outs as contingent consideration. The acquirers for these deals were Disney, Facebook, and Google.

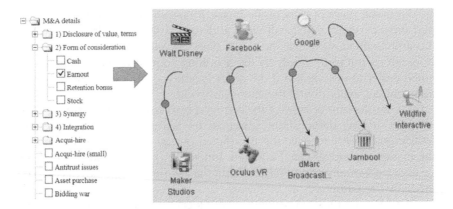

FIGURE 11.1 Sample deals involving earn-outs

DISNEY In 2014, Walt Disney acquired Maker Studios in what was viewed as a major move by Disney in entering the world of short-form online video. Maker was one of the largest multi-channel networks on YouTube. In a 10-Q statement, Disney stated the following about the Maker deal:

> On May 7, 2014, the Company acquired Maker Studios, Inc. (Maker), a leading network of online video content on YouTube, for approximately $500 million of cash consideration, subject to certain conditions and adjustments. Maker shareholders may also receive up to $450 million of additional cash if Maker achieves certain performance targets for calendar years 2014 and 2015. The Company has recognized a $198 million liability for the fair value of the contingent consideration (determined by a probability weighting of potential payouts)

Note certain key elements of the earn-out agreement between Disney and Maker:

- The potential earn-out of $450 million was sizable, amounting to almost 50 percent of total possible deal consideration ($950 million).
- Any additional consideration from the earn-out would be paid in cash, not stock.
- The earn-out period involved performance targets over *two* calendar years. Earn-out agreements have a starting and ending date during which the seller is eligible for the earn-out. If all else is equal, a longer term agreement is more valuable than a shorter one, but there also is more opportunity for the relationship between buyer and seller to sour.

- Upon the close of the transaction, Disney booked a liability for the fair value ($198 million) of the earn-out or contingent consideration. Accounting rules currently require earn-outs to be valued and booked as a liability if any additional payout is to be in cash. (We'll see later in this chapter that retention bonuses are handled differently.)
- Disney valued the earn-out using a probability weighting of potential outcomes. As mentioned earlier, this type of valuation approach is considered superior to simply discounting best-case estimates of future cash flows.
- In the disclosure, Disney does not state the specific performance objectives upon which the earn-out would be based. For competitive or confidentiality reasons, such objectives are often kept secret. However, these performance metrics are generally tied to drivers that will enable the acquirer to reach the synergy goals established for the deal.

FACEBOOK   In 2014, Facebook announced an agreement to acquire Oculus, the maker of a virtual reality gaming headset branded as Oculus Rift. In a 10-Q statement Facebook stated the following about the Oculus deal:

> *In March 2014, we entered into an agreement to acquire Oculus VR, Inc. (Oculus), a privately-held company developing virtual reality technology, for 23,071,377 shares of our Class B common stock and approximately $400 million in cash.... Further, up to an additional 3,460,706 shares of our Class B common stock and $60 million in cash would be payable upon the completion of certain milestones. The earn-out portion that would be payable to employee stockholders is also subject to continuous employment through the applicable payment dates.*

Note certain key elements of the earn-out agreement between Facebook and Oculus:

- Unlike the Disney/Maker earn-out where additional consideration would be paid in cash, the Facebook/Oculus agreement provides that additional consideration would be paid out as a combination of cash and stock.
- The potential earn-out was 15 percent of the guaranteed purchase price consideration. The 15 percent applied to both the stock and cash consideration reflected by the guaranteed purchase price. This earn-out on a percentage basis was notably smaller than the Disney/Maker agreement.
- The earn-out to employee stockholders was contingent upon these stockholders being in the continuous employment of Facebook during

the earn-out period. Although this agreement was not structured solely a retention bonus, it did include an employee retention element as one condition.

- As was the case with the Disney/Maker agreement, the specific performance goals relating to the earn-out were not disclosed.
- Although in a press release announcing this deal, Facebook placed a preliminary valuation of $300 million on the earn-out (15 percent of the guaranteed consideration), the value of the earn-out would likely be adjusted upon deal close based on more detailed analysis of the range of likely outcomes.

GOOGLE In this section, we'll examine two of the three Google deals (Jambool and Wildfire) shown in Figure 11.1. Although media sources estimated earn-outs for these transactions, Google did not disclose purchase price consideration regarding these acquisitions, either at close or potentially resulting from an earn-out. (Refer to Chapter 9 for our discussion of when such consideration is disclosed.)

Google did disclose earn-out information relating to dMarc, the third Google acquisition appearing in Figure 11.1. We will discuss the dMarc transaction in some detail later in this chapter.

In 2010, Google acquired Jambool, which developed payment technology to enable micropayments in online game or social network applications. According to TechCrunch, the deal value was $55 million with an additional $15 million to $20 million structured as an earn-out.[6]

Then in 2012, Google acquired Wildfire, a social marketing software developer that enabled companies to serve ad campaigns on services such as Facebook, Google+, and Twitter. According to TechCrunch, the consideration for this deal was $350 million in cash plus $100 million in earn-outs and retention bonuses.[7]

Note the following concerning these two Google deals that purportedly included earn-outs:

- It was third-party media that reported on these earn-outs. Google did not disclose details of these deals in its 10-K filings. There are major efforts made by media and other sources to attempt to uncover additional details about the M&A activity of leading technology companies.
- Such reporting by the media may or may not be completely reliable as it often relies on unnamed sources. As mentioned in Chapter 9, principals and their representatives are often legally bound by confidentiality agreements not to disclose the details of an acquisition.
- With these caveats, note that the reported earn-out associated with the Jambool deal represented about one-third of the guaranteed purchase

price. The reported earn-out and retention bonus reported for the Wild-fire deal also amounted to approximately one-third of the guaranteed purchase price.

- Although earn-outs and retention bonuses can be lumped together and intertwined by the media, for our purposes these two forms of potential deal consideration are better regarded as distinct aspects of additional deal consideration. In particular, as we'll see shortly, Google has migrated away from using earn-outs and has embraced retention bonuses as a major mechanism for stimulating *semi-organic growth*.

Retention Bonuses

Retention bonuses (also known as stay bonuses) associated with an acquisition can assume a number of purposes:

1. Encouraging employees to stay until deal close
2. Motivating employees to stay on after deal close in order to work on performance goals that are directly tied to an earn-out agreement
3. Rewarding employees to stay on after deal close to engage in work that may involve blending buyer and seller technologies, but also possibly work on additional projects for the acquirer. Assume there is no earn-out associated with this purpose. (If there also is an earn-out, the retention bonus is typically carved-out from potential consideration associated with the earn-out.)

In this section, we will focus on the third form of retention bonus listed above. In other words, our attention will be directed to arrangements that provide for extra compensation for founders and/or target employees after their company is acquired. And such compensation is to be provided contingent solely on the target team continuing to work on behalf of the acquirer, often to achieve *semi-organic growth*.

Retention Bonus Recognition

Recall that earn-outs are to be considered part of the purchase price of an acquisition. Earn-outs are typically valued using a probabilistic weighting of outcomes associated with the deal.

Retention bonuses in the form of additional compensation (as per above) are handled differently. For accounting purposes, these stay bonuses are not considered part of the purchase price, but instead are treated as wages to be recognized over the life of the retention period, usually one to four years.

Since this form of retention bonus may not have specific target performance goals attached to it (as is the case with an earn-out), it's important for the acquirer to gain the commitment of target employees to engage in efforts that will benefit the buyer. With technology knowledge workers in particular, it's vital for the acquirer to avoid a phenomenon known as *stay and play*. More on the stay and play challenge later in this chapter.

Retention Bonus Examples

Figure 11.2 pictures sample acquisitions that included retention bonuses. The acquirers for these deals were Apple, Facebook, and Google.

In 2014, Apple acquired Beats Electronics (Beats), which marketed consumer headphones as well as a streaming music subscription service. According to an Apple 10-Q, the consideration involved $2.6 billion in cash and $400 million in Apple stock that would vest over an unspecified time period based on continued employment of certain executives of Beats.

Note the following regarding the stay bonus associated with Beats deal:

- Apple CEO Tim Cook stated that growing Beats' existing businesses was "not the reason for doing the deal." According to the *Wall Street Journal*: "The deal was about recruiting the right people for Apple, which revolutionized music consumption with the iPod and its iTunes digital-music store but has risked falling behind in newer businesses such as streaming."[8]

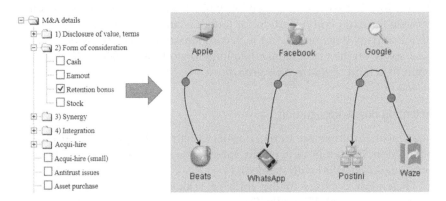

FIGURE 11.2 Sample deals involving retention bonuses

- The retention bonus of $400 million amounted to approximately 15 percent of the direct purchase price consideration.
- In announcing the deal, the vesting period for the retention bonus was not explicitly stated.
- The retention bonus would be paid in Apple stock. Using Apple stock in an M&A transaction was extremely rare behavior for Apple, and signaled a very important talent-related *semi-organic* acquisition for the company.

In 2014, Facebook agreed to acquire WhatsApp. According to a 10-Q Facebook filing: "In February 2014, we entered into an agreement to acquire WhatsApp Inc. (WhatsApp), a privately-held cross-platform mobile messaging company, for 183,865,778 shares of our Class A common stock and approximately $4 billion in cash.... Upon closing, we will also grant 45,966,445 RSUs to WhatsApp employees."

Note the following regarding the stay bonus associated with WhatsApp deal:

- The purchase price was initially pegged at $16 billion, consisting of $12 billion in Class A shares, $4 billion in cash. In addition, the retention bonus associated with the RSUs (restricted stock units) was initially valued at $3 billion.
- As initially valued, the retention bonus amounted to approximately 25 percent of the stock-based consideration of the direct purchase price, or about 19 percent of the total direct purchase price consideration. The second percentage could change based on the valuation of Facebook stock at deal close.
- The retention bonus involves stock-based compensation. With RSU-based compensation the stock is not received immediately, but according to a vesting plan that requires the employee to remain with the acquirer. The RSUs to be granted to WhatsApp founders and employees would vest over four years.
- The WhatsApp acquisition was viewed as an extremely lucrative deal for WhatsApp engineers, with very high incentive to stay with Facebook after the deal closed. According to one analysis, a senior engineer could stand to gain some $2.3 million over the four-year vesting period from the RSUs alone.[9] How about that for designing a deal to achieve talent stickiness?

Next, let's examine the two Google deals shown in Figure 11.2 for which retention bonus information was disclosed or reported.

In 2007, Google acquired Postini, a provider of on-demand communications security and compliance solutions. The purchase price was

$545.7 million. In addition, Google disclosed in a 10-Q filing that it was "obligated to make cash payments of up to $44.8 million through 2011, contingent upon each employee's continued employment with us. These contingent payments will be expensed, when and if earned."

In 2013, Google acquired Waze, an Israeli crowd-sourced mapping and navigation company, for a purchase price of $966 million in cash as disclosed in a Google 10-K filing. In addition, Haaretz (an Israeli news website) reported that $120 million would be going to Waze workers over the next four years.[10] The $120 million included $45 million that would be exchanged for Waze options and shares that employees held, and another $75 million was to be paid as compensation. The $75 million compensation arrangement was, in part, designed to help retain recently hired Waze employees who were without options.

Note the following regarding the stay bonus agreements associated with the Postini and Waze deals:

- In the Postini transaction, the retention bonus amounted to about 8 percent of purchase price consideration.
- In the Waze transaction, the retention compensation of $75 million likewise reflected about 8 percent of the purchase price consideration.
- However, even though the retention bonus percentages in both transactions were around 8 percent, it should not be assumed that stay bonuses pools are simply formulaic. These pools vary considerably, given factors such as the state of the target's technology, the desire to retain key talent, and the amount of consideration given the target at close.
- In addition to the $75 million retention bonus pool structured as a result of the Waze acquisition, some Waze employees had added incentive to stay in the employ of Google in order to vest options earlier received from Waze. This is not uncommon in the acquisition of technology ventures.
- Over time, retention bonuses (as opposed to earn-outs) became the vehicle of choice that Google used to keep talent at the company and stimulate semi-organic growth. We'll now explore the main reasons why this change occurred.

Moving Away from Earn-outs

Google's founders loved earn-outs. After all, in theory this form of contingent consideration promised to be a powerful motivator that coupled added reward with achieving key success results on the part of the target. Earn-outs seemed to be a natural additive to a guaranteed purchase price that would result in improving the odds of keeping entrepreneurial founders committed to pursuing agreed-on goals after being acquired by Google.

So most of Google's early acquisitions had an earn-out component associated with the transaction. But this affection for specific milestone-based potential consideration was dampened. Google would later make a marked transition to time-based retention bonuses that did not contain specific performance metrics.[11]

But why the change? There are at least three reasons.

dMarc Broadcasting

First of all, the dMarc Broadcasting acquisition depicted in Figure 11.1 did not go well. In 2006, Google bought dMarc, a company that worked with radio advertisers in the sales, scheduling, and delivery of radio ads. According to the 2006 Google 10-K, the consideration was $97.6 million in cash plus up to $1.136 billion in cash contingent (earn-out) payments. Note that the earn-out reflected 92 percent of the total potential consideration! Here's an extract from this 10-K relating to the dMarc deal.

> *In addition, we are contingently obligated to make additional cash payments of up to $1.136 billion. Specifically, we are contingently obligated to make an additional cash payment of $25.0 million upon the achievement of a product launch milestone, and additional cash payments of up to $390.0 million in respect of 2007 and up to $721.0 million in respect of 2008 if certain net revenue and advertising inventory targets are met in each of those years.... Net revenue targets are generally calculated based on revenue recognized primarily from the distribution of radio advertisements, less the inventory acquisition costs associated with such revenue. Advertising inventory targets are calculated by reference to the average quarter hour listener counts of advertising spots available in our system during each quarterly period. Because these contingent payments are based on the achievement of performance targets, actual payments may be substantially lower.*

It turned out that actual contingent payments were *indeed substantially lower!* In February 2007 (only about one year after the deal was announced), Chad and Ryan Steelberg, dMarc's founders, left Google in an apparent conflict over the extent to which the radio ad process could be automated. Evidently, the dMarc founders wanted more salespeople than Google and were troubled about lower than expected revenue growth.[12] Writing about Google's hurdles in entering the radio advertising business, *The New York Times* reported: "Industry insiders cite everything from culture clashes to resistance in the radio industry, which relies heavily on sales representatives, to automate its advertising systems. But the hurdle mentioned most often is Google's apparent inability to secure enough air time, or inventory, to make its system attractive to advertisers."[13]

In 2009, Google pulled the plug on its radio advertising business and announced plans to sell off its Google Radio Automation.

Not only had the incursion into radio been a failure, but Google's relationship with dMarc's founders was acrimonious and open to possible litigation. As mentioned above, the massive earn-out constituted 92 percent of total potential consideration for the transaction, so a lot was at stake.

The frustration and tension associated with the dMarc deal would trigger a spontaneous extinction of Google's addiction to earn-outs.

Rewrites

Second, Google found that the initial draft of an earn-out agreement might not capture important performance metrics that would only emerge with the passage of time after deal close.

For example, the earn-out performance goals initially written relating to the acquisition of Android in 2005 changed as Google's vision for the Android mobile operating system evolved. In order to keep the Android team motivated in the right direction, the agreement needed to be rewritten. In fact, the Android earn-out goals were redrafted at least twice.

With rapidly changing technology markets, it's hard to predict what might emerge as important in the months after a deal closes. Key earn-out performance goals can morph.

Narrow Founder Focus

A third reason why Google moved away from structuring earn-outs as part of an acquisition agreement involved a tunnel-vision focus on earn-out metrics that founders tended to assume after the deal closed.

Just as students are prone to focus on what a professor suggests will be on an exam and disregard other important material, founders and employees of an acquired company *tend to focus on x if the earn-out is tied to achieving x*. Even if the target's talent comes to realize that something other than x (say y or z) is more important for achieving *semi-organic growth* for the acquirer, undue effort can still be exerted to reaching x.

Rest and Vest?

So based on these three reasons (the dMarc experience, necessary rewrites, and narrow founder focus), Google's senior management determined that the company should move away from earn-outs and embrace retention (stay) bonuses.

But stay bonuses had their own potential drawbacks. What would guarantee that the founders/employees of an acquired company would remain intensely committed to the goals important in achieving semi-organic growth objectives? If all that was necessary was "staying," what would keep the new Google employees from "playing"? Would "rest and vest" become a significant danger? (*vest* here refers not to stock, but rather, time-based cash payments, as almost all Google retention bonuses came to be paid out in cash). Google hoped that the excitement of working on meaningful projects, the company culture, and wanting to have the choice of staying on at Google after the stay bonus period was over would motivate employees to perform well.

For now, retention bonuses were in. Earn-outs were out. But the jury was also out on whether earn-outs would make a comeback.

Watch the Videos

www.wiley.com/go/semiorganicgrowth

To view videos relating to the content of this chapter, refer to (1) *Pitfalls in M&A Contingent Consideration* and (2) *Direct and Reverse Break-up Fees,* which accompany this book as a supplemental resource.

Notes

1. Robert F. Bruner, "Technical Note on Structuring and Valuing Incentive Payments in M&A: Earnout and Other Contingent Payment to the Seller," Darden Business Publishing, 2001.
2. "Earn-Out Agreements: Part 1—An Overview," http://moneysoft .com/earn-out-agreements-part-1-an-overview, *MoneySoft,* accessed

August 22, 2014. There are five parts to the *MoneySoft* series on earn-outs; all are well-worth reading.

3. Ibid.

4. Bruner, op. cit., pp. 1–2.

5. For a case discussion of using Monte Carlo simulation in earn-out valuation from the perspective of both buyer and seller, see "Printicomm's Proposed Acquisition of Digitech: Negotiating Price and Form of Payment," *Darden Business Publishing*. Case number UV0087.

6. Michael Arrington, "Another Piece to Google's Social Puzzle: To Acquire Jambool for $70 Million," *TechCrunch* (August 8, 2010).

7. Josh Constine, "Google Slaps $100M Golden Handcuffs on Wildfire to Retain Employees after $350M Acquisition." *TechCrunch* (August 6, 2012).

8. Hannah Karp, Ryan Dezember and Alistar Barr, "Apple Paying Less Than $500 Million for Beats Music Streaming Service," *Wall Street Journal* (May 30, 2014).

9. Andy Rachleff, "WhatsApp: What an Acquisition Means for Employees," *Wealthfront Knowledge Center* (February 21, 2014).

10. Amir Teig, "Waze Employees Clinch Most Lucrative Exit in Israeli History," *Haaretz* (June 13, 2013).

11. Tomio Geron, "Google Slowly Moving Away From Its 'Addiction' to M&A Earn-Outs," *Wall Street Journal*, March 2, 2010.

12. Paul Kedrosky, "dMarc Founders Leave Google, Complain about Kool-Aid Taste," *Infectious Greed*, February 9, 2007.

13. Miguel Helet, "Google Encounters Hurdles in Selling Radio Advertising," *New York Times*, February 10, 2007.

CHAPTER 12

Dimensions of M&A Integration and Semi-Organic Growth

S uccessfully integrating an acquisition is the primary process by which value is captured from the transaction. It is through integration efforts that revenue enhancements are achieved and cost efficiencies are realized. This realization has been consistently stated, starting with some of the earliest studies dealing with M&A. In a book written in 1962, Mace and Montgomery stated: "Many potentially valuable acquired company assets have been lost by neglect and poor handling during the integration process."[1]

As we've seen in earlier chapters, Google has not achieved success in all of its *M&A integration* efforts. Recall that problems arose as early as the 2003 Applied Semantics purchase, and in 2005 Google asked Applied Semantics' former CFO to lead an effort to design and implement more effective methods for M&A integration.

Some major integration challenges continued for Google in subsequent purchases. In Chapter 11, we saw how an earn-out associated with the dMarc Broadcasting transaction in 2006 created significant frustration and disagreement. And the integration efforts associated with the Zagat acquisition in 2011 were fraught with discontent and even anger.

Nevertheless, in spite of these and other hiccups, Google has been notably successful in integrating the majority of its acquisitions. Was there something in the company's core DNA that was making this so? Or had Google learned through experimentation what would tend to work well in M&A integration?

In this chapter, we'll explore classic strategic dimensions that provide a blueprint for M&A integration. We'll examine how Google's semi-organic pattern of acquisitions fits into this scheme. And we'll see how and why Google has been overall quite successful in executing a very challenging type of integration strategy.

Typologies for M&A Integration

Although many variants have emerged from the M&A typology put forth by Haspeslagh and Jemison[2] in 1991, their seminal work proposing key dimensions by which integration efforts can be characterized has persisted as a highly useful framework. The authors set forth two vital dimensions that yield a 2×2 grid for guiding M&A integration. These two dimensions are *autonomy* and *strategic interdependence* and suggest four possible integration strategies, as shown in Figure 12.1.

The dimension of autonomy is characterized by the degree to which the target will be left alone or tightly managed in determining its future direction. On the other hand, strategic interdependence reflects the degree to which the acquirer's and target's technologies, products, or services must be interrelated after deal close.

As shown in Figure 12.1, four major integration types (absorption, holding, preservation, and symbiosis) result from analyzing the two dimensions of this grid.

1. ***Absorption***. This may be the style that first comes to mind upon hearing word *integration*. Absorption is characterized by tightly assimilating the target into the acquirer and doing so in a one-way manner such that the acquirer's culture and business practices dominate. Absorption may be appropriate when there is a *low need for autonomy* and *a high need for strategic interdependence*. Cisco during the 1990s became famous for such integration as it built technology *solution stacks* via acquisition.

Acquisition Types and Integration Strategies

Need for Strategic interdependence

		Low	High
Need for Organizational Autonomy	High	Preservation (Berkshire Hathaway)	Symbiosis (Google semi-organic M&A)
	Low	Holding (Many private equity deals)	Absorption (Classic Cisco)

FIGURE 12.1 Four possible integration strategies
Adapted from Haspeslagh & Jemison, *Managing Acquisitions: Creating Value through Corporate Renewal* (Free Press, 1991).

In the words of CEO John Chambers: "In a merger you can't blend resources and cultures—only one can survive." (Cisco later modified its approach in many of its deals.)

In the extreme, absorption could be dubbed the *Borg strategy*. Here's a famous quotation from the Borg, a notoriously "acquisitive" alien species from the science fiction series *Star Trek*: "We will add your biological and technological distinctiveness to our own. Your culture will adapt to service us. Resistance is futile."

2. **Holding**. This is an integration style characterized by a *low need for autonomy* as well as a *low need for strategic interdependence*. This strategy may be adopted by a private equity company that actively makes changes in a target's management and operations in order to increase financial performance. In addition, the target becomes a portfolio company that may have little or no interrelationship with other companies in the portfolio.

3. **Preservation**. This style is characterized by a *high need for autonomy* coupled with a *low need for strategic interdependence*. Here the classic example is Berkshire Hathaway, with dozens of diverse business units obtained via acquisition that are largely operated independently. Warren Buffett has frequently stated that his targets must have their own management in place, as Berkshire Hathaway is not able to supply it. (Indeed, Buffett stated in his 2013 annual letter that there were only 24 men and women who worked with him at his corporate office in Omaha!) Buffett's core strategy has been to buy great companies with great management and then preserve (and support) them.

4. **Symbiosis**. A symbiotic integration style is characterized by *high need for autonomy* as well as *high need for strategic interdependence*. Core to this effort is a blending of the acquirer and target such that a meaningful reciprocal exchange of technology, talent, and capability ensues. This bidirectional, alchemic form of integration is perhaps the most challenging to perform well.[3]

As we'll see, Google has certainly used more than one of these integration styles in its M&A history. And the style initially utilized in an acquisition can morph as the post-acquisition period progresses. Nevertheless, how Google has attempted (and often succeeded) in achieving symbiosis will be of highest interest to us. Indeed, this form of integration effort is most closely aligned with *semi-organic growth*.

Google's Integration Styles

When Google bought Applied Semantics (ASI) in 2003 with the goal of expanding its advertising reach beyond paid search to contextual advertising throughout the Web, Google was a relative neophyte in the M&A integration game.

As we observed in Chapter 2, ASI had technology (CIRCA/AdSense) and talent that needed to be blended with Google's own technology (Phil) and talent in building a contextual ad system for analyzing content on webpages and suggesting ad placement.

Although the Google/ASI integration effort was not a failure, it was hardly a home run. The integration was more absorption than alchemy. Applied Semantics engineers and managers reported to Mountain View counterparts across strict functional lines, engineering to engineering, marketing to marketing, finance to finance, and so on. ASI entrepreneurial team interactions were degraded as the company was quickly placed within the hierarchy of the acquirer.

Undoubtedly, some Google short-run goals were well served by this style of integration. Technologies were efficiently blended, but such efficiency came with a price as ASI talent experienced some suboptimal consequences of being put into this blender. Google was integrating ASI on the line between absorption and symbiosis, but perhaps had slipped too quickly into absorption. Google probably would have been better served from a strategic perspective by allowing, at least for a while, more freedom for ASI to operate as a creative entrepreneurial team.

To Google's credit, the company realized that changes were needed in future M&A post-deal activity. Always the experimenter, Google was determined to discover a more effective way to integrate acquisition technology as well as talent.

Research has shown that autonomy tends to work better than centralization, especially for transactions in service and knowledge-intensive industries. In particular, autonomy given to targets in technology industries is correlated with higher talent retention.

For example, as Ranft and Lord noted:

Many acquisitions of high-tech firms are motivated by the acquirers' desire to enhance their strategic technological capabilities. However, these capabilities are likely to be embedded to a large degree in the tacit and socially complex knowledge of the acquired firms' individual and collective human capital. This presents a dilemma for acquirers because, unlike tangible or financial assets, the acquired firms' valuable human assets cannot be purchased or owned outright and they can leave the firm at any time. Retention therefore is likely to be of central importance during acquisition implementation in knowledge-intensive firms.[4]

Google was about to experiment with larger doses of autonomy with some of its major deals.

Preservation Deals

In August 2005, Google acquired Android, a small startup based in Palo Alto that was developing software for mobile phones. Google's acquisition of the company triggered rumors that Google would enter the mobile phone market, although it was unclear at the time how it would play in this market. Two key players in the creation of Android, Andy Rubin (co-founder of Danger) and Rich Miner (co-founder of Wildfire Communications, Inc.) joined Google.

To a remarkable degree, Google allowed Android to operate with autonomy, from being allowed to maintain separate facilities to enjoying unprecedented freedom to hire employees of Android's choosing. Android was essentially preserved, with Google resources standing behind it to fuel development efforts.

Although some Google executives, including David Lawee, former Google Vice President of M&A, initially were skeptical that the Android deal would generate results, these executives were turned to converts as Android (after several iterations) took off and assumed its position as the dominant mobile operating system.

Then in 2006, Google acquired YouTube. Following the acquisition, YouTube would operate independently, retaining its brand and all employees, including co-founders Chad Hurley and Steve Chen.

Eric Schmidt (Google CEO at the time) was personally proactive in defending YouTube's autonomy. Google did not want to ruin YouTube's product innovation and agile culture. A former Google Group Product Manager knowledgeable about the transition stated: "YouTube was growing so well that they were afraid to mess it up like big companies sometimes do when they acquire smaller ones." To that end, YouTube maintained its San Bruno office location rather than moving to Google company headquarters. And as late as 2014, there was no significant Google branding visible at YouTube's offices.

YouTube's engineering (run by Chen) was augmented and enriched by Google's engineering and data center resources. And Hurley welcomed the addition of other Googlers, especially those who fit well into YouTube's culture. But YouTube did not experience the same freedom enjoyed by Android to hire new employees at will, and "Hurley was frustrated when candidates he liked were nixed by Mountain View."[5]

Google was tweaking multiple variables and addressing numerous subtleties of M&A integration, at times enjoying some notable success. Overall, autonomy was being increased, and target preservation (at least for a while) was becoming more common.

Symbiosis and Semi-Organic Growth

Although every one of Google's acquisitions had distinctive characteristics that required individual consideration as to how the target would be integrated, overall Google appeared to be moving toward *symbiosis* as a dominant mode. There are several reasons why this seemed to be occurring.

First of all, Google's core DNA included a proclivity to encourage employees (especially engineers) to experiment. And such experimentation would require a significant dose of autonomy.

Note the sense of autonomy implicit in a statement of Brian McLendon, VP of Engineering at Google, responsible for Google Maps, Google Earth, and Streetview: "The appeal for founders acquired by Google is that they have an idea which they have narrowed to a startup, a fiscally possible exit, but what they really want to do is something much bigger. Google can pour rocket fuel on that fire. . . ."[6]

Rocket fuel on fire. The image conjures up one hell of a symbiotic blend. And the fuel Google typically provided to the alchemic mixture was not only financial resources.

For many, if not most, of the acquisitions, Google now had preexisting initiatives that related to the target's products or services. Recall from Chapter 2 that while similarity may be vital in obtaining efficiency-based synergies (scale or scope), it is complementarity that generates value from mutually supportive differences (enhancement-based synergies).

Complementary acquisitions with *interdependence* could be designed to yield *economies of fitness*, a key dimension of semi-organic growth. Founders and other employees of the target would be given significant amounts of autonomy to continue to work on their venture, but within the context of a Google portfolio of products and services that would provide fuel for symbiotic blends.

It's true that at times, engineering teams from the target were "simply" assigned to existing Google product teams with the target's products being killed. This form of acqui-hire was more acqui-Hire than Acqui-hire, a distinction we'll discuss in detail in the next chapter. But, for now, we're interested in deals where the goal was a rich interactive mixture of the seller's core venture initiatives with an existing or emerging product offering from within Google.

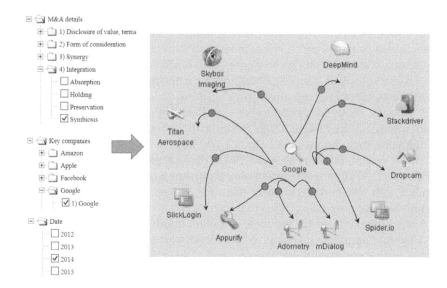

FIGURE 12.2 Examples of symbiotic integration during 2014

Consider a number of examples shown in Figure 12.2 from Google's M&A activity during 2014 that provide a flavor for this symbiotic pattern. We'll briefly describe these "alchemic" deals moving clockwise.

In a deal we've examined before, Google acquired DeepMind, an artificial intelligence company that built learning algorithms. DeepMind's employees reportedly included about a dozen of the world's experts in deep learning, a branch of artificial intelligence research that was tackling tasks such as recognizing faces in video or words in human speech. Although DeepMind had not yet released a product, but had made considerable progress in enabling computers to learn from very limited feedback.[7] From improving voice-activated search, to efficiently recommending new purchases, to enabling robots to navigate an external environment, the complementary interactions with existing and future Google's products and services were manifold.

Google acquired Stackdriver, which developed technology to support developers in monitoring apps and services running in the cloud. The company's technology provided visibility into errors, performance, behavior, and operations. The Stackdriver team would work on integrating its technology with the Google Cloud Platform. Adding Stackdriver was an attempt by Google to make its platform stand out in an increasingly competitive cloud computing market.

Google acquired Dropcam, which made Wi-Fi–connected video cameras and services that stream live video to mobile apps. In doing so, Google/ Nest added products and services in its push to become the dominant home operating system for all types of connected devices.

We next look at a series of acquisitions with significant symbiotic interaction with Google's core advertising business.

Google acquired Spider.io, a developer of technology to identify and weed out fraudulent clicks relating to online ads. Spider.io's seven employees, including founder Douglas de Jager would join Google. Three of these seven employees were PhDs. In completing the deal, Google posted: " ... [a] vibrant ecosystem only flourishes if marketers can buy media online with the confidence that their ads are reaching real people, that results they see are based on actual interest. To grow the pie for everyone, we need to take head on the issue of online fraud."

Google acquired mDialog, which developed technology that allowed large media companies to manage and deliver video advertising across a range of products, including iPhones and iPads, Android devices, and streaming products such as Xbox and Roku. In the short run, mDialog would continue to operate its service. However, Google planned to eventually fold the company's technology into DoubleClick.

Google purchased Adometry, which focused on online ad attribution, attempting to credit online ads for stimulating a user to click on an ad or buy a product. Google Analytics Premium supported websites in managing data, traffic, and ad reporting, and Adometry's technology would be used to facilitate the growth of that business.

And then there were ventures acquired with the expectation that they would be symbiotic with Android.

Google acquired Appurify, which offered technology that automated the testing and optimization of mobile apps and websites for developers. Appurify had 20+ employees who would join Google. Appurify would continue to offer its freemium cross-platform service, but would enjoy major adoption acceleration as it is integrated into Google's developer tool stack. Application testing and optimization was a big deal for Android, given its historic fragmentation problem arising from multiple flavors of the operating system.

Google acquired SlickLogin, which had developed technology that allowed users to authenticate password-protected accounts by placing a smartphone near a computer or tablet. SlickLogin's founders were formerly with the cybersecurity unit of the Israeli Defense Force, but now would be joining Google. Google hoped to leverage the SlickLogin team and technology by combining this authentication technology with a range of existing and future products.

Finally, there were acquisitions that were designed to interact with Google's services in the sky.

Google purchased Titan Aerospace, which was developing jet-sized drones designed to fly nonstop for years. Google reported that Titan's technology might be deployed to capture geo-images and provide Internet access to remote areas. Titan had about 20 employees (including CEO Vern Raburn) who planned to remain in New Mexico. Titan would work with Google's Loon, a project developing large, high-altitude balloons that provide Internet signals to remote locations as well as other emerging Google projects.

Google acquired Skybox Imaging, which designed small, relatively inexpensive satellites that gathered daily photos and video of the Earth. Their low-Earth orbit satellites are intended to stay in orbit for about four years. Skybox's 120 employees, including CEO Dan Berkenstock, would initially be assigned to the Google Maps area. For starters. Google was buying Skybox mainly for its image capabilities in support of Google Maps. However, Berkenstock also positioned Skybox as having a data mining capabilities that could allow investors and corporate clients obtain market intelligence from aerial photography. (Consider estimating Home Depot's quarterly sales by persistently monitoring the number of cars in its parking lot.)

This set of deals reflects only a small set of Google acquisitions that were designed to contain a significant symbiotic element. In each of these deals, the target would continue to operate with autonomy (varying degrees) on its technology, while strategically interacting with Google's current or emerging product/service offerings.

Making Symbiosis Work

Enabling founders and employees of a seller to continue working on what they are passionate about is a major contributing factor to achieving symbiosis. Assuming the target has been selected with a rich potential for strategic interactivity with the acquirer's offerings, the essential ingredients for symbiosis are in place.

But there are additional considerations if the alchemy is to actually work.

ATTITUDE   The right atmosphere must be present for successful integration. Haspeslagh and Jemison (1991) stressed the following atmospheric conditions, which are especially important in a symbiotic type of effort:

> ***Appreciation of respective organizational background and diff-erences***. This may be especially true for larger acquisitions, but also

applies to small acqui-hires with distinctive cultures. Kent Kresa, former CEO of Northrup Grumman and architect behind many noteworthy Northrup acquisitions, liked to compare M&A integration to dynamics found in New York City in the late 1800s. Although certainly not a perfect process, when immigrants from countries such as Ireland and Italy moved into the City, an alchemic process was occurring whereby the best of each culture could be amalgamated into a *new* New York. So it is with M&A combinations, where the best of each company should be appreciated and put forward in the new organization.

Willingness to work together. If interdependency is to be translated into reality, product teams within the acquirer must be ready to engage the technology and talent from the target. In cases where this has not occurred, the seller will remain isolated on the fringe of key company initiatives. Recall that in Chapter 8, we discussed Google's failed acquisition of Slide, apparently keeping Max Levchin on the fringes of the Google+ social networking initiative. Of course, reasons for such isolation can be placed at the feet of acquirer, target, or both.

Sufficient capacity to receive and transfer acquired capabilities. There must be enough slack resources on both the acquirer and target sides. Integration will not occur without the necessary effort and ability to make the blend happen. Boundary spanning integration teams must be in place. More about Google's evolution in the nature of such teams later in this chapter.

Ongoing communication relating to the purposes of the integration effort. Such purposes are subject to change over time as the acquirer and target learn more about each other and as market conditions evolve. Haspeslagh and Jemison stressed the potentially destructive attitude of "determinism," whereby initial deal metrics are stuck with despite overwhelming evidence that they should be changed. As discussed in Chapter 11, one reason why Google moved to stay bonuses (as opposed to earn-outs) was the need to change success metrics in M&A transactions, including Android.

Teerikangas and Joseph provide the following summary regarding attitudes and M&A integration: "Attitudes can bear positively or negatively on M&A. While fairness, experimentation, learning, ambition, and humility underlie experiences of successful integration, one must beware of the potential for destructive reactions in the post-acquisitive encounter of two organizations."[8]

Take particular note of the word *ambition* in the above quotation. At first glance, it hardly seems to fit in with other descriptors such as fairness and humility. However, in the amalgamation process of integrating a target, it is possible for the acquirer to be *too nice*. For example, when General Mills acquired Pillsbury in 2001, the company was criticized for overaccommodating the target during the post-acquisition process, with results appearing very slowly. Ambition is a necessary attitudinal dimension of successful organizational symbiosis.

TALENT MANAGEMENT As pointed out by Haspeslagh and Jemison, value leakage in any M&A transaction can be both economic and psychological.[9] Symbiotic deals driven primarily by the acquisition of technology and talent assets are especially subject to psychological leakage. Psychological leaks occur when the founders or employees of the seller are subject to undue stress and uncertainty. These intangible losses can be significant, as the acquirer is often dependent on the ongoing commitment of the target to meet the success metrics of the acquisition.

In technology acquisitions, maintaining the commitment of engineers is especially critical. Yet, if not carefully managed, integration efforts can have a disproportional negative effect on engineer or "inventor" types, given that their social networks may be more subject to disruption than other employee types. One research finding concluded that "inventors who provide skills that differ from those in the acquiring firm are most vulnerable to disruption of their routines, even though they might be highly attractive to the acquirer precisely because of their non-overlapping capabilities."[10]

Thus, in highly symbiotic semi-organic growth initiatives, there is considerable risk associated with leakage of talent commitment. It's critical to assess whether or not newly acquired talent is working under policies or norms that are well-suited to their expertise.

For a number of the symbiotic acquisitions shown in Figure 12.2, a relatively small team of engineers continued to work on technologies developed prior to acquisition by Google, often without management change. This type of arrangement minimizes the potential psychological leakage, especially if boundary spanning efforts to existing or future Google products and services are thoughtfully designed.

Google enlarged the capabilities of integration teams and augmented their composition beyond process managers to members with the influencing skills, business acumen, and technical expertise needed to manage integrations designed to achieve substantial amalgamation.

Although some psychic M&A value leakage may be inevitable, surveys given to acquired Googlers that capture meaningful information relating to their integration experiences are regularly given in order to improve onboarding of talent. Here again, ongoing progress achieved though experimentation and understanding is the goal.

SUBTLETIES IN SPEED AND TIMING   It's a mistake to assume that any given acquisition should be statically assigned to one position on the grid shown in Figure 12.1. For example, a Google acquisition that starts out primarily in a *preservation* model, over time may need to be more aggressively amalgamated as time passes in order to achieve *symbiotic* goals.

Haspelagh and Jamison stress that knowing: (1) Where to start with an integration, (2) how fast to proceed, and (3) knowing the best path to the desired success metrics are all critical aspects of M&A success. But as already noted, success metrics should not be viewed as endpoints carved in stone, but, rather, as objectives subject to modification given experimentation, discovery, and changing market dynamics.

Considering these three steps and using Haspelagh and Jamison's basic framework, let's examine how the plan for symbiotic integration might proceed for a couple of Google acquisitions. Refer to Figure 12.3.

In the case of DeepMind, we might start with preservation, initially doing everything possible to keep the unique AI talent in place in order to minimize psychological leakage. Of course, we would influence the team to address problems of particular importance to Google. As a particular solution emerges for a product or services (relating to search or robotics, for example) at two years $(t + 2)$ after deal close, we would amalgamate the technology and possibly talent into the specific Google offering. The path(s) to success may be more apparent than the precise speed of movement. A key

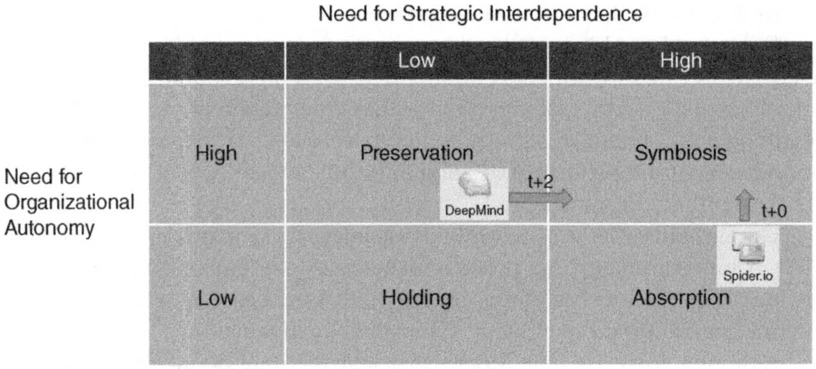

Need for Strategic Interdependence

	Low	High
High	Preservation DeepMind → t+2	Symbiosis ↑ t+0
Low	Holding	Absorption Spider.io

(Need for Organizational Autonomy — rows: High, Low)

FIGURE 12.3 Starting point and movement with an integration

point, however, is that as we move towards amalgamation, we move in a manner that minimizes operational control, but maintains strategic direction of the target.

In the case of Spider.io, acquired technology and talent has a logistical place within a Google service from the start. Spider.io's fraudulent click-detecting solution naturally belongs within the DoubleClick unit. It may work well to assign Spider.io's team into DoubleClick and direct their efforts into enhancing Google's advertising platform from day one (t+0) of the deal close. Here the goal is to move to amalgamation as quickly as possible from a position starting on the border of absorption and symbiosis.

These two scenarios are only high-level simulations of integration plans. Of course, micro dynamics that include personality variables within the buyer and seller teams and geographic distance of target from the acquirer must be considered in any integration plan.

There is continuing debate in academic literature about tradeoffs in the speed of integration. On the one hand, speed is an important consideration, given that more rapid receipt of cash-flow benefits yields higher present value for an acquirer. In addition, there often is a window of opportunity during which change on the part of the target may be more readily accepted.

On the other hand, rapid integration before the target is fully under-stood by the acquirer may result in decision-making mistakes that lead to value leakage, both economic and psychological. As one research study concluded: "There are, however, also negative effects of speed. A slower integration might minimize conflicts between partners, enhance trust build-ing, and reduce disruption of existing resources and process in both firms. . . . Hence, speed comes at a cost, and there may be situations in which the costs of speed outweigh the benefits."[11]

In summary, the successful acquirer will establish a starting point, path to the desired objectives and likely speed on the integration path for each transaction. It is unlikely that one play will work for all acquisitions. A play-book that can handle a variety of circumstances and subtleties is a better way to think about M&A integration. One size doesn't fit all.

Microanalysis Necessary

In an insightful conclusion to a paper summarizing research related to post-deal integration, Teerikangas and Joseph[12] state: "What this synthesis implies is that M&A integration research is conducted primarily through a macro-organizational, static, linear, descriptive, and prescriptive lens. This view omits the micro-organizational (i.e., individual actors, behaviors, atti-tudes, etc.), the dynamic, the emergent, the practice-based aspects of M&A."

Given its intense acquisition activity, Google represents perhaps the richest laboratory setting for analyzing M&A integration dynamics. Understanding these dynamics requires being able to take not only a macro perspective that includes high-level frameworks, but also a micro view that includes personality variables of teams and even individuals.

Perhaps M&A is better viewed as a courtship and not a takeover. As is the case with marriage, not all integrations work. But the chances of success will be increased if an acquirer is sensitive to the attitude, talent management, and timing dimensions addressed in this chapter.

Watch the Video

www.wiley.com/go/semiorganicgrowth

To view a video relating to the content of this chapter, refer to *M&A Integration—Not One Size Fits All*, which accompanies this book as a supplemental resource.

Notes

1. M. L. Mace and G. Montgomery, *Management Problems of Corporate Acquisitions*, (Boston: Harvard University Press, 1962), p. 230.
2. Haspeslagh and Jemison (1991).
3. See S. Teerikangas and R. Joseph, "Post-Deal Integration," in *The Handbook of Mergers and Acquisitions*, Chapter 14, Faulker, Teerikangas, and Joseph (Eds.), Faulkner, Teerikangas and Joseph, 2012, for an excellent review of symbiosis as well as other integration typologies.
4. A. Ranft and M. Lord, "Acquiring New Knowledge: The Role of Retaining Human Capital in Acquisitions of High-Tech Firms," *The Journal of High-Tech Management Research*, 11, no. 2 (2000): 295–319.
5. Levy (2011), p. 250.
6. Ben Popper, "Failure Is a Feature: How Google Stays Sharp Gobbling up Startups," *The Verge* (September 17, 2012).
7. Antonio Regalado, "Is Google Cornering the Market on Deep Learning?," *MIT Technology Review* (January 29, 2014).
8. Teerikangas and Joseph, p. 356.

9. Haspeslagh and Jemison.

10. S. Parachuri, A. Nerkar, and D. Hambrick, "Acquisition Integration and Productivity Losses in the Technical Core: Disruption of Inventors in Acquired Companies," *Organization Science* (October 2006), pp. 545–562.

11. Bauer and Matzler (2014).

12. Teerikangas and Joseph, p. 365.

CHAPTER 13

Acqui-Hires Enhancing Google Offerings

In earlier chapters, we demonstrated how Google's acquisitions can be associated with market-related activity. For example, in Chapter 4 we developed an MIT (media, Internet, technology) category tree that enabled us to categorize, search for, and analyze deals that fell within a given market segment.

However, while investors might think in terms of markets, customers do not. Customers buy products and services. And corporate business development executives must often determine how M&A activity can create or support specific products or services that *reach customers*.

In this chapter, we'll expand our market model to include a major category tree branch that can be used to identify Google's major product and services. We'll then analyze how a given acquisition might enhance one or more of these offerings.

Next, we'll identify four forms of acqui-hires that an organization can make to support the development of both existing and new products and services. Each form represents a distinct blend of the talent/technology of the target with the acquirer.

Finally, we'll explore major events in the lives of 16 Google M&A alumni, company founders who sold their companies to Google and later decided to pursue new avenues. Unlike acquired technologies, people are not bought for a lifetime. Talent obtained in an *acqui-hire* may decide to stay with a company or move on. Google's M&A alums are a particularly interesting group to monitor.

Why Products to Reach Customers Should Drive M&A Activity

Robert Bruner (2004)[1] provides a matrix for GE Power Systems (now GE Energy) that maps market segmentation against products that can reach customers. In Figure 13.1, we present a sample matrix adapted from Bruner's work.

The vertical dimension of Figure 13.1 breaks down segments and sub-segments of interest to GE Energy. This type of breakdown is similar in structure to the category tree developed for Google in Chapter 4, which identified segments and subsegments in media, Internet, and technology (MIT) platform markets.

Note that a major energy segment such as renewables is further broken down into more detailed subsegments that include biomass gas engines, hydroturbines, generators, solar cells and modules, and wind turbines. Of course, as was the case with our MIT market model, this sample energy market segmentation is dynamic and subject to continual update. And further (third, fourth, and even further) level subsegment delineation is often useful.

Next consider the horizontal dimension of Figure 13.1. This dimension details products and services for reaching customers. Here we are moving away from the more abstract concept of market to a more specific delineation of product or service offerings for selling into one or more market subsegments. For example, energy management software or field services might be two such product/service offerings.

Finally, note that some rectangles defined by market/product interactions of the grid have been designated as *target areas*, while others have been identified as *hot target areas*. These spaces represent especially important regions identified by executives or corporate development managers where growth is strategically important. Acquisitions in these areas may build on or enhance the acquirer's existing product/service platform (in a *semi-organic* sense) and thereby lead to new offerings by the acquirer.

Sample Google Product/Service Tree

Let's now develop an additional main branch of our market model that allows for the analysis and planning for semi-organic growth relating to Google's products and services. Figure 13.2 presents a sample snapshot from a sample category tree consisting of many of Google's offerings.

Note that in Figure 13.2, Google, as well as some of its key competitors, are depicted, with Google expanded so that its product areas are visible. Listed are some products and services ranging from Android to Google knowledge graph. (As we'll see, other products are in this categorization, but extend beyond what is shown in the figure.)

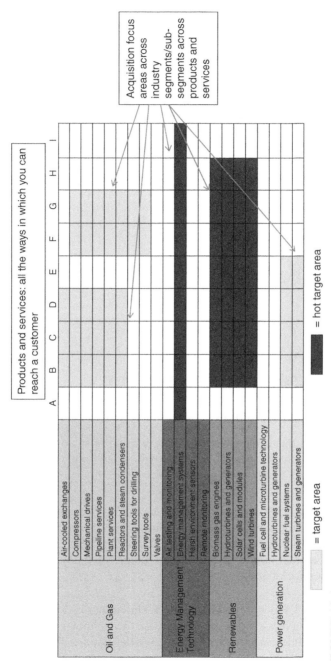

FIGURE 13.1 Mapping segments against products

Adapted from Bruner, *Applied Mergers and Acquisitions* (2004).

FIGURE 13.2 Google product and service category tree

Some M&A Product-Related Deals

After developing this category tree, we are now in position to analyze and plan for acquisitions in support of the growth of any one of these Google product lines. Let's consider some examples.

CLOUD In Figure 13.3, we have selected Google Cloud and generated an infographic showing sample Google acquisitions related to this service.

As you read the brief description for each of these three deals shown in Figure 13.3, consider how each deal helps Google reach potential customers of its cloud service offering:

  ▪ In March 2013, Google bought Talaria Technologies, a developer of Web application servers. Google planned to use the technology to enhance its cloud capabilities. Talaria's technology was designed to allow developers

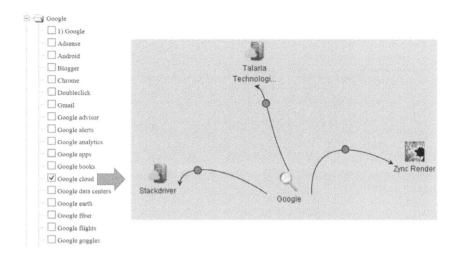

FIGURE 13.3 Google acquisitions in support of cloud services

to "handle more users with fewer boxes, without changing a line of code."

■ In May 2014, Google acquired Stackdriver, which designed technology to support developers in monitoring apps and services running in the cloud. The company's technology provided visibility into errors, performance, behavior, and operations. The Stackdriver team would work on integrating its technology with the Google Cloud Platform.

■ In August 2014, Google acquired Zync Render, a visual effects cloud rendering technology behind film productions such as *Star Trek Into Darkness* and *Looper*. Zync's technology had been used in dozens of feature films and hundreds of commercials. In commenting on the deal, Zync stated: "The scale and reliability of Google Cloud Platform will help us offer an even better service to our customers—including more scalability, more host packages, and better pricing (including per-minute billing)." Zync had previously been optimized for work on Amazon's EC2 cloud service.

GOOGLE X Next consider acquisitions in support of Google X, the company's research lab. Figure 13.4 shows some of these deals.

As with Google Cloud, once again note that this analysis is not focused on an overall market segment, but is centered on a unit within Google. Although Google X is not a specific offering per se, acquisitions attached to

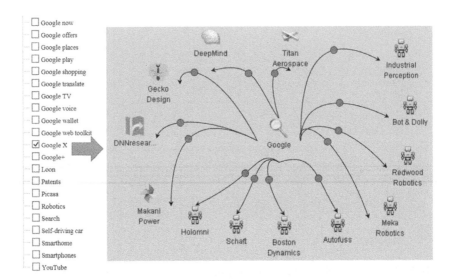

FIGURE 13.4 Acquisitions in support of Google X

this area are intended to help Google reach customers by enhancing existing products or yielding new ones. Therefore, it is an important Google facility to monitor and analyze.

As we've discussed a number of the purchases depicted in Figure 13.4 in earlier chapters, here we describe only a couple of these transactions:

- In March 2013, Google acquired DNNresearch, which developed a system for image search based on deep learning and convolutional neural networks. The technology was developed by Professor Geoffrey Hinton's group at the University of Toronto. DNN's technology was used for photo search in Google+, with an enhanced search capability being developed about six months after the deal closed.
- In August 2014, Google acquired Gecko Design, a mechanical engineering and product-design firm, with expertise in developing consumer-electronic products. Gecko typically worked with a customer's engineers prior to the start of manufacturing. Jacques Gagné (president) and Gecko's four other employees would join Google X. Google X wanted to enhance its design expertise to support its pipeline of consumer and commercial products that included Google Glass, Iris smart contact lens, and Project Loon high-altitude balloons for Internet access.

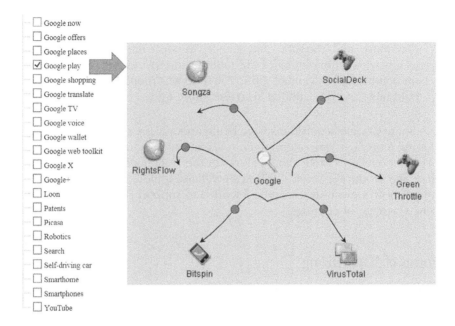

FIGURE 13.5 Acquisitions in support of Google Play

It's important to note that these acquisitions associated with Google X were being used to reach customers with a range of products across a diversity of market segments.

GOOGLE PLAY Finally, let's examine some of the acquisitions relating to Google Play, which was a fast-growing Android market where users could buy and download mobile apps, music, and games. Figure 13.5 depicts some of these deals. We'll summarize a couple of the music-related deals in order to get a flavor for how these transactions would support Google Play.

- In December 2011, Google bought RightsFlow, a company that tracked and processed royalty payments to songwriters and music publishers. The acquisition would give Google Play and YouTube technology help to manage its relationship with the fragmented music publishing industry.
- In July 2014, Google acquired Songza, a music-streaming service that developed Android and iOS apps for delivering human-curated music stations based on individual mood and activity. The company built data and algorithms that predicted what users would enjoy listening to given

geography, time of day, weather, or current activity—from sleep to sex. Google planned to use Songza's expertise in other products like Google Play Music and YouTube, and stated: "We view the Songza acquisition as a way to further enhance our radio feature by adding their expertise on context." In November 2014, YouTube was preparing its launch of a paid music service dubbed YouTube Music Key.

Some Google acquisitions were being undertaken with the goal of supporting more than one offering in our classification scheme. Therefore, our market modeling system should allow for the assignment of a deal to more than one product or service. Doing so will give a more comprehensive picture of how a given deal may be intended to support semi-organic growth across a range of offerings.

Forms of Acqui-Hiring

Recall that we have defined *acqui-hiring* as the process of acquiring a company to recruit its talent, with or without being interested in the target's technology, products, and services.

Although acqui-hiring has been around for decades, in recent years this phenomenon has been made prominent by Google and other leading technology companies. However, the term *acqui-hiring* has been used for acquisitions that vary in structure and purpose.

It is noteworthy that in spite of Google's obsession with recruiting top talent (apart from any M&A activity), the company has perhaps been the most active acqui-hirer in corporate history.[2] After all, unique capabilities and talent can often be discovered in entrepreneurial ventures founded by leaders with a change-the-world mentality.

In this section, we identify four forms of acqui-hiring in an attempt to give more precision to this practice.

Form I: Buy Company, Kill Technology, Reassign Talent

In an article on acqui-hiring, Coyle and Polsky describe the use of this practice as a talent centric, technology apathetic deal: "Facebook, Google, and other leading technology companies in Silicon Valley have been buying startup companies at a brisk pace. In many of these transactions, the buyer has little interest in acquiring the startup's projects or assets. Instead, the buyer's primary motivation is to hire some or all of the startup's software engineers."[3]

The authors argue that the pace of acqui-hiring has increased with the flourishing of technology startups in recent years given developments that include these factors:

- The costs associated with launching a new tech venture have fallen dramatically, given the significant cost reductions associated with open source software and cloud computing.
- Plentiful sources of startup capital have become available from business incubators, angel investors, venture-capital firms, and elsewhere.
- Given the technology cost savings and the availability of seed funding, startups are able to offer compensation packages that are more competitive with those offered by larger technology firms.[4]

Although many technology ventures flounder, first-class engineering and even managerial talent may reside in the company. Such talent can become an attractive "asset" to redeploy via acquisition within companies such as Apple, Facebook, or Google, especially if the target has been working in an area of general interest to the acquirer.

A Form I acqui-hire (we'll also call this an *acqui-Hire*) occurs when a venture is acquired, its products/technology are almost immediately shuttered, and its team is reassigned to work with a product team of the buyer, perhaps on related technology products.

Most of Google's acqui-hires in recent years have not been of Form I, as Google has typically wanted technology that it can deploy for semi-organic growth as opposed to being interested in a pure talent play. Nevertheless, Figure 13.6 depicts several Google acquisitions that might be viewed as approximating Form I acqui-Hires.

- In September 2013, Google acquired Bump, a mobile application that allowed two smartphones to connect wirelessly to send contact information, photos, and files between devices. When the acquisition was announced, Bump indicated that its apps would continue to exist as standalone products. However, on December 31, 2013, Bump announced that its team would now focus on new projects within Google. Bump and Flock would be discontinued and removed from the Apple App Store and Google Play. With only three months elapsing between acquiring Bump and the shutdown of its products, it appeared that this was more of an acqui-Hire of Bump's talent than a technology-acquisition deal.
- In May 2014, Google acquired Rangespan, a UK-based online shopping retailer. The company was founded in 2011 by Ryan Regan and

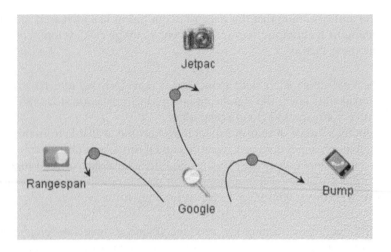

FIGURE 13.6 Form I *acqui-Hires*

Matt Henderson, two former Amazon executives. Rangespan provided back-office services to companies (such as Tesco) that included real-time analytics to support retailers in dynamically determining product offerings. Rangespan would wind down its offerings to retailers and suppliers as its team worked within Google to develop shopping services.

- In August 2014, Google acquired Jetpac, a developer of an app that made destination recommendations by analyzing shared Instagram photos. Recommendations were made for a wide range of venues such as bars where women frequented or for scenic views. Jetpac employees would join the Google Knowledge team, which was charged with developing a more sophisticated understanding of the real world that could be incorporated search results. The Jetpac app was removed from Apple's App Store a month after the company was acquired.

Form II: Buy Company for Product Fit as Well as Talent

"Gone are the days of acquiring companies strictly for talent, like coding Ruby. Now there needs to be a product fit."[5] Although perhaps slightly overstating the matter, Jacob Mullins, CEO of San Francisco-based Exitround, a marketplace for buyers and sellers of tech companies, was aptly describing a Form II acqui-hire. We term this form an *Acqui-hire*.

These types of deals abound, as exemplified by the crowded spaghetti-like infographic shown in Figure 13.7. (Given the popularity of this form,

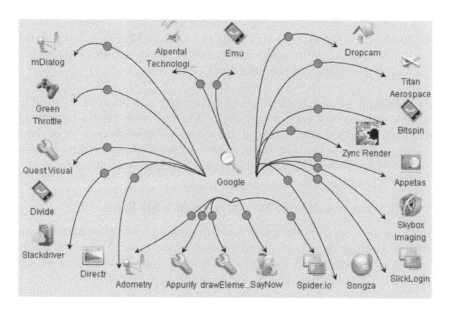

FIGURE 13.7 Form II *Acqui-hires*

we could have readily generated a diagram of such deals crowded to the point of complete illegibility!)

In order to illustrate the flavor of Form II, let's describe three of these deals occurring in 2014 (We've seen a number of the deals in Figure 13.7 in other contexts.):

1. In June 2014, Google acquired mDialog, which developed technology that allowed large media companies to manage and deliver video advertising across a range of digital devices. In the short run, mDialog would continue to operate its service. However, Google planned to eventually fold the company's technology into DoubleClick.

2. Also in June 2014, Google acquired Alpental, which was working on inexpensive, high-speed wireless Internet service using the 60GHz band of spectrum. Alpental's technology might be utilized in building out Google's delivery of fast Internet in remote locations, including as part of Project Loon, Google's initiative to power the Internet through balloons.

3. In August 2014, Google acquires EMU, a developer of a mobile instant application that included a virtual assistant to analyze conversations and then automate everyday tasks such as scheduling appointments,

managing reminders, making restaurant reservations, or sharing a location with a friend. Although EMU per se would be shut down as the result of the acquisition, Google would likely use its features to enhance existing services like Hangout and Google Now.

A Form II Acqui-hire blends both technology and talent in an effort to achieve *semi-organic growth*, and the technology must have a high probability of persisting after the deal close within some product or service. For Google, use of this form of acquisition goes back to its early days as evidenced by the Applied Semantics transaction featured in Chapter 2.

Form III: Major Acquisition of Technology, Product, and Talent

Although the term *acqui-hire* may typically conjure up images of a relatively small acquisition, there is another form that involves a large transaction with technology, product, and talent that has already enjoyed significant market acceptance. We dub this type of deal Form III or *ACQUI-HIRE*.

The companies depicted in Figure 13.8 should be quite familiar, as they have appeared and have been discussed often in earlier chapters. These deals reappear once again in order to provide examples of the Form III ACQUI-HIRE.

- In the $1.65 billion purchase of the YouTube video sharing site, Google not only retained the talent of company co-founders Chad Hurley and

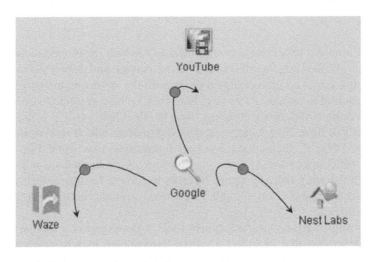

FIGURE 13.8 Form III *ACQUI-HIRES*

Steve Chen, but also a technology, brand and service against which Google had not been able to effectively compete.

- In the $966 million purchase of Waze, the crowd-sourced navigation company, Google not only extended the reach of Google Maps but it also added another dimension of consumer engagement. A significant deal term allowed Waze to continue to operate independently for three years, not requiring Waze employees to relocate from Israel. Once again, technology, product, and talent were all part of this large transaction.
- In the $3.2 billion purchase of Nest Labs, the smart-home device company, Google obtained a leading seller of Internet of Things consumer products. Google also obtained the services of Nest CEO Tony Fadell, a former Apple executive, instrumental in developing the iPod. Fadell would continue to run Nest, initially as a direct report to Larry Page.

In two of these three deals (YouTube and Nest), Google would achieve a major presence in markets where its own efforts had been struggling or were nascent at best. In the case of Waze, Google acquired a service with tens of millions of users in the mapping market where it already enjoyed substantial presence, but was eager to enhance social engagement.

All of these acquisitions were among Google's largest, and all involved technology, product, and talent to be used to fuel company growth in a major way.

Form IV: Talent to Be Utilized across Multiple Products

The final form of acqui-hire we have identified is Form IV: *acqui-HIRE*. In this form of deal the talent obtained may, in fact, be world-class and expected to have substantial impact across multiple Google products or services. Let's look at a couple of illustrations of a Form IV transaction (see Figure 13.9).

- As noted earlier, when Google acquired DeepMind in 2014, it obtained an artificial intelligence team of some 50 people considered to include

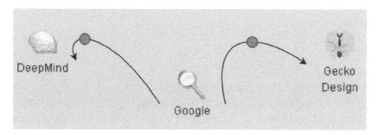

FIGURE 13.9 Form IV *acqui-HIRES*

leading thinkers in the field of deep learning. DeepMind's team could become involved in a wide range of Google initiatives ranging from improving Google Now search to developing critical components in robotics and driverless cars.

- When Google purchase Gecko Design in 2014, it obtained a much smaller team than that of DeepMind. Gecko's group consisted of Jacques Gagné (president) and four other employees. Nevertheless, Gecko, as a mechanical engineering and product-design firm with noted expertise in developing consumer-electronic products, could be utilized in a broad range of cutting-edge initiatives from Google Glass to modular smartphones.

The defining characteristic of Form IV acqui-HIRES is the broad-reaching potential product impact of the talent that comes with the deal.

Google M&A Alumni

What happens to founders who sell their companies to Google, often in an acqui-hire type deal? Do they stay on for a period of time tied to the contingent consideration term of the transaction and then leave? Do they leave sooner than anticipated? Or do they stay on with Google beyond the time period associated with any stay bonuses from the deal?

As you might anticipate, the answer is all of the above. But given that talent acquisition is such an important aspect of an acqui-hire, let's consider a sample of 16 founders/entrepreneurs who sold their companies to Google and explore what transpired in the lives of these *M&A alumni* after deal close. Although our analysis is limited to these 16 acquisitions, we'll make some generalizations about the post-acquisition professional moves by key talent associated with these purchases.

Let's briefly describe the post-acquisition lives of founders associated with the 16 companies shown in Figure 13.10. We'll move around this infographic by year of acquisition in a clock-wise direction starting with Pyra Labs.

2003

- Google acquired Pyra Labs, which had developed Blogger, a Web service that fueled the early growth of blogging. Evan Williams, Pyra's CEO, and six staff members were assigned to an existing Google engineering team. Williams left Google in October 2004. In 2007, he co-founded Twitter as a distinct entity (it previously had been bundled together with

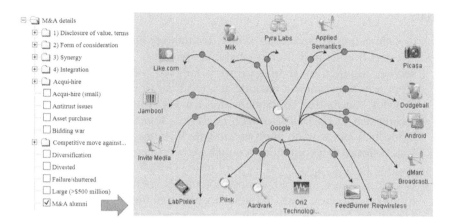

FIGURE 13.10 Google M&A alumni

other assets), providing a significant amount of Twitter's early funding and serving as the company's first chairman. Then in 2012, Williams co-founded Medium, a social journalism platform where people could share ideas and stories longer than 140 characters. In 2014, Google Ventures participated in Medium's $25 million financing round.

- As discussed in detail in Chapter 2, Google acquired Applied Semantics, a developer of semantic text processing and online advertising technology. Gil Elbaz, co-founder of Applied Semantics served as engineering director at Google from 2003 to 2007. In 2007, Elbaz founded Factual, a location platform that enabled personalized mobile experiences by enriching mobile location signals with global data. Factual's Global Places data covered some 75 million local businesses and points of interest in 50 countries.

2004

- Google acquired Picasa, a service that enabled users to organize, edit, and share digital photos on the Web. Picasa founder Lars Perkins joined Google and remained with the company until 2006. In 2011, Perkins founded Relive, a smart photo-sharing app that allowed users to share photos privately. Relive made it easier to share photos at events such as weddings, conferences, birthday parties, and vacations. You could invite people to join an event or share pictures from the event. When participants arrived, they opened the app and sharing automatically began.

2005

- Google acquired Dodgeball, whose technology allowed people to text selected friends and friends of friends within a 10-block radius. The service, founded by Dennis Crowley, targeted users wanting a convenient way to organize a meeting at a local bar or other venue. In 2009, Crowley co-founded FourSquare after leaving Google two years earlier, feeling that Dodgeball had been neglected. FourSquare was similar to Dodgeball, but with an improved mobile Web user interface. Some analysts believed that FourSquare could have been a centerpiece of Android, had the technology moved forward inside Google.
- Google acquired Android, its now-ubiquitous operating system software for mobile phones. Andy Rubin, a key player in the creation of Android, joined the team. By 2014, Android powered over one billion smartphones and tablets around the world. In 2013, Rubin still employed by Google, assumed control of the company's robotics division. In 2014, Google announced Rubin would be leaving the company to start an incubator for technology hardware products.

2006

- Google bought dMarc Broadcasting in an attempt to expand into radio advertising. As discussed in Chapter 8, the acquisition did not go well. In 2007, a little over one year after the deal close, Chad and Ryan Steelberg, dMarc's founders, left Google after disagreeing over the extent to which the radio ad process could be automated. Also in 2007, the Steelberg's founded Brand Affinity Technologies, focused on engaging and monetizing sports and entertainment fans.
- Google acquired Reqwireless (announced in 2006), which made Web browser and rich email software for wireless devices. After managing the Google-Waterloo engineering office for some three years, Roger Skubowius, founder of Reqwireless, left Google. In 2010, Skubowius founded Picowireless, a mobile app company for content publishers.

2007

- Google acquired FeedBurner, a distributor of RSS syndicated content for blogs and other media websites. The FeedBurner team was immediately transitioned into Google, and FeedBurner did not continue to operate independently. Dick Costolo (CEO of FeedBurner) assumed a product leadership role as group product manager on the Ads team. In 2009,

Costolo left Google and two months later joined Twitter as its COO and eventually became its CEO.

2009

- Google acquired On2 Technologies, a developer of video compression software and related video services. In 2010, Matt Frost, former On2 CEO, became head of Strategy and Partnerships for Google's Chrome Media team.

2010

- Google acquired Aardvark, a social search service that allowed users to ask questions and find information from people in their network. In 2013, Max Ventilla (co-founder of Aardvark) left Google to found AltSchool, a school that geared learning to a specific child's needs rather than on a fixed curriculum based on standardized test results.
- Google acquired Plink, which developed a graphic search engine developer to identify art and other visual objects. Plink's founders, Mark Cummins and James Philbin, both joined Google to work on Google Goggles, developing a mobile search application that would utilize some of the functionality of PlinkArt. From April 2010, through May 2013, Mark Cummins (PhD, Oxford), co-founder of Plink, was a software engineer at Google working on computer vision issues for products such as Goggles, Translate, Drive, and Google+. In 2014, Cummins was working on a new startup.
- Google acquired LabPixies, a publisher of mobile applications such as calendars, to do lists, news feeds, games, and entertainment. LabPixies founders joined the iGoogle team and operated out of Google Israel's Research and Development Center. In 2013, three LabPixies founders (including former CEO Ran Ben-Yair) left Google to establish ubimo, a mobile location–based ad platform.
- Google acquired Invite Media, which operated a demand-side media buying platform for the display marketplace. In 2012, Nat Turner and Zach Weinberg, Invite co-founders, left Google to start a health-care company. Turner acknowledged that he did not feel the same passion for ad tech as he did for health care. In 2013, Turner's new venture, Flatiron Health, raised $8 million in venture financing, including money from Google Ventures. Flatiron provided big data analytics services for oncology. The goal of Flatiron was to improve the data quality of the 96 percent of cancer patients unable to participate in clinical trials.

- Google acquired Jambool from Vikas Gupta and Reza Hussein. Jambool offered a payment API that enabled micropayments in online game or social network applications. In 2012, Vikas Gupta became co-founder of Play-I, which was designing toy robots that taught young children how to program. In 2013, Play-I (later named Wonder Workshop) raised seed-round financing from investors that included Google Ventures.
- Google acquired Like.com, a clothing and consumer goods visual search website. In 2011, Munjal Shah, Like co-founder, left Google. In 2013, Shah co-founded HealthEquity Labs, established on the principle that the best way to improve the world's health was not to focus on the unhealthy, but to celebrate those who take care of their health.

2012

- Google purchased Milk, a mobile app incubator established by Digg founder Kevin Rose. Google acqui-hired (Form I, as discussed earlier) Rose and members of Milk's product development team, reportedly to work on projects related to Google+. However, only months after the acquisition, Rose became a general partner at Google Ventures, the company's corporate venture capital arm. In 2014, Rose cut back on most of his duties at Google Ventures and started North Technologies.

M&A Alumni Takeaways

Here are insights that we can draw by analyzing this set of 16 Google M&A alumni as of 2014.

1. 69 percent (11 of 16) of these entrepreneurs had stayed in Google's employ for about two or three years post acquisition. 19 percent stayed longer than three years, and another 12 percent left before two years. Undoubtedly, stay bonuses associated with the acquisition (see Chapter 11) was one factor making two to three years a departure sweet spot.
2. Only one entrepreneur (Matt Frost) remained in Google's full-time employ in late 2014, with Andy Rubin leaving after having the longest tenure of almost 10 years.
3. A large percentage (88 percent, or 14 of 16) of the alumni went on to found new ventures after leaving Google. Another alumnus (Dick Costolo) went on to become non-founding CEO of Twitter.
4. While many of these new ventures were highly related to Google's traditional core markets, a notable number were in other areas that included health care/health-tech, and education/ed-tech.

5. Google Ventures (Google's corporate venture capital arm) had invested in a number of the new ventures formed by Google alumni.

We could have included other prominent M&A alumni beyond the 16 just discussed. (For example, Mike Cassidy, co-founder of Ruba, a travel-related ventured that Google acqui-hired in 2010, went on to become a lead for Google's Project Loon, helium-balloons for remote Internet access.) But these 16 suffice to illustrate the vibrancy of Google's M&A alumni network.

As Reid Hoffman, former CEO of LinkedIn, and co-authors have written: "The first thing you should do when a valuable employee tells you he is leaving is try to change his mind. The second is to congratulate him on the new job and welcome him to your company's alumni network."[6]

Google appeared to share the philosophy of Hoffman and of McKinsey, a consulting company renowned for caring about and building its alumni network. Although certainly not all post-acquisition relationships remained cordial, a large percentage of entrepreneurs appeared intent on maintaining genial professional connections with Google after leaving the company. And Google was reciprocating, realizing that a vibrant M&A alumni network might just bring future opportunities for semi-organic growth.

Notes

1. Bruner (2004), p. 917.
2. See the chapter titled "Talent—Hiring Is Most Important Thing You Do" in Schmidt and Rosenberg (2014) for a thorough discussion of Google's hiring practices apart from M&A.
3. J. Coyle and G. Polsky, "Acqui-hiring," *Duke Law Journal* (November 2013), p. 281.
4. Ibid., pp. 292–293.
5. Robert Hof, "Attention Startups: Here's How to Get Acqui-Hired by Google, Yahoo or Twitter," *Forbes* (December 4, 2013).
6. Reid Hoffman, Ben Casnocha, and Chris Yeh, "Tours of Duty: The New Employer-Employee Compact," *Harvard Business Review* (June 2013).

CHAPTER 14

Competitive Deal Constellations and Ecosystem Synergy

I n August 2014, Twitch, the popular e-sports streaming site, announced that it had been acquired by Amazon. With a purchase price of $970 million in cash, the deal was the largest in Amazon's history. The transaction surprised many analysts and reporters. During the preceding months, numerous media sources, including *Variety*, had been reporting that it would be Google that was about to "hitch" Twitch.

The Twitch deal highlighted the belief that the intensity of competition between Amazon and Google would be heading to new levels. In sectors that included digital devices, robotics, streaming video, cloud computing, and, perhaps most importantly, digital advertising and Web commerce, these two companies appeared to be moving toward direct conflict.

In this chapter, we'll demonstrate how battles such as the Amazon/ Google contest for market control can be better understood by examining competitive M&A *deal constellations.*

We'll then go on to illustrate how the concept of *ecosystem synergy* can strengthen competitive positioning. With ecosystem synergy, semi-organic growth not only occurs with an acquirer's core, but also between its acquisitions. In this sense, it is *second-order synergy.* We'll see how some Google acquisitions have achieved this higher degree of synergy.

Competitive Constellations: Google versus Amazon

In Chapter 3, we used Google and Apple to introduce dyadic M&A cascading where two companies engage in a series of tit-for-tat M&A transactions. In this section, we extend the notion of dyadic cascading and show how acquisitions by a company can be used to support an entire *ecosystem* that enhances the company's position against a specific competitor.

We'll examine select acquisitions by Amazon and Google during 2012–2014 to explore how these deals were instrumental in developing *control-based* competing ecosystems. These acquisitions, when viewed as a constellation, portray how each company was making offensive advances or bolstering defensive positioning against its competitor.

Amazon Acquisition Constellation for Positioning against Google

Figure 14.1 shows a number of Amazon acquisitions between 2012 and 2014, which, taken as a whole, can be viewed (at least in part) as positioning against Google. Note that we are selecting on three database dimensions in generating this infographic: (1) competitive move against; (2) key company; and (3) date. We'll describe these deals beginning with Peritor and moving clockwise.

- **Peritor (cloud services).** In January 2012, Amazon acquired Peritor, an IT consulting company that developed Scalarium, a Web-based cloud management platform. The platform automated server configuration and initial application setup. In 2013, Amazon Web Services (AWS) added OpsWorks. This offering was based on Peritor and enabled AWS users to configure and manage applications more easily without resorting to custom tools.
- **Kiva Systems (robotics).** In March 2012, Amazon signed a definitive agreement to acquire Kiva Systems. Kiva developed robotic technology to perform warehouse tasks. The company offered a Mobile-robotic

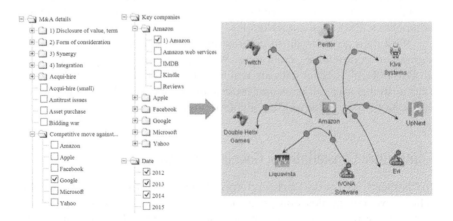

FIGURE 14.1 Amazon M&A positioning constellation against Google

Warehouse Automation System: an order fulfillment solution for inventory control, forward replenishment, picking, packing, shipping sortation, finishing, and quality control. Kiva robots were being used by two companies that Amazon previously acquired: Zappos.com (shoes) and Diapers.com (baby products). Kiva's robots could locate items in a customer's order, move the products around warehouses, and help get packed boxes to a loading dock. At $678 million, Kiva became the second-largest acquisition in Amazon's history, behind the 2009 purchase of Zappos. (Both deals would be surpassed by the 2014 Twitch deal.) Amazon's share price rose about 4 percent on the Kiva announcement.

- **UpNext (3-D mapping).** In July 2012, Amazon acquired UpNext, which developed mobile 3-D map applications for over 50 cities, including New York; Chicago; Boston; Washington, DC; Austin; San Francisco; Philadelphia; and Portland. The company's applications offered subway lines, real-time feeds, and venue information, enabling users to physically discover cities, as well as explore virtually. UpNext used vector-based 3-D images to recreate virtual buildings, in contrast to the photo-based technology used by Google's map offerings.
- **Evi (language recognition/search).** In November 2012, Amazon acquired the Evi search application, available for Apple's iOS and Google's Android. Evi responded to voice and text queries with spoken answers delivered in plain English. Users could also schedule events, make calls, and send texts and emails. The Evi app was similar in concept and scope to Apple's Siri voice assistant and the Google Now technology.
- **IVONA (language processing).** In January 2013, Amazon acquired IVONA Software, which developed text-to-speech and voice command technology for use in interfaces on mobile and other devices. With this acquisition, Amazon signaled that it intended to move beyond low-end hardware and compete against Apple's iPad and higher-end Android tablets.
- **Liquavista (mobile display).** In May 2013, Amazon acquired Liquavista from Samsung Electronics to support its efforts in developing new displays for mobile devices. Liquavista developed color e-paper video screens that could work with or without a backlight using electrowetting technology.
- **Double Helix Games (game developer).** In February 2014, Amazon acquired Double Helix Games, a game studio formed in 2007 through the merger of The Collective and Shiny Entertainment. The company created games for consoles and PCs, focusing on large-scale action titles. A few months later, Amazon introduced Fire TV, a set-top box that could

be used for video streaming, but also supported gaming as a primary function with the addition of a game controller.

- **Twitch (game streaming).** As mentioned in the opening of this chapter, in August 2014, Amazon acquired Twitch. Twitch was an extremely popular e-sports streaming site. The site provided functionality for gamers to host live game strategy sessions and enabled individual gamers to broadcast their game matches to followers interested in learning and discussing game strategy. The site was fostering a new type of "athlete"—a gaming superstar. The $970 million deal became the largest in Amazon's history. Widespread rumors suggested that Google was about to acquire Twitch. Sources that included *Forbes* reported, however, that Google became concerned about possible antitrust hurdles. Evidently, Google and Twitch were unable to agree on a reverse break-up fee if the deal did not pass regulatory muster. Twitch claimed to have more than 55 million unique users, with more than one million members who uploaded videos each month. Amazon's acquisition of Twitch would capture highly engaged users, which could result in substantially more advertising revenue for Amazon, including in-game advertising. Twitch enjoyed the 4th largest website traffic in the United States.

Although Amazon was using M&A to help build an ecosystem to compete with Google across a number of fronts from mapping to robotics, it was the Twitch deal that perhaps would strike closest to Google's core. Amazon, with notoriously low margins, was salivating at the possibility of high-margin digital advertising revenue from video streaming placed inside games. Google/YouTube lusted after the same revenue, but had been frustrated in this particular pursuit.

Google Acquisition Constellation for Positioning against Amazon

During the same time that Amazon was building its competitive acquisition constellation, Google was reciprocating. Figure 14.2 shows some clusters of Google acquisitions between 2012 and 2014 that at least in part can be viewed as positioning moves against Amazon. Given that we've discussed a number of these deals in earlier chapters, we'll provide only high-level information regarding the acquisitions here.

- **Zync Render, Talaria, and Stackdriver (cloud services).** Zync Render would be integrated into the Google Cloud Platform and offer film studios per-minute billing for services. Talaria would allow Google to enhance its cloud technology, enabling developers to "handle more users

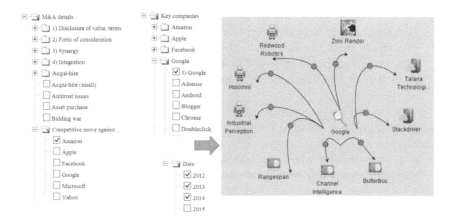

FIGURE 14.2 Google M&A positioning constellation against Amazon

with fewer boxes, without changing a line of code." Stackdriver's technology would support developers in monitoring apps and services running in the cloud. These three deals would work together to enhance Google's positioning against Amazon Web Services.

- **BufferBox, Channel Intelligence, and Rangespan (e-commerce).** During 2012–2014, Google acquired these three e-commerce companies. BufferBox delivered e-commerce goods to physical kiosks in grocery and convenience stores in Canada. BufferBox's services were similar to those of Amazon Lockers. Channel Intelligence supported clients in promoting their products across the Web by helping retailers manage their product listings on comparison shopping sites. Some one-third of shoppers were starting searches on Amazon, compared to only 13 percent on a search engine. Google hoped that Channel Intelligence might help change these statistics. Rangespan was a UK-based shopping retailer founded by two former Amazon executives. It provided back-office services, including real-time analytics for dynamically determining product offerings, to large retailers such as Tesco.

- **Industrial Perception, Holomni, and Redwood Robotics (robotics).** In 2013, Google purchased at least eight robotics companies. Industrial Perception was developing software that helped robots locate and identify objects. Applications included loading and unloading trucks, where robots could get to and grab items efficiently. Holomni was reportedly focusing on developing omnidirectional wheels and vehicles that have robotic applications. Redwood Robotics was working on the next generation of robotic arms, with the goal of using robots "to reduce the stress of dull and repetitive tasks." Redwood Robotics, Holomni, and Industrial Perception (among other robotics deals) could potentially work together to contribute to Google's Express (shop local stores online and get same-day delivery) in item selection, delivery, and as well as in other aspects of Google's venture into *e-commerce.*

Google and Amazon appeared to be meeting at the crossroads of *digital advertising* and *e-commerce.* Google was the digital advertising king, while Amazon occupied the e-commerce throne. The companies were jostling to be at the top of mind when you had any given purchase need.

Google hoped you would use its search engine to meet your needs, so it could show you related paid ads. But Amazon's website and mobile apps made it easy to find, purchase, and receive product with only one or two clicks. Now Amazon wanted a larger share of revenue from high-margin product ads. Each company was building a constellation of M&A transaction to help its efforts prevail.

Ecosystem Synergy

In Chapters 1 and 2, we stressed the importance of synergy analysis as an essential ingredient in M&A strategy, valuation, and integration. Recall that synergy involves the interaction of two or more agents such that their combined effect is greater than the sum of their individual effects. An assertion of deal synergy is regularly one the most exaggerated claims in corporate strategy. Interestingly, we saw that the origin of the use word *synergy* in M&A involves, perhaps appropriately, Irish coffee—a blending of hot coffee, Irish whiskey, and brown sugar, topped with thick cream.

We've seen that Google's deals typically anticipate *revenue synergy* that the company expects to occur in the near or distant future. Much of this projected revenue synergy involves creating new products or services or enhancing existing ones across a wide range of markets.

We've noted how *complementarity* between Google and its targets is vital in stimulating semi-organic growth. While similarity may be useful in obtaining efficiency-based synergies, complementarity is more closely aligned with enhancement-based synergies.

Ecosystem synergy takes complementarity to a new level. We'll use Google as a case study to understand this *second-order synergy,* whereby semi-organic growth can extend beyond the company's core to interactions with its other acquisitions.

Hal Varian, Google economist, has characterized the present era as one of *combinatorial innovation,* whereby Internet components (mainly in the form of bits) are blended to stimulate invention. This notion can be extended to apply to talent and technology acquired in M&A transactions. Combinatorial blends of thoughtfully selected targets can trigger innovation and favorably skew the odds of successful outcomes. Of course, this assumes that an appropriate integration strategy is selected (see Chapter 12) and is executed within a hospitable organizational culture.

Rise of Ecosystems

Products and services have become increasing complex and interrelated, requiring an ever-changing diversity of pieces that include technologies, applications, and content, all coupled with design capability. It is extremely rare for all necessary pieces to reside within one organization. An organization can no longer operate in relative isolation, but must be willing and able to operate outside its organizational boundaries to influence or control the necessary pieces to complete a product puzzle.

In short, an organization must design and execute its own organizational *ecosystems*. This may involve structuring *influencing* "activities and interactions between businesses that can be quickly and flexibly reconfigured."[1] Or it also may involve *controlling* activities that may lead to an ongoing series of acquisitions to acquiring necessary pieces designed to improve or create novel product offerings.

In either case, given that relevant knowledge, capabilities, and intellectual property are likely to be dispersed among many players, ecosystem thinking has become indispensable in modern corporate strategy.

Two Key Issues in Ecosystem Design

Although there are many issues that must be considered in designing a company ecosystem, for our purposes we focus on only two.

First of all, to what extent does a company plan to use *influence or control* in building an ecosystem? Taking an influence approach implies emphasizing partnership or minority investment arrangements, whereas control suggests acquisition or majority ownership.

Successful ecosystems have been built using both approaches. In fact, an ecosystem can combine both influence and control. For example, in 2014, Google's Android ecosystem comprised alliances with handset partners that included Samsung and Lenovo, semi-conductor companies such as Broadcom and Qualcomm, mobile operators such as Sprint and T-Mobile, as well as tens of thousands of unique mobile app developers. However, as we've seen before (see, for example, Figure 7.2), Google had also acquired numerous companies that helped make up this ecosystem.

A second key issue involves whether or not a lead company in an ecosystem creates more value than it captures for itself. Is value being fairly shared in the ecosystem so as to perpetuate its long-term existence?

There's no question that Apple created enormous value for itself as it developed its *influence-based* digital music ecosystem for iPod/iTunes with companies that included major music companies such as Universal and Sony starting in 2003. But it was far from clear that Apple created enough value for its partners in the process. As the music industry shifted a decade later, Apple was scrambling to reposition itself with the acquisition of companies such as Beats. Furthermore, Apple was being viewed with a *fox in the chicken coop* mentality by a number of media companies as it attempted to perpetuate its hold on digital music and extend its reach into digital video.

On the other hand, if a company (such as Google) desires to build an ecosystem that is largely control-based, then designing mechanisms to fairly share potential value created from acquisitions must be put in place if such efforts are to succeed in the long run. We addressed some important aspects of this topic in Chapter 11.

Strategic Approaches to Ecosystems

Ecosystem design varies across companies as well within the same company. Here are some examples of ecosystems that differ across the dimension of influence versus control.

APPLE'S APP STORE: REVENUE SHARING   While Apple has traditionally utilized a highly integrated (controlled) approach in hardware design, the company has created an influence-based ecosystem for developers in its App Store. The App Store is a digital distribution center for iOS applications running on devices such as the iPhone and iPad. Typically, developers receive 70 percent of revenue generated from apps, with 30 percent going to Apple.

Apple's App Store was launched in 2008 as an extension to iTunes, and by 2014 had grown to contain almost 1.5 million applications, with total downloads approaching 100 billion. In 2013, Apple customers spent over $10 billion at the store. The App Store was viewed as a vital extension of Apple's mobile smartphone and tablet offerings and represented one of the most successful examples of an influence-based ecosystem in history.

INTEL CAPITAL: MINORITY EQUITY INVESTMENTS   In his 1996 book titled *Only the Paranoid Survive*, Andy Grove (former CEO of Intel) highlighted the "power, vigor, and competence of *complementors*." Grove defined complementors as companies whose well-being is tied to your activities or "fellow travelers" with common interests.[2]

Historically, Microsoft had been Intel's mega-complementor. For more than a decade, Intel and Microsoft had been partners in what Grove liked to depict as an upward business spiral, with each company on one side of the spiral working together to drive revenue growth. Microsoft released "fatter" office software, which required "faster" Intel processors, which enabled to even fatter office applications, and so on. A perpetuating sales cycle was driven by this duopolistic ecosystem.

As this ecosystem started to lose vitality, Intel's vision of complementarity expanded, leading the company in 1996 to start ratcheting up a corporate minority equity investment program. Intel would move well beyond dyadic complementarity and make corporate venture capital investments in a myriad of companies designed to stimulate the growth of its core products.

Intel Capital was formed, and by 2014 this corporate venture capital arm had invested over $11 billion in some 1,400 investments. Apart from generating financial returns, these deals over the years were designed to build strategic Intel-centric ecosystems in markets that ranged from Wi-Fi chips to digital media to the Internet of Things.

Unlike Apple, Intel's influence driver for its ecosystem development was not revenue sharing, but growth capital in the form of corporate venture investments.

GOOGLE: AN M&A-DRIVEN ECOSYSTEM   Although the word *ecosystem* may not be commonly attached to clusters of M&A activity, doing so is appropriate. Ecosystem M&A synergy exists where target acquisitions have synergy with each other and not only with the acquirer. Consider an example. Google has engaged in a series of advertising-related acquisitions that have helped the company cover the entire value chain of advertising. Some of these acquisitions include Invite Media, DoubleClick, and Admeld. See Figure 14.3.

In 2008, Google fended off opposition from companies such as Microsoft and gained FTC approval to acquire DoubleClick. DoubleClick is an exchange that provides services and products for advertising agencies, marketers, and Web publishers to support marketing programs. Next, in 2010, Google purchased Invite Media, which operated a media-buying platform with optimization technology for purchasers of display advertising. Finally, in 2011, Google bought Admeld, which had developed advertising optimization technology for online publishers (providers of online advertising space).

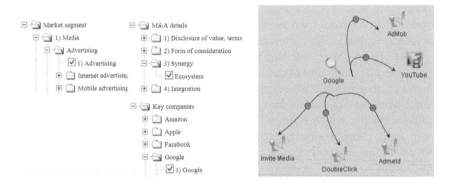

FIGURE 14.3 M&A ecosystem synergy in advertising

In the digital world, ads typically start with the advertiser, going from an ad agency to a demand-side platform (Invite Media), then to an ad exchange (DoubleClick), which also interacts with a supply-side platform (Admeld). Ultimately, ads reach users through services such as YouTube or AdMob, another acquisition that provided Google with one of the largest mobile advertising networks.

Google's M&A cluster of advertising companies is a vibrant example of ecosystem synergy—where target acquisitions enjoy synergies with each other and not only with the initial core of acquirer.

M&A Ecosystem Synergy: Description and Examples

Acquisition ecosystems such as Google's deals across the advertising value chain can be viewed not only as positioning constellations against competition, but can also be seen as generating *second-order synergy* within a company.

As discussed in Chapter 1, synergy involves the notion (often fanciful) that the value of combined enterprises will exceed the sum of their individual values. Revenue synergies are anticipated top-line enhancements that will come from use of the acquirer's superior distribution capability, cross-selling of companies' products, effective integration across an industry value chain, or creation of an enhanced or even novel product or service. The list of possible revenue synergies is long. Sometimes such synergies are real; often they are optimistically imaginative.

Recall that synergy can be represented by the equation $V(A + T) > V(A) + V(T)$, where $V(A)$ is the value of the acquirer and $V(T)$ is the value of the target.

But with *ecosystem synergy*, we're now considering what could be an additional dimension of M&A synergy. Research findings suggest that initiation of a series of acquisitions as part of a strategic M&A program is associated with value creation for buyers.[3] This is especially true when ecosystem synergy can be realized.

Ecosystem synergy exists where target acquisitions have synergy with each other and not only with the acquirer. In other words, $V(A + T_1 + T_2) > V(A + T_1) + V(A + T_2)$, where A stands for the acquirer, and T_1 and T_2 stand for distinct targets that enjoy synergies with each other in addition to synergies with acquirer.

We now consider two additional examples of realized and *potential* ecosystem synergy in select pairs of Google's acquisitions. In one example, the ecosystem synergies have been achieved. The other example is highly speculative. We start with the moonshot.

ENERGY DISTRIBUTION AND USE: MAKANI AND NEST Consider Google's 2013 purchase of Makani Power (AWTs or airborne wind turbines) and 2014 acquisition of Nest (Wi-Fi–enabled, self-learning home devices). The Nest and Makani deals could interact with each other on three possible levels[4]:

1. *Internet of Things.* Potential synergy between Makani and Nest could derive from an implementation of the Internet of Things (IoT), where the Internet extends into the physical world and embraces everyday devices, systems, and services. Ubiquitous computing and sensor technology enable connectivity and learning, utilizing frameworks that focus on real-time data working with many "things" interacting in a controlled environment. Applications include urban planning, environmental sensing, emergency response, smart product management, and home automation. In a grand Google scheme of IoT, Makani's turbines generating energy and Nest's portfolio of devices automating homes, could become two "smart" nodes in the network.

2. *Technical complementarity.* Nest could provide insight into the standing challenges Makani is facing in critical areas such as:
   - Obtaining permission to fly with unmarked, unlit tethers
   - Having to observe a setback from any trunk power lines
   - Being unable to fly in adverse conditions

   Nest could help by providing advanced sensor technology and machine learning. AWTs could become smart devices that recognize objects, avoid avian mortality, and become capable of reacting to environmental conditions. This could help deal with regulation constraints and risks involving tethers, a major bottleneck in applying Makani's technology. It could also decrease the probability of damage from unanticipated events and reduce maintenance costs.

3. *Energy distribution*. Google could position itself on both the supply side and demand side of an energy ecosystem. The Makani experiment is about energy production. The power, simplicity, and scalability of its approach attempts to transform energy creation from a material/capital-intensive process to a flexible, modular, and software-driven technology.

Nest involves potential energy savings, including Nest Energy Services, which helps homes save on energy bills by curbing power consumption during peak hours. Nest enables need-based energy creation as well as efficient energy distribution between individual homes and a networked smart grid, whether traditional or novel, such as what could emerge from Makani Power.

VIDEO ADVERTISING: APPLIED SEMANTICS AND YOUTUBE   In illustrating ecosystem synergy between Applied Semantics (ASI) and YouTube, we return to Google's watershed purchase of ASI in 2003. Recall from Chapter 2 that the ASI deal led to AdSense, software that could mine webpages for meaning, parsing content, and recommending what type of ads would work well on a particular page.

After the 2006 YouTube acquisition. Google began placing ads in videos or on page feeds for videos using AdSense technology. The ads were contextual, based on metadata contained in a given YouTube video. Searching for a video about Florence, Italy, could not only bring up pasta ads next to the video search results but also embed a relevant travel banner ad within the video when viewed.

Ads could travel with the video, so if it was served on another site, additional revenue would flow to the creator and to Google. Working together, AdSense and YouTube were generating synergy as part of a video advertising ecosystem.

Creators of popular YouTube videos were urged to sign up for AdSense accounts in order to participate in this algorithmic matching magic. Google's AdSense promised to provide YouTube channels with ads relevant to viewers and target audiences, thereby increasing the likelihood that ads would be viewed.

Ecosystem Synergy and Semi-Organic Growth

Perhaps Google's ecosystem synergy and related semi-organic growth should be compared to how one newspaper described Thomas Edison's

Menlo Park lab well over a century ago. Edison's lab had expanded to occupy two city blocks and had "a stock of almost every conceivable material." This 1887 newspaper article gasped that the lab contained: "eight thousand kinds of chemicals, every kind of screw made, every size of needle, every kind of cord or wire, hair of humans, horses, hogs, cows, rabbits, goats, minx, camels ... silk in every texture, cocoons, various kinds of hoofs, shark's teeth, deer horns, tortoise shell ... cork, resin, varnish and oil, ostrich feathers, a peacock's tail, jet, amber, rubber, all ores ... "[5]

Opportunities for technology and talent combinations abound inside Google's "labs." The company's experimental culture pursues known and yet-to-be discovered M&A synergies, both direct and ecosystem-based. The campus is constantly refueled by a steady flow of new acquisitions.

As Google extends its product and service reach via technology and talent acquisitions, the prospect for semi-organic growth continues to flourish.

Watch the Video

www.wiley.com/go/semiorganicgrowth

To view a video relating to the content of this chapter, refer to *Minority Equity Investments versus Acquisitions,* which accompanies this book as a supplemental resource.

Notes

1. Williamson and De Meyer (2012).
2. Andrew S. Grove, *Only the Paranoid Survive* (New York: Bantam Doubleday Dell Publishing Group, 1996).
3. See, for example, Fuller, Netter, and Stegemoller (2002).
4. I am indebted to Miao Wang for her analysis of this speculative ecosystem synergy between Makani and Nest.
5. Quoted in Seth Shulman, *Owning the Future* (New York: Houghton Mifflin Company, 1999), pp. 158–160.

References

Akbulut, M., and J. Matsusaka. 2010. "50+ Years of Diversification Announcements." *Financial Review* 45: 231–262.

Akbulut, M. 2013. "Do Overvaluation-Driven Stock Acquisitions Really Benefit Acquirer Shareholders?" *Journal of Financial and Quantitative Analysis* 48 (4): 1025–1055.

Bauer, F., and K. Matzler. 2014. "Antecedents of M&A Success: The Role of Strategic Complementarity, Cultural Fit, and Degree and Speed of Integration." *Strategic Management Journal* 35: 269–291.

Boeker, Warren. 1989. Strategic Change: The Effects of Founding and History. *Academy of Management Journal* 32 (3): 489.

Bruner, Robert. 2004. *Applied Mergers and Acquisitions*. Hoboken, NJ: Wiley Finance.

Catmull, Ed. 2014. *Creativity Inc*. New York: Random House.

Cloodt, M., J. Hagedoorn, and V. Van Kranenburg. 2006. "Mergers and Acquisitions: Their Effect on the Innovative Performance of Companies in High-Tech Industries." *Research Policy* 35 (5): 642–654.

DePamphilis, Donald M. 2014, *Mergers, Acquisitions, and Other Restructuring Activities*, 7th ed. San Diego: Academic Press.

Faulkner, David, Satu Teerikangas, and Richard Joseph. 2012. *The Handbook of Mergers and Acquisitions*. Oxford: Oxford University Press.

Frick, Kevin A., and Alberto Torres. 2002. "Learning from High-Tech Deals." *The McKinsey Quarterly* 1.

Fuller, K., J. Netter, and M. Stegemoller. 2002. "What Do Returns to Acquiring Firms Tell Us? Evidence from Firms that Make Many Acquisitions." *The Journal of Finance* 57 (4): 1763–1793.

Geis, George T., and George S. Geis. 2001. *Digital Deals*. New York: McGraw-Hill.

Gomes, Emanuel, Duncan N. Angwin, Yaakov Weber, and Shlomo Yedidia Tarba. 2013. "Critical Success Factors through the Mergers and Acquisitions Process: Revealing Pre- and Post-M&A Connections for Improved Performance." *Thunderbird International Business Review* 55 (1) (January/February).

Haspeslagh, Philippe. C., and David. B. Jemison. 1991. *Managing Acquisitions: Creating Value through Corporate Renewal*. New York: The Free Press.

Herd, Thomas J., and Ryan McManis. 2012. "Who Says M&A Doesn't Create Value?" *Outlook*, 1.

Levy, Stephen. 2011. *In the Plex*. New York: Simon & Schuster.

Martynova, Marina, and Luc Renneborg. 2008. "A Century of Corporate Takeovers: What Have We Learned, and Where Do We Stand?" *Journal of Banking & Finance* 32: 2148–2177.

Milanov, H., and S. A. Fernhaber. 2009. "The Impact of Early Imprinting on the Evolution of New Venture Networks." *Journal of Business Venturing* 24 (1): 46–61.

Netter, J. M., M. Stegemoller, and M. B. Wintoki. 2011. "Implications of Data Screens on Merger and Acquisition Analysis: A Large Sample Study of Mergers and Acquisitions from 1992–2009." *Review of Financial Studies* 24: 2316–2357.

Rodrigues, Usha, and Mike Stegemoller. 2007. "An Inconsistency in SEC Disclosure Requirements? The Case of the 'Insignificant' Private Target." *Journal of Corporate Finance* 13: 251–269.

Rothaermel, Frank T., Michael A. Hitt, and Lloyd A. Jobe. 2006. "Balancing Vertical Integration and Strategic Outsourcing: Effects on Product Portfolio, Product Success, and Firm Performance." *Strategic Management Journal* 27: 1033–1056.

Schmidt, Eric, and Jonathan Rosenberg. 2014. *Google: How Google Works*. New York: Grand Central Publishing.

Sears, Joshua, and Glenn Hoetker. 2014. "Technological Overlap, Technological Capabilities, and Resource Recombination in Technological Acquisitions." *Strategic Management Journal* 35: 48–67.

Stinchcombe, Arthur L. 1965. Social Structure and Organizations. In J. G. March (ed.)., *Handbook of Organizations*, 142–194. Chicago: Rand-McNally & Co.

Thaler, Richard H. 1988. "Anomalies: The Winner's Curse." *Journal of Economic Perspectives* 2 (1): 191–202.

Williamson, P., and A. De Meyer. 2012. "Ecosystem Advantage: How to Successfully Harness the Power of Partners." *California Management Review* 55 (1): 24–46.

About the Website

This book is accompanied by a companion website at www.wiley.com/ go/semiorganicgrowth (password: wiley15). The website includes a short introductory video, *Introductory Video: Semi-Organic Growth and Corporate Business Development*, together with 14 additional videos, each about 10 minutes in length. The content of each video is designed to add to your understanding of key concepts found in a given chapter. You'll find these videos referenced at the end of each chapter. Note: Two chapters (3 and 11) have two videos, while two other chapters (7 and 13) do not have any videos.

Here are the titles of the 14 videos:

1. *When Not to Do an Acquisition*
2. *What's Distinctive about Semi-Organic Growth?*
3. *Contrasting Apple's Acquisition Strategy with Google's Acquisition Cascades*
4. *M&A Market Modeling for Target Acquisitions*
5. *M&A's Role in Building an Ecosystem*
6. *Contrasting Amazon's Acquisition Strategy with Google's*
7. No video
8. *M&A Financial Accounting Considerations*
9. *M&A Financial Disclosure Practices*
10. *Contrasting Facebook's M&A Consideration with Google's*
11. *Pitfalls in M&A Contingent Consideration Direct and Reverse Break-Up Fees*
12. *M&A Integration—Not One Size Fits All*
13. No video
14. *Minority Equity Investments versus Acquisitions*

About the Author

George T. Geis teaches at UCLA Anderson in the areas of corporate business development and entrepreneurship. He has been voted Outstanding Teacher of the Year at UCLA Anderson five times. Geis is currently faculty director of Anderson's Mergers and Acquisitions Executive program. Geis has also taught mergers and acquisitions at the Haas School, UC Berkeley. He has been a visiting professor at Bocconi University in Milan, Italy, as well as at the Darden School of Business at the University of Virginia.

Geis is an expert on M&A activity in technology, communications, and media markets. Geis's research interests include market modeling for M&A-related strategies.

A National Science Foundation and Woodrow Wilson Honorary Fellow, Geis has extensive consulting experience and has published dozens of professional articles and seven books. He is the recipient of the Financial Executives Institute Award for outstanding achievement in finance. In 2013, Geis was a Batten Fellow at the Darden School, University of Virginia.

Geis is the editor of a website that provides a visual analysis of M&A deals in technology, media, and communications markets at http://www.trivergence.com. He also writes an M&A blog at http://maprofessor.blogspot.com.

Geis graduated summa cum laude with a BS with honors in mathematics from Purdue University. He received an MBA from the University of California, Los Angeles, and a PhD from the University of Southern California.

Index

Printed and bound by CPI Group (UK) Ltd, Croydon, CR0 4YY

21/06/2023

03229091-0001